FORTHCOMING TITLES

V. Spike Peterson and Anne Sisson Runyan
Global Gender Issues

☐ ☐ ☐

Sarah Tisch and Michael Wallace
**Dilemmas of Development Assistance:
The What, Why, and Who of Foreign Aid**

☐ ☐ ☐

Bruce E. Moon
International Trade in the 1990s

☐ ☐ ☐

Ted Robert Gurr and Barbara Harff
Ethnic Conflict in World Politics

☐ ☐ ☐

Frederic S. Pearson
The Spread of Arms in the International System

INTERNATIONAL
HUMAN RIGHTS

Margaret Sutherland

DILEMMAS IN WORLD POLITICS

Series Editor
George A. Lopez, University of Notre Dame

Dilemmas in World Politics offers teachers and students of international relations a series of quality books on critical issues, trends, and regions in international politics. Each text examines a "real world" dilemma and is structured to cover the historical, theoretical, practical, and projected dimensions of its subject.

EDITORIAL BOARD

INTERNATIONAL HUMAN RIGHTS

■　■　■

Jack Donnelly

UNIVERSITY OF DENVER

Westview Press

BOULDER □ SAN FRANCISCO □ OXFORD

Dilemmas in World Politics Series

Copyright © 1993 by Westview Press, Inc.

Published in 1993 in the United States of America by Westview Press, Inc., 5500 Central Avenue, Boulder, Colorado 80301-2877, and in the United Kingdom by Westview Press, 36 Lonsdale Road, Summertown, Oxford OX2 7EW

Library of Congress Cataloging-in-Publication Data
Donnelly, Jack.
International human rights / Jack Donnelly.
    p.   cm. — (Dilemmas in world politics)
    Includes bibliographical references and index.
    ISBN 0-8133-8181-9. — ISBN 0-8133-8182-7 (pbk.)
    1. Human rights.   I. Title.   II. Series.
JC571.D753   1993
341.4'81—dc20   93-459
                                                                              CIP

Printed and bound in the United States of America

The paper used in this publication meets the requirements
of the American National Standard for Permanence of Paper
for Printed Library Materials Z39.48-1984.

10   9   8   7   6   5   4   3

Contents

□ □ □

Tables and Illustrations

xi

□ □ □

Acknowledgments

This book originated in an invitation from George Lopez, the series editor of Dilemmas in World Politics, and Jennifer Knerr, the supervising editor of the series at Westview Press. Throughout three major rewrites, which led to the final draft's arriving at the press a year and a half late, they both have been cheerful and supportive, and their suggestions of style, substance, and organization have greatly improved the manuscript. They have consistently asked for a good book later rather than an okay one now. I hope that they are pleased with the results of their patience and prodding. I also thank Michael Stohl, who reviewed the manuscript for Westview, for his helpful critical comments and suggestions; Marian Safran, whose careful copyediting smoothed out many rough edges; and Mark Jendrysik, Holloway Sparks, and Jacek Lubecki for their research assistance.

I owe a special debt to Rhoda Howard. Writing for a general audience of intelligent but not necessarily informed readers is very different from the academic writing I usually do. I knew this in theory before I started work on this book. I finally began to appreciate it in practice after her savage (but unfortunately accurate) dismantling of the first draft. If there are still passages that ask or assume too much of the reader, it's not because she didn't try to get me to change them.

Jack Donnelly

□ □ □

Acronyms

ACOA   American Committee on Africa
AI   Amnesty International
ANC   African National Congress
AOHR   Arab Organization for Human Rights
APDH   Permanent Assembly for Human Rights
ARENA   National Republican Alliance
CADHU   Argentine Human Rights Commission
CAT   Committee Against Torture
CEDAW   Committee on the Elimination of Discrimination Against
            Women
CELS   Center for Legal and Social Studies
CERD   Committee on the Elimination of Racial Discrimination
CIA   Central Intelligence Agency
COMADRES   Committee of Mothers of Political Prisoners, Disappeared,
            and Assassinated in El Salvador
CONADEP   National Commission on Disappeared Persons (Sábato
            Commission)
COPACHI   Committee of Cooperation for Peace
COSATU   Congress of South African Trade Unions
CSCE   Conference on Security and Cooperation in Europe
CVR   Commission for Truth and Reconciliation (Rettig
            Commission)
EC   European Community
ECOSOC   Economic and Social Council
EEC   European Economic Community
ERP   Revolutionary Army of the People
ESMA   Navy Mechanics School
FDN   Nicaraguan Democratic Forces
FDR   Democratic Revolutionary Front
FEDEFAM   Federation of Families of Disappeared Persons and
            Political Prisoners
FSLN   Sandinista National Liberation Front
GA   General Assembly

GATT	General Agreement on Tariffs and Trade
GDR	German Democratic Republic
ILO	International Labor Organization
IMF	International Monetary Fund
INGO	international nongovernmental organization
MEDH	Ecumenical Movement for Human Rights
NAACP	National Association for the Advancement of Colored People
NGOs	nongovernmental organizations
NSM	National Security Memorandum
OAS	Organization of American States
OAU	Organization of African Unity
ORDEN	Nationalist Democratic Organization
PRC	People's Republic of China
SERPAJ	Service for Peace and Justice
SWAPO	South-West Africa People's Organization
UK	United Kingdom
UN	United Nations

□ □ □

Introduction:
A Note to the Reader

This is a book about the international relations of human rights since the end of World War II, that is, the ways in which states and other international actors have addressed human rights. Although wide-ranging, the topic is narrower than some readers might expect.

Life, liberty, security, subsistence, and other things to which we have human rights may be denied by an extensive array of individuals and organizations. "Human rights," however, are usually taken to have a special reference to the ways in which states treat their own citizens. For example, domestically, we distinguish muggings and private assaults, which are not typically considered human rights violations, from police brutality and torture, which are. Internationally, we distinguish terrorism, war, and war crimes from human rights issues, even though they both lead to denials of life and security. Although the boundaries are not always entirely clear—for example, disappearances became an important form of human rights abuse in the 1970s (see Chapter 3) when perpetrators attempted to obscure the nature of their actions by operating at the boundary between private violence (murder) and state terrorism—the distinction is part of our ordinary language and focuses our attention on an important set of political problems.

No single book can cover all aspects of the politics of human rights. My principal concern in this book will be *international* human rights policies, a vital and increasingly well established area of policy and inquiry. This does not imply that international action is the principal determinant of whether human rights are respected or violated. In fact, much of the book demonstrates the limits of international action.

Nonetheless, one of this book's distinctive features, as opposed to most other discussions of international human rights, is its substantial attention to the domestic politics of human rights. Chapter 3 provides a relatively detailed look at human rights violations in the Southern Cone of South America. In addition, briefer domestic case studies of South Africa and Central America appear in Chapters 4 and 5.

Another distinctive feature of this book, along with the other volumes in the Dilemmas in World Politics series, is a relatively extensive emphasis on theory. Chapter 2 addresses philosophical issues of the nature, substance, and source of human rights; the place of human rights in the contemporary international society of states; and the theoretical challenges posed to the very enterprise of international human rights policy by arguments of radical cultural relativism and political realism (realpolitik, "power politics"). Like the domestic case studies, this discussion may appear to be more than is strictly necessary in a book on international human rights. I would submit, though, that both the case studies and the theory provide important background, context, and insights. I encourage the reader at least to look them over, even—perhaps especially—if at the outset those issues do not seem central to his or her own concerns.

I have tried to write a book that assumes little or no background knowledge. Anyone with an interest in the topic, regardless of age or experience, should find this book accessible. I have tried, however, not to write a *textbook*, a term that has justly acquired pejorative overtones. I have tried not to "write down," either in style or in substance. Furthermore, although I have made an effort to retain some balance in the discussion, I have not expunged my own views and interpretations.

Textbook presentations of controversial issues—when they are not entirely avoided—tend to involve bland and noncommittal presentations of "the two sides" to an argument. By contrast, I have often laid out and defended one interpretation and given lesser (or even scant) attention to alternative views. I have made great efforts to be accurate and fair. But there is no false pretense of "objectivity." And I draw the reader's attention to the discussion questions for each chapter, which appear at the end of the book. They often frame alternative interpretations and help to highlight controversial claims in the main body of the text, especially in Chapters 2 and 6.

Unlike many authors of introductory books, I have not set out with the principal goal of providing information—although there is a lot of straightforward factual information for the reader to absorb. Neither do I aim to convey the received wisdom on the subject—although this book does provide an overview of the kinds of issues typically addressed, and some important perspectives that have been commonly adopted, in the study of international human rights. Rather, I hope to get the reader thinking about why and how human rights are violated, what can (and cannot) be done about such violations through international action, why human rights remain such a small part of international relations, and what might be done about that. These are pressing political issues that merit, even demand, thought and attention.

ONE

□ □ □

Human Rights as an Issue
in World Politics

Before World War II, the issue of human rights rarely appeared on international political agendas. Most states violated human rights systematically. Racial discrimination pervaded the United States. The Soviet Union was a totalitarian secret-police state. Britain, France, the Netherlands, Portugal, Belgium, and Spain maintained colonial empires in Africa, Asia, and the Caribbean. And the political history of most Central and South American countries was largely a succession of military dictatorships and civilian oligarchies. Although such phenomena troubled many people in other countries, they were not considered a legitimate subject for international action. Rather, human rights were viewed as an entirely internal (domestic) political matter, an internationally protected exercise of the sovereign prerogatives of states.

As we will see in more detail in Chapter 2, for the past three centuries international relations has been organized around the principle of sovereignty. States, the principal actors in international relations, are seen as **sovereign,** that is, as political units that do not recognize a higher authority. The right of **sovereignty** has a correlative duty: **nonintervention,** the principle that other states are obliged not to interfere in matters that are essentially within the domestic jurisdiction of sovereign states. Human rights, which typically involve a state's treatment of its own citizens in its own territory, were thus excluded from international scrutiny.

In the nineteenth and early twentieth centuries, the European Great Powers and the United States did occasionally intervene in the Ottoman and Chinese empires to rescue nationals caught in situations of civil strife or to establish or protect special rights and privileges for Europeans and Americans. Rarely, though, did they intervene to protect foreign nationals from their own government. In fact, human rights were seldom even a topic of diplomatic discussion. Likewise, the "humanitarian law" of war, expressed in documents such as the 1907 Hague Conventions, limited only what a state could do to *foreign* nationals, not the ways a state treated its own nationals (or peoples over whom it exercised colonial rule).

The principal exception was the nineteenth-century antislavery campaign. As early as the Congress of Vienna in 1815, major powers recognized an obligation to abolish the slave trade. At the Brussels Conference of 1890, a comprehensive treaty to abolish the slave trade was finally concluded. But even slavery (as opposed to international trade in slaves) was treated as largely an internal matter. A major international treaty to abolish slavery was not drafted until 1926.

After World War I, the International Labor Organization (ILO) began to deal with some workers' rights. In addition, the League of Nations was given limited powers to protect ethnic minorities in areas where boundaries had been altered following the war.[1] With these marginal exceptions, before World War II broke out in 1939, human rights had not been a topic of international relations. In assessing current international human rights activity, we must keep in mind this starting point.

THE EMERGENCE OF
INTERNATIONAL HUMAN RIGHTS NORMS

Often a problem becomes a subject of international action only after a dramatic event crystallizes awareness. For example, the discovery of the Antarctic ozone hole contributed significantly to the recent upsurge of international environmental action. The catalyst that made human rights an issue in world politics was the Holocaust, the systematic murder of millions of innocent civilians by Germany during World War II.

The human rights record of the victorious Allies was anything but exemplary. Before the war, and in its early days when action was still possible, little was done to aid Jews trying to escape from Germany and the surrounding countries. In fact, some who were able to flee were denied refuge by Allied governments, including the United States. During the war, no effort was made to impede the functioning of the death camps, let alone rescue their victims. For example, the Allies did not even bomb the railway lines that brought hundreds of thousands to the slaughter at Auschwitz. The world watched—or, rather, turned a blind eye to—the genocidal massacre of six million Jews and a half million Gypsies, and the deaths of tens of thousands of Communists, social democrats, homosexuals, church activists, and just ordinary decent people who refused complicity in the new politics and technology of barbarism.

Only as the war came to an end were Allied leaders and citizens, previously concerned exclusively with military victory, willing to begin to confront this horror. But when people dealt with the Holocaust in international organizations, they were forced to face it armed only with their moral sensibilities. As we have seen, international law and diplomacy before the war had not addressed human rights.

The first step in filling this void came with the Nuremberg War Crimes Trials (1945–1946), at which leading Nazis were prosecuted under the novel charge of crimes against humanity. Many have seen this as ex post facto prosecution, punishment for acts that although clearly immoral were not legally prohibited at the time they were committed. The process also had the appearance of bias: losers were punished, but there was no inquiry into the crimes of the winners. Nonetheless, Nuremberg was an important step toward international action against human rights violations.

Human rights really emerged as a standard subject of international relations, though, in the United Nations (UN). The Covenant of the League of Nations did not mention human rights. The Preamble of the Charter of the United Nations, by contrast, includes a determination "to reaffirm faith in fundamental human rights." Article 1 lists "encouraging respect for human rights and for fundamental freedoms for all" as one of the organization's principal purposes. And the United Nations moved quickly to elaborate strong international human rights standards.

On December 9, 1948, the Convention on the Prevention and Punishment of the Crime of Genocide was opened for signature (see Box 1.1). On the following day, the General Assembly unanimously adopted the **Universal Declaration of Human Rights,**[2] the 1948 General Assembly resolution that provides the most authoritative statement of international human rights norms. This vital document is reprinted as the Appendix, and its main provisions are included in Table 1.1. Most countries celebrate December 10, the anniversary of its adoption, as Human Rights Day.

FROM COLD WAR TO COVENANTS

The rise of the **cold war,** the ideological and geopolitical struggle between the United States and the Soviet Union, brought this initial progress to a halt. After the descent of the Iron Curtain in Central and Eastern Europe in 1948, and the final Communist victory in China in 1949, human rights became just one more area of superpower struggle. For example, in the late 1950s the United Nations Commission on Human Rights, which was under Western (U.S.) control, extensively discussed the right to free-

BOX 1.1   Treaties as a Source of International Law

Law-making treaties such as the 1948 Genocide Convention and the 1966 International Human Rights Covenants typically are drafted by an international organization or conference and then presented to states for their consideration—or, as international lawyers put it, they are "opened for signature and ratification." Neither the drafting of a treaty nor its approval by the United Nations or another international organization gives it legal effect. For a treaty to be binding, it must be accepted by sovereign states. And it is binding only on those states that have formally and voluntarily accepted it.

Signing a treaty is a declaration by a state that it intends to be bound by the treaty. That obligation, however, only becomes effective after the treaty has been *ratified* or acceded to according to the constitutional procedures of that country. (In the United States, the president signs a treaty and then transmits it to the Senate for ratification, for which a two-thirds vote is required.) States that have ratified or acceded to a treaty are said to be *parties* to the treaty. Typically a specified number of states must become parties before the treaty becomes binding. When sufficient ratifications have been filed, the treaty is said to enter into force.

dom of information (a right that the Soviets systematically violated) but completely ignored all economic and social rights, as well as most other particular civil and political rights. Conversely, the Soviets tried to focus attention on racial discrimination in the United States and unemployment throughout the capitalist West. Although each side pointed to serious violations, the superpowers rarely raised those issues out of an independent concern for human rights. Rather, charges of human rights violations were tactical maneuvers in a broader political and ideological struggle.

Furthermore, the international political practice of both superpowers regularly revealed a flagrant disregard for human rights. For example, in Guatemala in 1954 the United States overthrew the freely elected government of Jacobo Arbenz Guzmán, in part because of its redistributive policies that aimed to better implement economic and social rights. This ushered in thirty years of military rule that culminated in the systematic massacre of tens of thousands of Guatemalans by the armed forces and by semiofficial death squads in the early 1980s. Elsewhere as well, the United States not only tolerated gross and systematic violations of human rights in "friendly" (anticommunist) countries but often warmly embraced the responsible regimes. Likewise, the Soviets not merely embraced and encouraged, but forcibly insisted upon, one-party totalitarian dictatorships. For example, in 1956, Soviet tanks rolled into Hungary to put an end to liberal political reforms and (re)impose a totalitarian dictatorship.

TABLE 1.1   Internationally Recognized Human Rights

The International Bill of Human Rights recognizes the rights to:
  Equality of rights without discrimination (D1, D2, E2, E3, C2, C3)
  Life (D3, C6)
  Liberty and security of person (D3, C9)
  Protection against slavery (D4, C8)
  Protection against torture and cruel and inhuman punishment (D5, C7)
  Recognition as a person before the law (D6, C16)
  Equal protection of the law (D7, C14, C26)
  Access to legal remedies for rights violations (D8, C2)
  Protection against arbitrary arrest or detention (D9, C9)
  Hearing before an independent and impartial judiciary (D10, C14)
  Presumption of innocence (D11, C14)
  Protection against ex post facto laws (D11, C15)
  Protection of privacy, family, and home (D12, C17)
  Freedom of movement and residence (D13, C12)
  Seek asylum from persecution (D14)
  Nationality (D15)
  Marry and found a family (D16, E10, C23)
  Own property (D17)
  Freedom of thought, conscience, and religion (D18, C18)
  Freedom of opinion, expression, and the press (D19, C19)
  Freedom of assembly and association (D20, C21, C22)
  Political participation (D21, C25)
  Social security (D22, E9)
  Work, under favorable conditions (D23, E6, E7)
  Free trade unions (D23, E8, C22)
  Rest and leisure (D24, E7)
  Food, clothing, and housing (D25, E11)
  Health care and social services (D25, E12)
  Special protections for children (D25, E10, C24)
  Education (D26, E13, E14)
  Participation in cultural life (D27, E15)
  A social and international order needed to realize rights (D28)
  Self-determination (E1, C1)
  Humane treatment when detained or imprisoned (C10)
  Protection against debtor's prison (C11)
  Protection against arbitrary expulsion of aliens (C13)
  Protection against advocacy of racial or religious hatred (C20)
  Protection of minority culture (C27)

NOTE: This list includes all rights that are enumerated in two of the three documents of the International Bill of Human Rights or have a full article in one document. The source of each right is indicated in parentheses, by document and article number. D = Universal Declaration of Human Rights. E = International Covenant on Economic, Social, and Cultural Rights. C = International Covenant on Civil and Political Rights.

Although at the United Nations there was continued discussion of human rights, the momentum of the immediate postwar years was not sustained. The Universal Declaration of Human Rights is a resolution of the UN General Assembly, not a treaty. As such, it is not binding in international law (see Box 1.2). In fact, according to the text of the declaration, it is "a standard of achievement." Its drafters intended to follow the declaration with a treaty, or covenant, that would give human rights binding force in international law. Although drafting was largely complete by 1953, the covenant was tabled for more than a decade, primarily because of ideological rivalry over the status of economic and social rights. This stalemate aptly symbolizes the situation in the 1950s and early 1960s.

Decolonization was the principal exception to the pattern of UN ineffectiveness in the field of human rights after 1948. In 1945, when the United Nations was founded, most of Africa and Asia were Western colonial possessions. The process of decolonization that began in 1947 with the independence of Indonesia and India accelerated dramatically in Africa in the late 1950s and 1960s. As a result, UN membership doubled in barely a decade, and the character of the organization changed significantly.

By the mid-1960s, Afro-Asian states formed the largest voting bloc in the UN. These countries, which had suffered under colonial rule, had a special interest in human rights issues. They found a sympathetic hearing from some Western European and Latin American countries. The UN thus again began to give priority to human rights questions. For example, in 1965 the International Convention on the Elimination of All Forms of Racial Discrimination was opened for signature and ratification.

The **International Human Rights Covenants** were finally completed in December 1966. (In deference to the lingering cold war—particularly the desires of the United States—the single treaty envisioned in 1948 was broken into two, the International Covenant on Economic, Social, and Cultural Rights and the International Covenant on Civil and Political Rights.) The Covenants, together with the Universal Declaration, represent an authoritative statement of international human rights norms, standards of behavior to which all states should aspire. These three documents, which are sometimes referred to collectively as the **International Bill of Human Rights,** present a summary statement of the minimum social and political guarantees internationally recognized as necessary for a life of dignity in the contemporary world. They are listed in Table 1.1.

The Covenants, however, mark the high point of the UN's standards-setting work. Because of their very comprehensiveness, further major progress in international action on behalf of human rights would have to come primarily in the area of implementing (or monitoring the implementation of) these standards.

BOX 1.2   Sources of International Law

The two main sources of international law are treaties and custom. Other sources—for example, the writings of publicists, general principles of law recognized in the domestic law of most states, national and international judicial decisions, or *jus cogens* (overriding international norms, very much like the classical idea of the natural law)—are either of lesser importance or their status is a matter of controversy.

Treaties are essentially contractual agreements of states to accept certain specified obligations. The process by which treaties become binding is briefly discussed in Box 1.1.

Customary rules of international law are well-established state practices to which a sense of obligation has come to be attached. One classic example often used in teaching international law in the United States is the case of *The Scotia*. The U.S. Supreme Court decided in 1871 that it had become a binding customary practice of the international law of the sea that ships show colored running lights in a pattern originally specified by Great Britain, and the court awarded damages on the basis of this unwritten, customary law. In the area of human rights, a U.S. District Court held in the 1980 case of *Filartiga v. Peña-Irala,* brought by the family of a Paraguayan torture victim, that torture was a violation of customary international law.

Some lawyers have argued that the Universal Declaration of Human Rights has, over time, become a part of customary international law, or at least strong evidence of custom. Even if this is true, the Universal Declaration per se does not establish international legal obligations. That task was reserved by its drafters for a later treaty, which was ultimately adopted by the UN General Assembly in 1966, and entered into force in 1976.

THE 1970s: FROM STANDARD SETTING TO MONITORING

It might seem that the existence of international norms such as those in the Universal Declaration would give the United Nations authority to inquire into how states implemented (or did not implement) them. In fact, though, states agreed only that they ought to follow international human rights standards. They most definitely did *not* agree to let the UN investigate their compliance with these standards.

This began to change in the late 1960s. In 1967, Economic and Social Council Resolution 1235 authorized the Commission on Human Rights to discuss human rights violations in particular countries. In 1968, a Special Committee of Investigation was created to consider human rights in the territories occupied by Israel after the 1967 war. In the same year, the Security Council imposed a mandatory blockade on the white minority regime in Southern Rhodesia. The 1965 racial discrimination convention, which requires parties to file periodic reports on implementation, came into force in 1969. And in 1970 Economic and Social Council Resolution 1503 authorized the Commission on Human Rights to conduct confidential investigations of communications (that is, complaints) that suggested "a consistent pattern of gross and reliably attested violations of human rights and fundamental freedoms." This was called the 1503 Procedure.

Each of these efforts was limited or partial. Little of substance has been achieved through the 1503 Procedure, and the implementation provisions of the racial discrimination convention are extremely weak (see Chapter 4). The initiatives in Southern Africa and the Occupied Territories largely reflected the special political concerns of the newly dominant Afro-Asian bloc. Even Resolution 1235 qualified its application to "all countries" by stipulating a special concern with racial discrimination and colonialism. Optimists could argue that these developments provided precedents for stronger action. Their significance, though, was largely symbolic: the UN was at last beginning to move, however tentatively, from merely setting standards to examining, or monitoring, how those standards were implemented by states.

Modest monitoring progress continued in the 1970s. For example, the 1973 military coup in Chile, which removed the elected government of Salvador Allende and launched a brutal reign of terror that left Chile under repressive military rule for more than fifteen years (see Chapter 3), led the UN to create an Ad Hoc Working Group on the Situation of Human Rights in Chile. In 1976, the International Human Rights Covenants entered into force; that is, following the ratification of thirty-five states, the Covenants became binding legal obligations for those states.

However tentative, even timid, these new initiatives were, they came in an environment of severe structural constraints. The United Nations is an intergovernmental organization, established by a treaty (the UN Charter) among sovereign states. Its members are sovereign states. Delegates to the United Nations represent states, not the international community, let alone those individuals whose rights are violated by states. And the UN, like other intergovernmental organizations, has only those powers that states, the principal violators of human rights, give it. Its limited powers in the field of human rights are thus easily explained.

What is more surprising, or at least historically unprecedented, is that the UN actually did acquire these monitoring powers, however limited they are. For victims of human rights violations, this is of little comfort, more an explanation than a justification. Nonetheless, in evaluating the human rights achievements of the UN and other intergovernmental organizations, it would be naive, perhaps even irresponsible, to ignore the basic fact of sovereignty and the limits it imposes.

The 1970s also saw human rights explicitly introduced into the bilateral foreign policies of individual countries, beginning in the United States. U.S. foreign policy throughout the postwar period had used the language of democracy, with the United States presenting itself as the leader and defender of the "Free World." In some cases, rhetoric had been matched by reality, most notably in U.S. support for European reconstruction after World War II and for decolonization in Africa. More often, the rhetoric had meant no more than support for avowedly anticommunist regimes, irrespective of their human rights practices.

In the 1970s, human rights began to make some headway in U.S. foreign policy. In 1973, Congress recommended linking U.S. foreign aid to the human rights practices of recipient countries. In 1975 this linkage was made mandatory: U.S. foreign aid policy was required to take into account (although not necessarily be determined by) the human rights practices of recipient countries. Such legislation was both nationally and internationally unprecedented. When Jimmy Carter became president in 1977, the U.S. executive branch also became generally supportive of pursuing human rights in foreign policy. Although practice still often fell short of rhetoric, these initial American initiatives helped to open the way for new ways of thinking and new bilateral and multilateral policies (see Chapter 5).

The 1970s was also the decade in which human rights **nongovernmental organizations (NGOs),** private associations that engage in political activity, emerged as a notable international political force, as symbolized by the award of the Nobel Peace Prize to Amnesty International in 1977. Such groups typically act as advocates for victims of human rights violations by publicizing violations and lobbying to alter the practices of states and international organizations.

For example, Amnesty International (AI), which was founded in 1961 and had an international membership of more than 1 million people by the end of 1990, publishes an annual report, special reports on individual countries, and occasional reports on torture and other general issues of concern. Its representatives testify before national legislatures and intergovernmental organizations and publicize human rights issues through public statements and appearances in the media. AI's best known activity is its letter-writing campaigns on behalf of individual prisoners of conscience, people incarcerated for their beliefs or nonviolent political activities. In 1990, Amnesty International was active on behalf of some 3,000 prisoners, and in its first thirty years of operation, AI adopted or investigated the cases of over 42,000 individual prisoners.

The private status of human rights NGOs allows them to operate free of the political control of states. And unlike even states with active international human rights policies, human rights NGOs do not have broader foreign policy concerns that may conflict with their human rights objectives. As a result, they often are better able to press the issue of human rights violations. NGOs, however, must rely on the power of publicity and persuasion. They lack the resources of even weak states. States remain free to be unpersuaded. And many states have used their powers of coercion against the members of human rights NGOs, turning them into new victims.

One of the first important contributions of human rights NGOs was to help to legitimize international concern with human rights. Lobbying by nongovernmental organizations helped to assure that human rights language was included in the United Nations Charter. Since then, NGOs have become regular, active, and occasionally influential participants in the human rights work of the UN. For example, national and international lobbying by Amnesty International played an important role in UN initiatives on torture in the 1970s and 1980s.

NGOs have also helped to incorporate concern for human rights into the foreign policies of individual countries. For example, the Dutch section of Amnesty International was involved in the drafting of the 1979 White Paper that made human rights a formal part of the foreign policy of the Netherlands. In the United States, AI has been especially active on Capitol Hill, lobbying, testifying, and providing information and support to sympathetic members of Congress and their staffs. Furthermore, national human rights NGOs have been involved in the domestic politics of a large number of states.

In the mid- and late 1970s, both the number of human rights NGOs and the level of their activity increased dramatically. For example, in the United States the American Association for the Advancement of Science established a Clearinghouse for Persecuted Scientists in 1977, and in 1978 the International Human Rights Law Group was created and the Lawyers Committee for Human Rights began operating. Older groups were reinvigorated, such as France's International League for the Rights of Man. By the late 1970s, about 200 U.S. NGOs dealt in some way with international human rights. There was roughly the same number in the United Kingdom (UK). Thus in addition to states and intergovernmental organizations, private groups (NGOs) had become significant international actors on behalf of human rights.

THE 1980s: FURTHER GROWTH
AND INSTITUTIONALIZATION

Multilateral, bilateral, and nongovernmental human rights activity continued to increase, more or less steadily, through the 1980s. Several important normative instruments were completed by the United Nations. In

December 1979, the Convention on the Elimination of Discrimination Against Women was opened for signature and ratification. This wide-ranging treaty, addressing systematic discrimination against half the population of the globe, in every country of the world, was the first major human rights treaty to emerge from the UN since the Covenants in 1966. The Convention Against Torture and Other Cruel, Inhuman or Degrading Treatment or Punishment was opened for signature in 1984. The General Assembly adopted a Declaration on the Right to Development in 1986. The decade came to a close with the Convention on the Rights of the Child in November 1989.

In the area of monitoring, the Human Rights Committee began to review periodic reports submitted under the International Covenant on Civil and Political Rights. The Commission on Human Rights undertook "thematic" initiatives on disappearances, torture, and summary or arbitrary executions. The Committee on Economic, Social, and Cultural Rights was created in 1986 to improve reporting and monitoring in this important area. In addition, a larger and more diverse group of countries than had heretofore been the case came under public scrutiny in the Commission on Human Rights.

The process of incorporating human rights into bilateral foreign policy also accelerated in the 1980s. The Netherlands and Norway have had particularly prominent international human rights policies. A number of other European countries have also explicitly incorporated human rights into their foreign policies, as did Canada (see Chapter 5). Both the Council of Europe and the European Community have introduced human rights concerns into their external relations (see Chapter 4). A few Third World countries, such as Costa Rica, have also emphasized human rights in their foreign policies.

Perhaps more surprising was the persistence of the issue of human rights in U.S. foreign policy. Ronald Reagan campaigned for the presidency in 1980 against Carter's human rights policy, and his revival of the cold war against the Soviet "evil empire" led many people to fear (or hope) that human rights would again be forced to the sidelines, as it had been in the 1950s. U.S. international human rights policy did become less evenhanded and more contentious in the 1980s. Nonetheless, when George Bush took office in 1989, human rights had a secure (although hardly uncontroversial) and well-institutionalized place in U.S. foreign policy. The Bureau of Human Rights and Humanitarian Affairs was increasingly seen as an integral part of the State Department rather than as an unwanted intrusion, and regular, continuing action on behalf of international human rights had considerable bipartisan support in Congress.

The 1980s also saw a dramatic decline in the fortunes of repressive dictatorships. Throughout Latin America, military regimes that had appeared unshakable in the 1970s crumbled in the 1980s. By 1990, elected governments held office in every continental country in the Western Hemisphere (although the democratic credentials of some, such as Paraguay, remained extremely suspect). In addition, there were peaceful transfers of power after elections in several countries, including Argentina, Brazil, El Salvador, and Uruguay in 1989, Nicaragua in 1990, and Guatemala in 1991.

Even more striking changes occurred in Central and Eastern Europe. Soviet-imposed regimes in East Germany and Czechoslovakia crumbled in the fall of 1989 in the face of peaceful mass popular protests. In Hungary and Poland, where liberalization had begun earlier in the decade, Communist party dictatorships also peacefully withdrew from power. Even Romania and Bulgaria ousted their old Communist governments (although their new governments include numerous old Communists with tenuous democratic credentials). In the USSR, where *glasnost* (openness) and *perestroika* (restructuring) had created the international political space for these changes, the Communist party fell from power after the abortive military coup of August 1991, and the Soviet Union was dissolved four months later.

In Asia, the personalist dictatorship of Ferdinand Marcos was overthrown in the Philippines in 1986. South Korea's military dictatorship was replaced by an elected government in 1988. Taiwan moved from a one-party state to something approximating a multiparty democracy. After the death of General Zia in Pakistan, Benazir Bhutto was elected president, in December 1988, ending a dozen years of military rule. In Bangladesh, competitive elections led to a peaceful transfer of power in February 1991.

Asia, however, also presented the most dramatic human rights setback of the decade, the June 1989 massacre in Beijing's Tienanmen Square. With peaceful protest violently repressed and even modest liberalization foreclosed, the People's Republic of China (PRC) has forcefully reaffirmed the continuing vitality of Stalinist totalitarianism in one country. Popular pressures for democratization also seem to have been defeated by military repression in Burma. In North Korea, there was not even the temporary liberalization of the Tienanmen Spring. Only modest liberalization took place in Vietnam (although that country did withdraw its troops from Cambodia, which it had occupied for almost a decade) and Indonesia. A military coup ended Thailand's most recent experiment with democratic civilian rule in 1992. In the Philippines, human rights violations increased significantly in 1990 and 1991.

Dictatorial governments in Sub-Saharan Africa had largely escaped the initial wave of democratization in the 1980s. By the end of the decade, though, Africa too was touched by a wave of liberalization. South Africa began significant steps toward liberalization in 1989; the last vestiges of official apartheid were eliminated in 1991; and the March 1992 plebiscite seems to have decisively closed the door on official racial separation and domination. Furthermore, liberalization and democratization came to many of the countries of black Africa in the early 1990s, in contrast to the one-party and no-party states that were the norm in the 1970s and 1980s.

Opposition parties won open, multiparty elections in São Tomé and Príncipe in January 1991 and in Cape Verde in February 1991. In March 1991, Benin's Nicephore Soglo became the first candidate in the history of mainland Africa to defeat an incumbent president in a democratic election. Even more dramatic was the November 1991 defeat of Kenneth Kaunda, Zambia's president for the first quarter century of its independence.

In fall of 1990, however, contested elections in the Ivory Coast (Côte d'Ivoire) and Gabon were marred by massive official fraud. In a number of other countries, such as Kenya and Zaire, popular pressures for liberalization have so far been successfully resisted. And even where political change or liberalization has taken place, both its depth and its persistence usually remain questionable. For example, the latter half of 1991 in Togo was marked by a series of inconclusive attempted coups by the forces of former-dictator Gnassingbe Eyadema. Nonetheless, political space opened in most of the countries of Africa for the first time in one, two, or even three decades.

The Middle East, however, presents an almost universally discouraging regional human rights picture. Iran and Iraq fought and finally concluded an extraordinarily vicious and costly war, but peace has brought little or no reduction in repression. A cynic might even suggest that all it did was allow Saddam Hussein to turn his rapacious sights on the apparently easier target of Kuwait. Hafiz al-Assad's dictatorial rule continues in Syria, where the massacre of tens of thousands of civilians in the town of Hama in 1982 was one of the most brutal acts of internal repression anywhere in the world during the entire decade. The Gulf States, including recently liberated Kuwait, remain as closed and undemocratic as ever. And the Palestinian *intifada*, the uprising against Israeli occupation that began in December 1987, has led to greater Israeli violations of Palestinian human rights and greater internal pressure on Israeli democracy.

Despite these limits, though, the 1980s and early 1990s have established new expectations, both nationally and internationally, and created new problems and opportunities for international human rights activity. We will return to this new context in the final chapter of this book.

TWO

□ □ □

Theories of Human Rights

The preceding chapter provided a brief overview of some of the more important developments in international human rights over the past fifty years. This chapter addresses several theoretical issues connected with human rights. We begin with philosophical theories of human rights. We then turn to the theory of international relations and the place of human rights in the international society of states. Finally, we look at two theoretical challenges to the entire enterprise of international human rights policies, namely, political realism and cultural relativism.

THE NATURE OF HUMAN RIGHTS

The very term **human rights** indicates both their nature and their source: they are the rights that one has simply because one is human. They are held by all human beings, irrespective of any rights or duties one may (or may not) have as citizens, members of families, workers, or parts of any public or private organization or association. In the language of the 1948 declaration, they are universal rights.

If all human beings have them simply because they are human, human rights are held equally by all.[1] And because being human cannot be renounced, lost or forfeited, human rights are inalienable. Even the cruelest torturer and the most debased victim are still human beings. In practice, not all people *enjoy* all their human rights, let alone enjoy them equally. Nonetheless, all human beings *have* the same human rights and hold them equally and inalienably.

What exactly does it mean to have a right? In English, "right" has two principal moral and political senses. "Right" may refer to what *is* right, the right thing to do. Thus we say that it is right to help the needy or wrong (the opposite of right) to lie, cheat, or steal. "Right" may also refer to a special entitlement that one has to something. In this sense we speak of having, claiming, exercising, enforcing, and violating rights.[2] There are many things to which people do not *have* a (human) right that it would nevertheless *be* right for every human being to have or enjoy, for example, to be treated with consideration and respect by strangers, or to have the chance to develop one's artistic abilities.

Both rights and considerations of righteousness create relations between people who have a duty and people who are owed or benefit from that duty. Rights, however, involve a special set of social institutions, rules, or practices. Rights place right-holders and duty-bearers in a relationship that is largely under the control of the right-holder, who ordinarily may exercise her right more or less as she sees fit. Furthermore, claims of rights ordinarily take priority over ("trump") other kinds of demands, such as utility or righteousness.

Rights do not have absolute priority over other considerations. They do, however, ordinarily take prima facie priority. Right-holders do not have absolute discretion in how they exercise their rights. Discretionary exercise, however, is a central and distinguishing feature of rights. In fact, the power and control of rights in ordinary circumstances are precisely what makes them so valuable to right-holders.

Human rights are a special type of right. In their most fundamental sense, they are paramount moral rights. In the preceding chapter we saw that human rights are also recognized in international law. Most countries also recognize many of these rights in their national constitution, legislation, or legal practice. As a result, the same "thing"—for example, food, protection against discrimination, or freedom of association—often is guaranteed by several different types of rights.

One "needs" *human* rights principally when they are not effectively guaranteed by national law and practice. If one can secure food, equal treatment, or free association through national legal processes, one is unlikely to advance human rights claims. One still has those human rights, but they are not likely to be used (as human rights). For example, in the United States racial discrimination is prohibited by both constitutional and statutory law. Protection against discrimination on the basis of sexual preference is much less clearly established in most jurisdictions. Therefore, gay rights activists claim a human right to nondiscrimination with considerable frequency. Racial minorities, by contrast, more often claim legal and constitutional rights—"civil rights."

The language of human rights is fundamentally that of the oppressed or dispossessed. The principal use of human rights claims is to challenge or seek to alter national legal or political practices. Claims of human rights thus aim to be self-liquidating. To assert one's human rights is to attempt to change political structures and practices in ways that will make it no longer necessary to claim those rights (as human rights). For example, the struggle for human rights in South Africa has been a struggle to change South African laws and practices so that average South Africans would no longer need to claim human rights. Rather, they would be able to turn to the South African legislature, courts, or bureaucracy should they be denied, for example, equal protection of the laws, political participation, or health care.

Human rights thus provide a moral standard of national political legitimacy. Chapter 1 suggested that they are also emerging as an international political standard of legitimacy. Only when citizens no longer need to assert their human rights regularly against their government is that government likely to be considered legitimate in the contemporary world.

THE SOURCE OR JUSTIFICATION OF HUMAN RIGHTS

How does being human give rise to rights? To answer this question we need a theory of human nature. Although I despair of being able to offer such a theory, I can point out some basic distinctions that provide useful insights.

A theory of human nature deals with how we define, or what it means to be, human. In a very crude way, we can say that a scientific approach to human nature involves an empirical investigation of the psychobiological makeup of human beings. A moral or philosophical approach focuses on what it means to be a person, a *human* being capable of reflective action and subject to the constraints of morality. Although moral theories of human nature may be constrained or even partially determined by scientific theories, they address different issues.

Those who seek to ground human rights in a scientific theory of human nature usually speak of basic human needs. Unfortunately, any list of needs that can make a plausible claim to be scientifically (empirically) established provides a clearly inadequate list of human rights: life, food, protection against cruel or inhuman treatment, and not much else. Whether because of contingent failings in our current scientific procedures or knowledge, or because science is in principle incapable of providing an appropriate theory of human nature, few specific human rights can be grounded in the psychological, physiological, and biochemical sciences. We have human rights not to what we need for health but to what we need for human dignity.

A social-scientific or anthropological approach that seeks to ground human rights on cross-cultural consensus faces problems that are just as serious. History is replete with examples of societies based on hierarchies of birth, gender, wealth, or power. Likewise, many cultures have sanctioned slavery, infanticide, blood feuds, and the execution of dissidents. In U.S. history one can point to systematic torture and execution of religious deviants (witches); enslavement of and then legal discrimination against African Americans; denial of political participation, property rights, and even legal personality to women; and repression of political dissidents (especially Communists).

The human nature that is the source of human rights rests on a moral account of human possibility. It indicates what human beings might become rather than what they have been, or even what they "are" in some scientifically determinable sense. Human rights rest on an account of a life of dignity to which human beings are "by nature" suited and the kind of person worthy of and entitled to such a life. And if the rights specified by the underlying theory of human nature are implemented and enforced, they should help to bring into being the envisioned type of person. The effective implementation of human rights should thus result in a self-fulfilling moral prophecy.

Unfortunately, no philosophical theory of human nature has ever achieved widespread acceptance. Consensus is no measure of truth. Without it, however, any particular theory—and any international action based on it—is vulnerable to attack. The problem is even more severe when we consider that many moral theories, and their underlying theories of human nature, deny the very existence of human rights.

For example, Marxism explains moral beliefs and doctrines in terms of class structure and struggle, which are determined by the means and mode of production. Radical behaviorists see human personality as the result of conditioning. In both cases, "human nature" is the result of historical processes that shape human beings into socially prescribed molds, rather than the reflection of an inherent essence or potential. For adherents of either theory, it is pointless to speak of equal and inalienable rights held by all people simply because they are human. "Simply because they are human" probably makes no sense to Marxists or behaviorists. It certainly has so substantive moral implications.

Utilitarianism, which achieved its classic formulations in the works of Jeremy Bentham and John Stuart Mill in the first half of the nineteenth century, is also fundamentally at odds with human rights. Utilitarians hold that the moral quality of an act is a function of its good or bad consequences (utility). Good and bad, in turn, are a matter of pleasure and pain (which utilitarians usually define in very subtle and expansive ways). The principle of utility, or what Bentham called the greatest happiness principle, requires us to act so as to maximize the balance of pleasure over pain. For a utilitarian, statements about human rights are at most a convenient shorthand for noting the tendency of certain acts to produce pleasure or pain, a practical convenience to save us the bother of calculating utilities.

Furthermore, any moral or political theory that places extreme emphasis on the differences between moral communities is also likely to be incompatible with the idea of human rights. For example, during the classical Greek period, Hellenic peoples considered themselves to be inherently superior to "barbarians" (non-Greeks), who were not entitled to the same treatment as Greeks. The American notion of manifest destiny or the British colonial ideology of the white man's burden justified barbarous treatment of nonwhite peoples on the grounds of the superior virtue or moral development of Americans or Englishmen. Nazi Germany provides an even more extreme version of the denial of rights to "inferior races" on grounds of moral and political superiority.

There are also, of course, a variety of bases for justifying human rights. For example, human rights have often been held to be given to human beings by God. A classic example is John Locke's *Second Treatise of Government*, which was published immediately after the English revolution of 1688 and is often seen as the first major work in the history of political thought based on a conception of natural (or, as we would say today, human) rights. Many contemporary Catholic and Protestant theologians similarly ground human rights in natural law or divine donation.

Human rights might also be seen as a political specification of Immanuel Kant's **categorical imperative.** In his *Grounding for the Metaphysics of Morals,* first published in 1785, Kant argued that there is one supreme principle of morality, namely, the duty to treat people as ends, never as means only. This duty, or imperative, Kant argued, is categorical; that is, it holds at all times, in all places, without exception. A list of human rights can be seen as a political specification of what it means to treat all human beings as ends.

Alan Gewirth has recently presented a theory based on the premise that we have human rights to those things that are necessary in order to act as a moral agent.[3] Human rights might also be seen as a political specification of the social practices necessary to human flourishing and a life of virtue. In my own work I have tried to give an account of human rights as the social and political guarantees necessary to protect individuals from the standard threats to human dignity posed by the modern state and modern markets.[4]

We thus have a considerable variety of possible moral justifications for human rights, as well as a no-less-considerable array of theories that deny or radically devalue the very idea of human rights. In what follows I will assume that there are human rights, that we have accepted some sort of philosophical defense. Whatever the theoretical problems posed by this assumption, the fact that almost all states do acknowledge the existence of human rights makes the assumption sufficient for studying international human rights.

LISTS OF HUMAN RIGHTS

Despite the absence of philosophical consensus, there is, as we saw in the preceding chapter, an international *political* consensus on the list of rights in the Universal Declaration of Human Rights and the International Human Rights Covenants (see Table 1.1 and the Appendix). This consensus can also draw theoretical support from the fact that it can be derived from a plausible and attractive philosophical account, namely, the requirement that the state treat each person with equal concern and respect.[5] Consider the Universal Declaration of Human Rights.

One must be recognized as a person (Universal Declaration, Article 6) in order to be treated with any sort of concern or respect. Personal rights to nationality and to recognition before the law, along with rights to life and to protection against slavery, torture, and other inhuman or degrading practices can be seen as legal and political prerequisites to recognition and thus respect (Articles 3, 4, 5, 15). Rights to equal protection of the laws and protection against racial, sexual, and other forms of discrimination are essential to *equal* respect (Articles 1, 2, 7).

Equal respect for all persons will be at most a hollow formality without personal autonomy, the freedom to choose and act on one's own ideas of the good life. Freedoms of speech, conscience, religion, and association, along with the right to privacy, guarantee a private sphere of personal autonomy (Articles 12, 18–20). The rights to education and to participate in the cultural life of the community provide a social dimension to the idea of personal autonomy (Articles 26, 27). The rights to vote and to freedom of speech, press, assembly, and association guarantee political autonomy (Articles 18–21).

Rights to food, health care, and social insurance (Article 25) are also needed to make equal concern and respect a practical reality rather than a mere formal possibility. The right to work is a right to economic participation very similar to the right to political participation (Article 23). A (limited) right to property may also be justified in such terms (Article 17).

Finally, the special threat to personal security and equality posed by the modern state requires legal rights to constrain the state and its functionaries. These include rights to be presumed innocent until proven guilty, due process, fair and public hearings before an independent tribunal, and protection from arbitrary arrest, detention, or exile (Articles 8–

11). Anything less would mean that the state may treat citizens with differential concern or respect.

The idea of equal concern and respect certainly is philosophically controversial. It does, however, have a certain inherent plausibility. It is closely related to the basic fact that human rights are equal and inalienable. It even offers an attractive interpretation of the common claim that human rights derive from the inherent dignity of the human person.

There are also powerful practical reasons for taking seriously the list of human rights in the Universal Declaration and the Covenants. To act internationally on the basis of a different list would risk the charge of imposing one's own biased preferences, as opposed to widely accepted international standards. It is thus not surprising that almost all states have explicitly endorsed this list—whatever their actual practices may be.

There have been two principal exceptions in recent years. Some fundamentalist Muslim states have denounced the principle of not making legal and political distinctions on the basis of sex. Such objections raise issues of cultural relativism that will be considered in general theoretical terms below. In addition, many Western, and especially U.S., conservatives have questioned the status of economic, social, and cultural rights. Such objections in their strongest form involve a general claim that economic, social, and cultural rights "belong to a different logical category," that is, are not really *human* rights.[6]

Such critics argue that **economic, social, and cultural rights,** entitlements to socially provided goods and services such as food, health care, social insurance, and education, are less important than **civil and political rights,** such as due process, equal protection of the laws, freedom of speech, and the right to vote. The right to paid holidays (Universal Declaration, Article 24) is an often-cited example. This right certainly is far less important than, say, the right to life. But the full right recognized in the Universal Declaration—the right to "rest, leisure, and reasonable limitation of working hours and periodic holidays with pay"—is very important. Consider, for example, the horrors of sixty-hour work weeks, fifty-two weeks a year, in nineteenth-century factories, or twentieth-century "sweat shops" in the U.S. garment industry.

In addition, one can point to even more minor civil and political rights. For example, Article 10 of the International Covenant on Civil and Political Rights proclaims the right of juveniles to separate prison facilities. In every country of the world, far fewer people have suffered from penal confinement as juveniles in the company of adult criminals than from the denial of reasonable rest and leisure. In any case, the right to paid holidays is hardly the typical economic and social right. Consider, for example, the rights to food, housing, health care, work, and social security.

Arguments of practicality, which are often advanced against economic and social rights, are more complex. For example, Maurice Cranston argued that "there is nothing especially difficult about transforming political and civil rights into positive rights," but that in most countries it is "utterly impossible" to realize most economic and social rights.[7] The victims of repression in countries such as South Africa, Paraguay, Romania, and North Korea, however, have in fact found it extremely difficult to transform internationally recognized civil and political rights into effective rights in national law.

Conversely, many of the impediments to implementing economic and social rights are political. For example, there is already enough food in the world to feed every person. Universal implementation of the right to food would "only" require redistributing existing supplies. Of course, health care and social services at the level provided in much of Western Europe cannot be universally implemented. That level has yet to be reached even by the United States. Nonetheless, almost all countries can make major improvements in the realization of virtually all economic and social rights at relatively modest cost.

It is also often argued that there is a qualitative difference between "negative" civil and political rights and "positive" economic and social rights. Negative rights require only the forbearance of others to be realized. Violating a negative right thus involves actively causing harm, a sin of commission. Positive rights require that others provide active support. Violating a positive right involves only failing to provide assistance, a (presumably lesser) sin of omission.

All human rights, however, require both positive action and restraint by the state if they are to be effectively implemented. Some rights, of course, are relatively positive and others are relatively negative. But even this distinction does not correspond to that between civil and political and economic and social rights.

The (civil and political) right to vote requires extensive positive endeavors, not forbearance, on the part of the government. So do the rights to due process, trial by a jury of one's peers, and access to legal remedies for violations of basic rights. Even the right to nondiscrimination, which at first glance might seem to require nothing more than refraining from discriminating, in many cases requires extensive, difficult, and costly state intervention (e.g., affirmative action) if individuals are truly to be protected against discrimination. "Simply" refraining, or abstaining—or, more accurately, assuring that certain things are not done—often requires considerable work over an extended period of time. In fact, if it really were easy to abstain, the right in question probably would not be very important (at least in that context).

FIGURE 2.1 Leah Levin, *Human Rights: Questions & Answers* (Paris: UNESCO, 1981). Reprinted by permission of UNESCO Publishing.

The (social) right to marry and found a family is no less negative than the right to freedom of religion. The rights to participate in the cultural life of the community and to share in the benefits of science and technology are as negative (or as positive) as the right to nondiscrimination. The right to food often could be better implemented if governments would simply stop encouraging the production of cash crops for export. Arguments for the efficiency of markets imply that governmental restraint may contribute significantly to realizing economic and social rights.

The moral basis of the positive-negative distinction is also questionable. Does it really make a moral difference if one kills someone through neglect or by positive action? What if the neglect is knowing and willful? Consider, for example, leaving an injured man to die; refusing to implement relatively inexpensive health care or nutrition programs for needy and malnourished children; or the fact that a black infant in the United States is twice as likely to die as a white infant. The central moral issue, I would suggest, is the destructive impact on lives, not the means used to achieve it.

Another way to approach the question of the status of economic, social, and cultural rights is to ask what a life with only civil and political rights would look like. Without certain minimum economic and social guarantees, a life of dignity is clearly impossible, at least in modern market economies. Even strong conservatives in the Reagan administration stressed the importance of a "safety net" of economic and social rights for the "deserving poor."

Finally, we should note that most critics of economic and social rights effectively destroy their own arguments by defending a right to property. This is an *economic* right, not a civil and political right—and a rather extravagant economic right at that. Furthermore, the standard defenses of a right to property also support other economic and social rights. For example, rights to work and social insurance no less than a right to private property provide a sphere of personal economic security.

There are, of course, differences between economic and social rights and civil and political rights. But there are no less important differences within each broad class of rights, as well as important similarities across these classes. For example, we noted strong analogies between the civil and political rights that guarantee political participation and the economic participation guaranteed by the right to work. Likewise, the (civil and political) right to life and the (economic and social) right to food can be seen as different means to protect the same value.

HUMAN RIGHTS
AND THE SOCIETY OF STATES

Having surmounted, or at least disposed of, some of the more pressing philosophical questions, we can now turn to the place of human rights in the theory of international relations.

Sovereignty, Anarchy, and International Society

The modern international system is often dated, somewhat arbitrarily, to 1648, when the Treaty of Westphalia ended the Thirty Years' War. As we have seen, however, human rights has been an issue in international relations for less than fifty years (Chapter 1). It was no accident, though, that the issue of human rights was absent from modern international relations for its first three centuries. That was the direct result of a system of world order based on the sovereignty of territorial states.

To be sovereign is to be subject to no higher power. In other times and places, such as early modern Europe, sovereignty was a personal attribute of rulers. Elsewhere, as in medieval Europe, no (earthly) power was considered to be sovereign. In modern international relations states are sovereign.

International relations is structured around the legal fiction that states have exclusive jurisdiction over their territory, its occupants and resources, and the events that take place there. Practice typically falls far short of precept, as is usually the case with political principles. Nonetheless, most basic international norms, rules, and practices rest on the premise of state sovereignty. Even many characteristic violations of sovereignty, such as illegal interventions by powerful states, can be traced back to the absence of political power or legal authority above states that is the essence of sovereignty.

Nonintervention is the duty correlative to the right of sovereignty. Other states are obliged not to interfere with the internal actions of a sovereign state. A state's actions are a legitimate concern of other states only if those actions intrude on their sovereignty. Because human rights principally regulate the ways states treat their own citizens within their own territory, international human rights policies would seem to involve unjustifiable intervention.

A principal function of international law, however, is to overcome the initial presumption of sovereignty and nonintervention. A **treaty** is a contractual agreement by states to accept certain obligations to other states, that is, specified restrictions on their sovereignty. For example, a treaty of alliance may oblige a state to come to the aid of an ally that is attacked. In such cases, the state is no longer (legally) free to choose whether or not to go to war. Through the treaty, it has voluntarily relinquished a part of its sovereign freedom of action. International law is the record of restrictions on sovereignty accepted by states.

The centrality of sovereignty is simply another way of saying that international relations is anarchic, a political realm without hierarchical relations of authority and subordination. States are seen as formally equal sovereign entities, initially free of obligations to one another, interacting in the absence of higher political authority. But **anarchy,** the absence of hierarchical political rule, does not necessarily imply chaos, the absence of order. In addition to international law, states have established other means, such as the rules and procedures of diplomacy and the recognition of spheres of influence, to regulate their interactions. This body of formal and informal restrictions on the original sovereignty of states creates an international social order. International relations takes place within an anarchical society of states.[8] Although there is no international government, there is rule-governed social order.

The international society of states of the eighteenth, nineteenth, and early twentieth centuries typically gave punctilious respect to the sovereign prerogative of each state to treat its own citizens as it saw fit. As we saw in the preceding chapter, though, there is a substantial body of international human rights law. States have become increasingly vocal in expressing, and sometimes even acting on, their international human rights concerns. In addition, human rights NGOs, which seek to constrain the freedom of action of rights-violating states, have become more numerous and more active.

This reflects (and has helped to create) a transformed understanding of the place of the state and of individuals in international relations. States have traditionally been the sole subjects of international law. Only states have legal standing, the right to bring actions in international tribunals. The rights and interests of individuals traditionally could be protected only by states acting on their behalf. Even the International Bill of Human Rights does not empower individuals to act against states. Nonetheless, contemporary international human rights law, which is discussed in more detail in Chapter 4, has given individuals and their rights a place in international law and relations and has introduced a new conception of international legitimacy.

Traditionally, a government was considered legitimate if it exercised authority over its territory and accepted the international legal obligations that it and its predecessors had contracted. What it did at home was largely irrelevant. Today, however, human rights provide a standard of moral legitimacy that has been partially (although very incompletely) incorporated into the rules of the international society of states.

Consider the almost universal negative reaction to the Tienanmen massacre in 1989, when Chinese troops fired on unarmed student demonstrators and brutally crushed the PRC's emerging democracy movement. The resulting diplomatic isolation of the PRC reflected this new, human rights–based understanding of international political legitimacy. But China's isolation lasted only a year. The Bush administration did not let its concern over continuing repression stand in the way of more or less regular diplomatic relations, including special trading privileges for the PRC. Although human rights concerns can no longer be completely dismissed in the foreign policy of the United States and most other countries, such concerns have been only incompletely incorporated into contemporary international relations and usually remain subordinated to considerations of power and sovereignty.

This tension is characteristic of the current state of international human rights. The future of international human rights activity can be seen as a struggle over balancing the competing claims of sovereignty and international human rights and the competing conceptions of legitimacy that they imply.

Three Models of International Human Rights

The universality of human rights fits uncomfortably in a political order structured around sovereign states. Universal moral rights on their face seem better suited to a cosmopolitan conception of world politics, which sees individuals more as members of a single global political community ("cosmopolis") than as citizens of states. Instead of thinking of international relations (the relations between nation-states), a "cosmopolitan" thinks of a global political process in which individuals and other nonstate actors are important direct participants. We thus have three competing theoretical models of the place of human rights in international relations, each with its own conception of the international community and its role in international human rights.

The traditional **statist** model sees human rights as principally a matter of sovereign national jurisdiction. Contemporary statists certainly admit that human rights are no longer the exclusive preserve of states, and that the state is no longer the sole significant international actor, if it ever was. Statists nonetheless insist that human rights remain principally a matter of sovereign national jurisdiction and a largely peripheral concern of international (interstate) relations. For statists, there is no significant, independent international community. In particular, there is no international body with the right to act on behalf of human rights.

A **cosmopolitan** model starts with individuals rather than states, which are often "the problem" for cosmopolitans. Cosmopolitans focus on challenges to the state and its powers both from below, by individuals and NGOs, and from above, by the truly global community (not merely international organizations and other groupings of states). They often see international organizations, and even some transnational NGOs, as representatives of an inchoate global community of humankind above the society of states. International action on behalf of human rights is relatively unproblematic in such a model. In fact, cosmopolitans largely reverse the burden of proof, requiring justification for *non*intervention in the face of gross and persistent violations of human rights.

If the statist and cosmopolitan models lie at the end points of a continuum of international orders, the space toward the center of that continuum is occupied by what we can call **internationalist** models. Internationalists stress the evolving consensus (among states and nonstate actors alike) on international human rights norms. Without denying the continued centrality of states, internationalists focus attention on the international society of states, which imposes only limited restrictions on states.

The "international community," in an internationalist model, is essentially the society of states (supplemented by NGOs and individuals, to the extent that they have been formally or informally incorporated into international political processes). International human rights activity is permissible only to the extent authorized by the formal or informal norms of the international society of states. Because such authorization varies considerably with the character of particular international societies, we need to distinguish further between strong and weak internationalism, based on the distance from the statist end of the spectrum.

Each model can be viewed as resting on descriptive claims about the place that human rights do have in contemporary international relations or prescriptive claims about the place they ought to have. For example, a statist might argue (descriptively) that human rights are in fact peripheral in international relations, or. (prescriptively) that they ought to be peripheral, or both.

The cosmopolitan model, however, has little descriptive power. States and their interests in fact still dominate contemporary international relations. The international political power of individuals, NGOs, and other nonstate actors is real, and it appears to be growing. But it is still relatively small—and power is an essentially relative notion. The global political community (as opposed to the international society of states) is at best rudimentary. The cosmopolitan model, to the extent that it is more than a prescription about what is desirable, is largely a prediction about the direction of change in world politics.

The statist model, although it was accurate until World War II, is at best a crude and somewhat misleading first approximation today. Some sort of internationalist model provides the most accurate description of the place of human rights in contemporary international relations. I already began to lay out the evidence for this claim in Chapter 1. Much of Chapters 4, 5, and 6 in effect show that a relatively weak internationalist model, with modest international societal constraints on state sovereignty, describes the nature of international human rights policies over the past half century and is likely to continue to do so throughout the 1990s.

The current descriptive power of an internationalist model, however, does not mean that it will necessarily remain accurate in the future. It is not obviously the best, or even a good, way to treat human rights in international relations. Nonetheless, the reality that we face today is one of considerable state sovereignty, with modest limits rooted in the international society of states.

REALISM AND HUMAN RIGHTS

Before leaving the discussion of theory, we need to consider two common theoretical challenges to the limited, but nonetheless real, concern with international human rights characteristic of the contemporary society of states, namely, political **realism,** or **realpolitik** (power politics), and certain forms of cultural relativism. The theory of realpolitik is an old and well-established theory of international relations. It is typically traced back to figures such as Machiavelli in the early sixteenth century and

Thucydides, whose *History* chronicles the great wars between Athens and Sparta in the final decades of the fifth century B.C. Even today, realism remains the most prominent theoretical perspective in the study of international relations.

Realism stresses "the primacy in all political life of power and security."[9] This focus arises from an account of human nature that emphasizes self-interest and the egoistic passions and an account of international relations that emphasizes the constraints imposed by international anarchy. Because men are egoistic and evil and because international anarchy requires states to rely on their own resources even for defense, "universal moral principles cannot be applied to the actions of states."[10] To pursue a moral foreign policy would be not only foolishly unsuccessful but also dangerous because it would leave one's country more vulnerable to the power of self-interested states.

Rather than morality, realists argue that considerations of the national interest should guide foreign policy. And the national interest, for the realist, must be defined in terms of power and security. For example, George Kennan, one of the architects of postwar U.S. foreign policy and one of the most respected recent realist writers, argued that a government's "primary obligation is to the *interests* of the national society it represents ... its military security, the integrity of its political life and the well-being of its people." "The process of government ... is a practical exercise and not a moral one."[11] As for international human rights policies,

> it is difficult to see any promise in an American policy which sets out to correct and improve the political habits of large parts of the world's population. Misgovernment ... has been the common condition of most of mankind for centuries and millennia in the past. It is going to remain that condition for long into the future, no matter how valiantly Americans insist on tilting against the windmills.[12]

Such arguments do contain a kernel of truth. The demands of morality often do conflict with the national interest defined in terms of power. But *all* objectives of foreign policy may compete with the national interest thus defined. For example, arms races may contribute to the outbreak of war. Alliances may prove dangerously entangling. Realists, however, rightly refuse to conclude from this that we should eschew arms or allies. They should also abandon their categorical attacks on morality in foreign policy.

Realist arguments against morality in foreign policy also appeal to the special office of the statesman. For example, Herbert Butterfield argued that although an individual may choose to sacrifice himself in the face of foreign invasion, "it is not clear that he has a socially recognizable right to offer the same sacrifice on behalf of all his fellow-citizens or to impose such self-abnegation on the rest of his society."[13] But nonmoral objectives as well may be pursued by statesmen with excessive zeal—and equally deadly consequences. For example, Germany's alliance with Austria-Hungary dragged it into World War I. In fact, the European alliance system transformed a regional dispute between Austria-Hungary and Russia into a devastating world war that led to the elimination of Austria-Hungary from the map. Despite such examples, realists would (again rightly) never think of excluding alliances from foreign policy. Once more, a valuable caution against moralistic excess has been wildly exaggerated.

Most moral objectives can be pursued at a cost far less than national survival. This certainly is true of many international human rights goals. For example, the United States could reduce or eliminate aid to most Third World countries on human rights grounds with little or no discernable impact on U.S. national security or major U.S. economic interests.

In addition, there is no reason why a country cannot, if it wishes, include human rights or other moral concerns in its definition of the national interest. Security, independence, and prosperity may be unavoidable necessities of national political life, but a government need not limit itself to the pursuit of these necessities. Even if the primary obligation of a government must be to the national interest defined in terms of power, this need not be its *sole*, or even ultimate, obligation.

An appeal to the anarchic structure of international relations will not rescue realist amoralism. For example, Robert Art and Kenneth Waltz claimed that "states in anarchy cannot afford to be moral. The possibility of moral behavior rests upon the existence of an effective government that can deter and punish illegal actions."[14] This is obviously false, even if we set aside their confusion of morality and law. Just as individuals may behave morally without government enforcement of moral rules, so moral behavior is possible in international relations.

The costs of moral behavior are typically greater in an anarchic system of self-help enforcement. Nonetheless, states often can act on moral concerns with safety, and sometimes even with success. In particular instances there may be good policy reasons to pursue an amoral, or even immoral, policy. There are, however, no good general theoretical reasons why such a policy ought to be required, or even the norm.

CULTURAL RELATIVISM
AND UNIVERSAL HUMAN RIGHTS

Realist arguments are often reinforced by **relativist** arguments that moral values are historically or culturally specific rather than universal. For example, Kennan argued that "there are no internationally accepted standards of morality to which the U.S. government could appeal if it wished to act in the name of moral principles."[15] Many nonrealists, however, also share such a relativist skepticism. Thus it is often claimed that there are a variety of distinctive and defensible conceptions of human rights that merit our respect and toleration even if we disagree with them.

One standard form of such arguments has been the claim that there are "three worlds" of human rights.[16] The "Western" (First World) approach, it is asserted, emphasizes civil and political rights and the right to private property. The "socialist" (Second World) approach emphasizes economic and social rights. The "Third World" approach emphasizes self-determination and economic development. Furthermore, both the socialist and the Third World conceptions are held to be group oriented, in contrast to the fundamental individualism of the "Western" approach.

The reality of Western practice over the past half century, however, has been quite different from this caricature. In Western Europe, economic and social rights are generally well guaranteed. Even in the United States, which has by far the worst record on economic and social rights of the major developed countries, a fairly extensive welfare state exists.

In the former Soviet bloc, citizens, given the opportunity, have demanded their civil and political rights in country after country. Civil and political rights, far from being a superfluous bourgeois luxury, seem to be viewed by Central and Eastern Europeans as no less essential to a life of dignity than Western Europeans do. And the dismal state of the economies of Central and Eastern Europe shows that the sacrifice of civil and political rights in the name of socialism probably has not even facilitated the long-term realization of economic and social rights.

The wave of liberalizations and democratizations throughout the Third World in the past decade likewise suggests that the so-called Third World conception of human rights has little basis in local aspirations or understandings. As in the former Soviet bloc, ordinary citizens in country after country in the Third World have found internationally recognized civil and political rights essential to protecting themselves against repressive economic and political elites. When given the chance, they have in effect declared that the sacrifices they made in the name of development, self-determination, or national security were most often imposed on them by force, and that their resistance was repressed through systematic violations of civil and political rights.

Political histories, cultural legacies, economic conditions, and human rights problems certainly differ in these three "worlds." For that matter, there is considerable diversity even within each "world," especially the Third World. Cultural relativity is a fact. Social institutions and values have varied, and continue to vary, with time and place. Nonetheless, I will argue that human rights are today essentially universal, requiring only relatively modest adjustments in the name of cultural diversity.

Moral relativism, the belief that moral values (and thus conceptions of human rights) are determined by history, culture, economics, or some other independent social force, is best seen as a matter of degree. At one extreme is a *radical relativism* that sees culture (or history, or economics) as the source of all values.[17] Such a position in effect denies the very idea of human rights, for it holds that there are no rights that everyone is entitled to equally, simply as a human being. Radical relativism can be ignored once we have decided, as we have above, that there *are* human rights, rights that all human beings have, independent of society and irrespective of their particular history or culture.

At the other end of the spectrum lies what we can call radical **universalism,** the view that all values, including human rights, are entirely universal, in no way subject to modification in light of cultural or historical differences. In its pure form, radical universalism holds that there is only one set of human rights, which applies at all times and in all places. Whatever the possible theoretical attractions of such a view, it has little practical relevance. For example, to insist that all human rights be implemented in precisely identical ways in all countries would be wildly unrealistic, if not morally perverse.

Rejecting the two end points of the spectrum still leaves us with a considerable variety of relativist positions. These can be roughly divided into two ranges.

Strong relativism holds that human rights (and other values) are principally, but not entirely, determined by culture or other circumstances. "Universal" human rights serve as a check on culturally specific values. The emphasis, however, is on variation and relativity. *Weak relativism* reverses the emphasis. Human rights are held to be largely universal, subject only to secondary cultural modifications. The position I want to defend here, on both descriptive and prescriptive grounds, is a form of weak cultural relativism.

Internationally recognized human rights represent a good first approximation of the guarantees necessary for a life of dignity in the contemporary world of modern states and modern markets. In all countries of the world, the unchecked power of the modern state threatens individuals, families, groups, and communities alike. Likewise, national and international economic markets, whether free or controlled, threaten human dignity in all countries of the contemporary world. The Universal Declaration and the Covenants provide a generally sound approach to protecting human dignity against these threats. For example, it is difficult to imagine defensible arguments in the contemporary world to deny rights to life, liberty, security of the person, or protection against slavery, arbitrary arrest, racial discrimination, and torture. The rights to food, health care, work, and social insurance are equally basic to any plausible conception of equal human dignity.

Universality, however, is only an initial presumption. Some deviations from international human rights norms may be justified—or even demanded. For example, the free and full consent of spouses in marriage (Universal Declaration, Article 16) reflects a historically and culturally specific conception of marriage that it would be unreasonable to apply everywhere without exception. This does not mean that we should approve of forced marriages. It does, however, suggest accepting certain notions of consent that would be unacceptable in the contemporary West.

The possibility of justifiable modifications, however, must not obscure the fundamental universality of international human rights norms. Deviations should be rare and their cumulative impact relatively minor. This suggests that as human rights are specified in greater detail, there is more latitude for legitimate variation.

We can very roughly distinguish three levels at which human rights can be specified. At the top are what we can call the "concepts," very general formulations such as the rights to political participation or work. Here very little cultural variability is justifiable.[18] Below these are what we can call "interpretations." For example, a guaranteed job and unemployment insurance are two interpretations of the right to work. Some interpretive variability seems plausible for most internationally recognized human rights. And at the third level, considerable variation in the particular form in which an interpretation is implemented may be justifiable.

Suppose that we interpret the right to political participation as a right to vote in open and fair elections. This leaves open many questions of form or implementation. For example, members of a national legislature might be chosen through winner-take-all elections in local districts or by a system in which people vote for party lists and assignment of seats is proportional to the national vote. Such variations of form usually should be considered permissible, as long as they tend to realize the aim of the governing concept and interpretation.

These guidelines will not provide clear answers in all important cases. They do, however, have strong and generally clear implications. Consider, for example, the claim of many Muslims that men and women do not have the same rights, that each sex has its own particular, and largely complementary, rights and responsibilities.

The weak relativist position sketched above would reject such an argument. The claim that because of ascriptive characteristics such as age, sex, race, or family one is not entitled to the same basic human rights as members of other groups is incompatible with the very idea of human rights.

This does not imply that all differences based on gender are incompatible with human rights. For example, dress codes to protect public morals and decency, such as the Muslim requirement that women wear veils in public or the Western requirement that women (but not men) cover their chests in public, clearly lie within the realm of permissible distinctions. But the claim that one group in society has radically different basic rights from another group—especially the group that is responsible for defining and enforcing such differences of rights—is not a culturally different conception of human rights, but a partial rejection of the very idea of *human* rights.

Such an argument does not imply wanton cultural imperialism. In fact, the Western legacy of imperialism demands that we show special caution and sensitivity when dealing with fundamentally clashing cultural values. Caution, however, must not be confused with inaction. Even if we are not entitled to impose our values on others, they are our own values. Sometimes they may demand that we act on them even in the absence of agreement by others. And if the values of others are particularly objectionable—consider, for example, societies in which it is traditional to kill the first-born child if it is female, or the deeply rooted tradition of anti-Semitism in the West—even strong social sanctions may deserve neither respect nor toleration.

THREE

□   □   □

The Domestic Politics
of Human Rights:
The Case of the Southern Cone

This book deals primarily with the international politics of human rights. In a world of sovereign states, though, national politics largely determines how human rights are protected or violated. A national-level case study can both illustrate this important point and provide concreteness and immediacy to the notion of "human rights violations." In this chapter, we will look in some detail at human rights violations in the Southern Cone of South America. In Chapters 4 and 5 we will look much more briefly at South Africa and two cases in Central America (Nicaragua and El Salvador). Although many different cases might have been chosen, these are the ones that have probably received the most international human rights attention in recent years, especially in the United States.

The geographical area known as the Southern Cone of South America includes the countries of Argentina, Chile, Paraguay, and Uruguay, as well as southern Brazil. In this chapter we will look at three of these countries, Argentina, Chile, and Uruguay, which for convenience I will refer to as the countries of the Southern Cone. All three suffered under a distinctive style of intensely repressive military rule in the 1970s and 1980s, and they served as a focal point for many important developments in international human rights policies.

POLITICS BEFORE THE COUPS

The Southern Cone's descent into brutal military dictatorship surprised most observers. In Chile, military rule had been rare from the mid-nineteenth century on. After World War II, a stable three-party democratic system had become institutionalized. And in 1970, Salvador Allende became the world's first freely elected Marxist president.

Allende dramatically intensified the economic and social reforms begun under his Christian Democratic predecessor, Eduardo Frei. Large agricultural estates were expropriated. Key private industries and banks were nationalized, including Chile's (largely U.S.-owned) copper industry. Social services were expanded. These changes were both lavishly praised and reviled, within Chile and abroad. The resulting ideological polarization helped to set the stage for the military coup of September 11, 1973, that killed Allende, removed his government from power, and installed a repressive military regime that ruled until 1990.

In Uruguay, the military had not intervened in politics since the 1860s. Furthermore, in the first two decades of the twentieth century, President José Batlle y Ordoñez began a series of social and political reforms on behalf of women, children, and labor. These policies were extended by Batlle's successors, creating a widely admired democratic welfare state that provided education and health care for all. Nonetheless, in the late 1960s and early 1970s, Uruguay suffered a gradual but complete political collapse.

Uruguay's government was weakened by a political stalemate between its two dominant parties. The economy was beset by high inflation and persistent labor unrest. And the Tupamaros, one of Latin America's most dramatic and successful urban guerrilla groups, were waging a war of terrorism against the Uruguayan state and society. Civil liberties were temporarily suspended in 1968, 1970, and 1971 to permit unrestricted military action against the guerrillas. In 1972, the government declared an even more stringent state of internal war and passed a new Law of National Security, which created special security offenses. In June 1973, President Bordaberry unilaterally suspended most remaining constitutional rights and closed the National Assembly. For the next three years he was the public face of the military government, until he too was forced from office.

Argentina's political history was more checkered. In the decades after 1821–1822, when Argentina won independence from Spain, Argentine politics was marked by violent struggles among provincial bosses (caudillos) and no less brutal struggles for leadership in the capital, Buenos Aires. Later in the century, however, a considerable degree of order was achieved. Argentina even experienced a period of democratic rule from 1916 until 1930.

After World War II, the populist leader Juan Perón ruled Argentina as an elected president for a decade. In 1955, however, he was overthrown in a military coup. Civilian governments were prevented from completing their terms in office by military coups in 1966 and 1973. But the military was not even able to impose its preferred candidates when the country returned to civilian rule. Marcelo Cavarozzi aptly characterized this alternation of ineffective civilian and military regimes as the "failure of 'semidemocracy.'"[1]

In the mid-1970s, an already-unstable political situation was made much worse by the incompetence and corruption of the civilian government. Meanwhile, the Montoneros and the Revolutionary Army of the People (ERP) were waging urban and rural guerrilla warfare against the Argentine state and society. The Argentine Right, with the support of the military and security forces, responded with assassinations of leftist students, lawyers, journalists, and trade unionists, in addition to guerrillas. In October 1975, five months before the overthrow of the civilian government, Army Commander-in-Chief Jorge Rafael Videla warned that "as many people will die in Argentina as is necessary to restore order."[2] The following year, Videla, who had become president, delivered on his promise of violence, if not order.

TORTURE AND DISAPPEARANCES

A distinguishing feature of repression in the Southern Cone was the extensive use of **disappearances,** that is, extrajudicial detentions, usually accompanied by torture, often followed by death.[3] The politics of disappearances was most highly developed in Argentina.

> Task forces of the armed services ... were detailed to arrest suspected subversives without warrant; to avoid identification of the captors; to take the detainees to clandestine detention camps, generally within military or police facilities; and to disclaim any knowledge of the whereabouts of their prisoners. In those camps, prisoners were interrogated under the most severe forms of torture. ... The camps were deliberately shielded from any judicial or administrative investigation so that the torturers could be free to use any methods, and to deny even the existence of their prisoners, without fear of punishment. ... The overwhelming majority of those who entered the system of "disappearances" were never seen alive again.[4]

After the return of civilian government, the Argentine National Commission on Disappeared Persons (CONADEP, the Sábato Commission) documented 8,960 disappearances, a figure that probably underestimates the total by one-third or more (see Figure 3.1). The commission identified 340 clandestine detention and torture centers, involving about 700 military officers and organized in 5 zones, 35 subzones, and 210 areas. The kidnappers operated with such impunity that only one disappearance in ten occurred in unknown circumstances. Three-fifths took place in the home of the victim, with witnesses present during the abduction. The mere passing of an unmarked green four-door Ford Falcon, the car of choice of the arresting squads, was enough to spread terror.

The Navy Mechanics School (ESMA) in Buenos Aires was Argentina's most important clandestine detention center. Torture at ESMA was so extensive that it became virtually a routinized, bureaucratic activity. A trip to ESMA typically began with "Caroline," a thick broom handle with two long wires running out the end. The victim was stripped and tied to a steel bed frame. "Caroline" was attached to a box on a table that supplied the current. Then the electricity was applied to the victim, who often was periodically doused with water to increase the effects.

> It was unhurried and methodical. If the victim was a woman they went for the breasts, vagina, anus. If a man, they favored genitals, tongue, neck. ... Sometimes victims twitched so uncontrollably that they shattered their own arms and legs. Patrick Rice, an Irish priest who had worked in the slums and was detained for several days, recalls watching his flesh sizzle. What he most remembers is the smell. It was like bacon.[5]

Children were tortured in front of their parents, and parents in front of their children. Some prisoners were kept in rooms no longer or wider than a single bed. And the torture continued for days, weeks, even months, until the victim was released or, more often, killed. The sadistic brutality did not always even end with the death of the victim. "One woman was sent the hands of her daughter in a shoe box." The body of another woman "was dumped in her parents' yard, naked but showing no outward signs of torture. Later the director of the funeral home called to inform her parents that the girl's vagina had been sewn up. Inside he had found a rat."[6]

Most bodies, however, were never recovered. At ESMA, which also served as a disposal site for other naval camps, corpses were initially buried under the sports field. When this was filled, the bodies were burned daily, at 5:30 in the afternoon, usually after having been cut up with a circular saw. Finally, those in charge of destroying the evidence of their crimes hit on the idea of aerial disposal at sea. Once they mastered the currents—at first bodies washed up in Buenos Aires, then in Montevideo—there was no trace to be found. Other units encased their victims in cement and dumped them in the river. The army's preferred method seems to have been to drive the corpses to the cemetery and register them as "NN," Name Unknown.

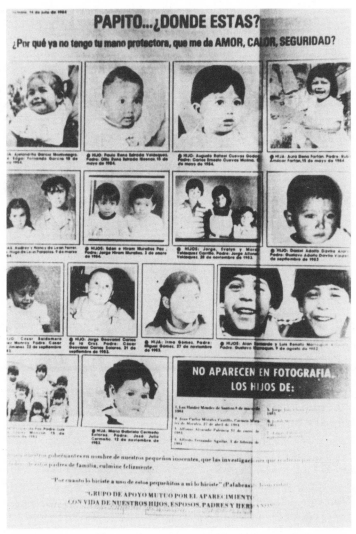

FIGURE 3.1 "Daddy ... where are you?" The fathers of the children pictured here had all "disappeared" in Guatemala. Amnesty International photo.

Repression in Chile was very similar, although the number of deaths was much lower. The Uruguayan style, however, was significantly different. Almost all the disappeared reappeared, usually in prison, after having been severely tortured. Only 44 Uruguayans who disappeared in Uruguay remained unaccounted for at the end of military rule. The per capita rate of permanent disappearances in Uruguay was only about one-fifth the Chilean rate and one-twentieth the Argentinean rate. But about 60,000 people, roughly 2 percent of the population, were detained, giving Uruguay the highest per capita rate of political prisoners and torture victims in all of Latin America.[7] Virtually everyone in the country at least knew of someone who had been detained. This was an extraordinarily powerful technique of state terror.

In Uruguay, there was a grotesque division of labor between the clandestine detention centers, which specialized in physical abuse, and the official prisons, which specialized in psychological abuse. The prison regimen was carefully calculated to dehumanize and break people who had already suffered excruciating physical torture. Prisoners were never referred to by name, always by number—or by insulting epithet: "cockroach," "rat," "*apesto*" (diseased one). Peepholes and listening devices were common, and broken prisoners were used as informants. Cell mates were often chosen on the basis of psychological profiles in order to cause one another the most annoyance. Even families were incorporated into the routine of torture. For example, children were sometimes permitted to visit their parents once a month, but only if the parent demonstrated no sign of affection.

Prisoners were allowed outside only one hour a day. When they were in their cells, they were often required to stand except during designated sleeping hours. Every aspect of existence was regulated by ominously arbitrary rules. Violations were typically punished by isolation in a windowless cell with a bare electric light bulb that burned twenty-four hours a day. In the most extreme case, nine top Tupamaro leaders, following months of the most brutal physical torture, were kept in complete solitary confinement for over a decade. One spent an extended period of his confinement at the bottom of a dry well. Mauricio Rosencof reported: "In over eleven and a half years, I didn't see the sun for more than eight hours altogether. I forgot colors—there were no colors."[8]

THE NATIONAL SECURITY DOCTRINE

Much of the brutality reflected pure sadism.

At ESMA the complete licence they [the torturers] had to do what they wanted with their prisoners seems to have acted on them like an addiction.

Sometimes they would stay in the torture room for a full 24 hours, never taking time off or resting; or else they would go home, and then return a couple of hours later, as though the atmosphere of cruelty and violence had drawn them back.[9]

But at least some of the brutality was the work of professionals pursuing what they saw as defense of the nation.

National security doctrines, which drew heavily on French and U.S. counterinsurgency doctrines, were first popularized in Brazil in the 1960s. They provided an all-encompassing ideological framework for the military regimes of the Southern Cone. The state was viewed as the central institution of society. The military in turn was seen as the central institution of the state, the only organization with the combination of insight, commitment, and resources needed to protect the interests and values of the nation.

The "Subversive" Threat

The nation and its values were seen as under assault from an international conspiracy that was centered on, but by no means limited to, international communism. For example, a diagram used at Argentina's Air Force Academy[10] depicts a tree of subversion with three roots: Marxism, Zionism, and Freemasonry. Progressive Catholicism appears at the top, and new growths at the bottom include human rights organizations, women's rights, pacifism, nonaggression, disarmament, the Rotary Club, Lions Club, and junior chambers of commerce. The main branches off the trunk are Communist parties, the extreme totalitarian right (nazism and fascism), Socialist parties, liberal democracy, revolutionary front parties, Protestants, sectarians and anti-Christians, armed revolutionary organizations, and "indirect aggression." The branches off the limb of "indirect aggression" are particularly striking: drug addiction, alcoholism, prostitution, gambling, political liberalism, economic liberalism, lay education, trade union corruption, "hippiness," pornography, homosexuality, divorce, art, newspapers, television, cinema, theater, magazines, and books.

To counter such a threat, all-out war was necessary. The process would not always be pretty, especially when applied to the agents of "indirect aggression." But even if many "subversives" were more misdirected or gullible than malicious, they were still guilty and had to be treated as such. As General Iberico Saint Jean, military governor of Buenos Aires, put it in May 1976, "First we will kill all the subversives; then we will kill their collaborators; then ... their sympathizers; then ... those who remain indifferent; and finally we will kill the timid."[11]

The metaphor of disease was also common. "Subversives" were an infection. The armed forces were the nation's antibodies. An infected member of the body politic had to be isolated (detained) to stop the spread of the disease. If a treatment was possible, so much the better—although even a cure might be painful (torture). If the member was beyond repair, though, permanent surgical removal (death) was demanded. What mattered was the long-run health of the body politic, not its individual members.

This paranoid vision helps to explain the wide range of victims. Violence and terror against terrorists was not unexpected; in both Argentina and Uruguay it had been official policy even before the coups. Most of the disappeared, though, had no connection at all to the guerrillas.[12] Yet they too were considered guilty because of their "dangerous" political views.

Uruguay carried this ideology to its totalitarian extreme. A scheme of political reliability ratings—Certificates of Democratic Background—was established. An "A" rating indicated political reliability. A "B," or suspect, rating subjected one to police scrutiny and harassment. Those rated "C"—sometimes for an "offense" as minor as having been involved in a protest march twenty years earlier—were absolutely banned from public employment, a serious penalty in a country where the state was the largest employer. Many had trouble finding even private-sector jobs because hiring a "C" (or even a "B") citizen often led to harassing government audits and ominous questions about the employer's own loyalty.

The military sought to penetrate and "purify" all aspects of Uruguayan social life. Each school received a new, politically reliable director, and each class was given a "teacher's aide" to take notes on the behavior of students and teachers. A permit was required to hold a birthday party. Elections for captains of amateur soccer teams were supervised by the military, which could veto the results. A public performance of Ravel's Piano Concerto for the Left Hand was banned because of its sinister title.

Economic Reform and Economic and Social Rights

National purification in the Southern Cone also had a major economic dimension. In Chile, the Pinochet government tried to reverse not only Allende's reforms, but those of Frei as well. In 1975 the junta applied what it called a "Shock Treatment" (*Plan Shock*). Government spending declined by more than a quarter and public investment was cut in half. Uruguay and Argentina pursued similar plans, although somewhat less vigorously. The aim was to privatize the economy and to weaken or destroy organized labor, which was seen as a major subversive threat.

The result of this forced march toward free markets was a rapid decline in living standards. For example, real wages and salaries in Chile were about one-third lower in 1976 than in 1970. In Argentina infant mortality increased dramatically.[13] The architect of Argentina's economic reforms, José Martínez de Hoz (whose niece was married to Lieutenant Enrique Yon, one of ESMA's torturers), became in his own way as well known as his military bosses.

After the initial shock, the economies of the Southern Cone began to recover, especially in Chile. Although most of the benefits of growth were concentrated in the hands of a small elite, employment and real wages did increase, and inflation declined. Economic success helped to calm at least some of the discontent with military rule. In fact, in all three countries the military counted on economic success to deflect attention from, or compensate for, repression.

It is fairly clear who were the economic and political victims of the national security state: the Left, trade unions, other autonomous social groups, and dissidents of all sorts, as well as ordinary citizens who were more or less accidentally caught in the system. But who were the beneficiaries?

Some members of the upper and middle classes certainly profited from the privatization of the economy and the lifting of government controls. Industrialists seem to have strongly supported military control over labor. In Argentina, as many as half of the disappeared were labor activists. But neither local industrialists nor multinational corporations seem to have had much influence on economic policies. Furthermore, the turn to free markets left local industrialists extremely vulnerable to foreign competition.[14] Likewise, although the military amply rewarded itself—for example, between 1968 and 1973, Uruguayan spending on education declined from 24.3 percent to 16.6 percent of the budget, while military spending rose from 13.9 percent to 26.2 percent[15]—economic advantage seems to have been a secondary concern.[16] In their economic policies as much as in their political strategies, ideology was central to the policies of the military regimes of the Southern Cone.

HUMAN RIGHTS NGOs

If the Southern Cone provides a particularly striking example of human rights violations, it also provides a moving example of resistance. On April 30, 1977, fourteen middle-aged women, frustrated in their search for their disappeared children through official channels, met publicly in the Plaza de Mayo, the main square of Buenos Aires, in front of the Casa Rosada, the president's residence and seat of government. Thus began the work of Argentina's Mothers of the Plaza de Mayo. Their weekly Thursday afternoon vigil—white scarves on their heads, silently walking around the square—became a symbol of both the cruelty of the military regime and the refusal of at least some ordinary people to bow to repression (see Figure 3.2).

Although subject to harassment and even attack—nine people associated with the mothers, including two French nuns, permanently disappeared on December 10, 1977, after evening mass—the mothers persevered and grew in numbers and in strength. By 1980, they had almost 5,000 members and were able to set up a small office.[17]

The Grandmothers of the Plaza de Mayo were organized in October 1977 to deal with one of the most bizarre aspects of Argentina's Dirty War, the traffic in children. Young children and infants were occasionally picked up with their parents. Others were born while their mothers were in captivity. The total numbered around 800. They were usually given or sold to childless military couples. One torturer estimated that about 60 babies passed through ESMA, and that all but 2—whose heads had been smashed against the wall in efforts to get their mothers to talk—were sold.[18] Even today, the grandmothers continue to try to trace and recover these victims.

Several other human rights NGOs operated in Argentina. For example, the Center for Legal and Social Studies (CELS) was established in the summer of 1979 to investigate individual cases involving the security forces. Within a year of its founding, CELS had become affiliated with both the Geneva-based International Commission of Jurists and the New York–based International League for Human Rights. The Argentine Human Rights Commission (CADHU) was formed in 1975 to protest right-wing death-squad killings. It was forced into exile in 1976 but opened branches in Geneva, Mexico, Rome, and Washington to spread information about the nature of the repression in Argentina. Adolfo Pérez Esquivel, a leader of the Service for Peace and Justice (SERPAJ), received the Nobel Peace Prize in 1980, three years after having been imprisoned and tortured by the military regime. Important work was also done by the Permanent Assembly for Human Rights (APDH) and the Families of Those Detained and Disappeared for Political Reasons.

The Argentine Catholic church, however, despite the disappearance or assassination of two bishops and twenty priests, nuns, and seminarians, was not a vocal critic of the military regime. Although SERPAJ was a religious organization, and the Ecumenical Movement for Human Rights (MEDH) was active, the Catholic church as an institution was not part of the opposition. In fact, some military chaplains actively participated in the system of torture.

In Chile, by contrast, the Church was at the center of the human rights movement. The Committee of Cooperation for Peace (COPACHI) was formed in October 1973, the month after the coup, under the joint leadership of the bishops of Chile's Catholic and Lutheran churches. A month

FIGURE 3.2 "Mothers of the Plaza de Mayo" demonstration in Argentina on behalf of the disappeared. Amnesty International photo.

later, a legal-aid organization was established in headquarters provided by the Catholic church. By August 1974, COPACHI had more than 100 employees in the capital city of Santiago alone.

When Pinochet ordered COPACHI dissolved in November 1975, the Catholic church responded by organizing the Vicaría de la Solidaridad (Vicariate of Solidarity).[19] The Vicaría provided aid and support for relatives of the disappeared and legal assistance to victims of state terror. Its Health Department organized soup kitchens and child-nutrition programs, especially in the poorer urban areas, which had been severely affected by Pinochet's economic reforms. The Campesino Program and the Labor Department sought to aid peasant organizations and unions, which had been special targets of repression. As military rule dragged on, the Vicaría also began an extensive program of documentation and analysis.

Some lay human rights groups were also active in Chile, particularly the Chilean Human Rights Commission, which was formed in November 1978. But in Chile, as in much of the rest of Latin America, the Catholic church could do things that were impossible for lay organizations and even other churches. And the Chilean Catholic church itself faced "the murder of priests; the detention of priests and nuns; attacks on priests and nuns; expulsion of priests from Chile; abductions of lay workers; police raids on Church premises; bombings and other attacks against parish houses, chapels and cathedrals; and instances of government interference in Church activities."[20]

In addition to aiding victims and their families, human rights NGOs were an important source of information. For example, Emilio Mignone, the founder of CELS, had worked for the Organization of American States (OAS) in Washington during the 1960s and put his contacts to good use. In fact, the lists of disappeared people prepared by CELS and APDH provided much of the factual basis for initial UN and OAS action. Given the efforts of the juntas to hide the scope of their violence, this may have been a significant achievement.

Human rights NGOs also allowed Argentineans and Chileans a limited opportunity to struggle against, rather than simply acquiesce in, military rule and the Dirty War. (In Uruguay the system of repression was so totalitarian that no effective local human rights NGOs were able to function until the final two or three years of military rule.) Their activities may have played a role in the failure to stablize military rule.

THE COLLAPSE OF MILITARY RULE

The Argentine military, ironically, finally fell from power after it lost a conventional war with Britain over control of the obscure Falkland Islands. Argentina had long protested British occupation and control of the Malvinas, as they are known in Latin America. In April 1982, the military junta decided to reclaim them by force. This decision largely arose from the government's need to deflect attention from the collapse of the economy in the wake of the global recession of the early 1980s.

The invasion, however, was decisively repulsed. Rather than rescue the military's reputation, the Malvinas debacle completed its humiliation. Having attacked its own people, brought the economy to the brink of ruin, and then embarrassed itself and the country before the entire world, the Argentine military had little choice but to permit a return to civilian government. On October 30, 1983, Raúl Alfonsin won an absolute majority in the national presidential election. He took office on December 10, the thirty-fifth anniversary of the adoption of the Universal Declaration of Human Rights.

In Chile as well, the economy collapsed in ruin in the early 1980s. In 1982, per capita gross domestic product declined 15.8 percent. By March 1983, one-third of the labor force was unemployed. Between 1981 and 1985, the legal minimum wage lost between one-fifth and one-half of its purchasing power. Close to one-half of the children in Chile were malnourished, an appalling situation in a country that had previously been relatively prosperous. A wave of bankruptcies brought hard times even to the middle and upper classes.

Working-class residential neighborhoods began to organize. The old political parties (especially the centrist Christian Democrats, which had never been forced entirely underground) began to act, cautiously, in public. As the junta approached its tenth anniversary in power, opposition increased in all sectors of society. In June 1983, strikes by truck drivers and copper miners represented labor's first major challenge since the coup. On July 2 and 3, a successful general strike was held. Between May and November a series of Days of National Protest culminated in a demonstration by close to one million people in downtown Santiago. And "1983 became known in Chile as 'the year when people lost their fear.'"[21]

The military, however, also found new resolve. As opposition grew, so did repression. Several deaths and over one thousand arrests accompanied the July general strike. Mass arrests increased dramatically, as did banishments, exiles, torture, and political deaths. By late 1984, the government was forced to reimpose a state of siege, and repression became more brutal. For example, two young Chileans were set on fire by the police during a protest demonstration, killing one and savagely maiming the other. Although the government claimed that the youths had accidentally set themselves aflame with a Molotov cocktail, a third victim was torched a week later, as if to remind opponents that it had been no accident.

Popular resistance, however, could not be crushed this time. On October 5, 1988, the military turned to a plebiscite to legitimate its rule. The majority of Chileans, however, rejected a new eight-year term for Pinochet. On December 14, 1989, an opposition alliance of seventeen parties, led by Patricio Aylwin, won the first relatively free elections in Chile in nearly two decades.

The Uruguayan military was also hit hard by the economic crisis of the early 1980s. By 1984, real wages were less than half of their 1968 levels, and more than 10 percent of the population had left the country, including one-seventh of the country's university graduates and close to one-fifth of the economically active population of the capital city of Montevideo.[22] The military, after some initial indecision, ultimately proved unwilling to adopt the Chilean strategy of increased repression in the face of growing opposition. Elections were held in 1984 and a freely elected civilian government returned to power in 1985, even without a Falklands-like blunder.

NUNCA MÁS: SETTLING ACCOUNTS WITH TORTURERS AND THE PAST

Elections, or at least the transfer of power from one elected civilian government to another (as occurred in both Argentina and Uruguay in 1989), are sometimes seen as the solution for human rights problems. But a nation that has suffered gross and systematic violations of human rights remains no less scarred than individual victims, their families, friends, and acquaintances. Furthermore, successor regimes face the problem of dealing with those responsible for human rights violations under the old order.

When the torture stops, it may not be entirely clear how to deal with the torturers and murderers and their superiors—especially when the guilty retain considerable political power and control the weaponry that once before supported their dictatorial rule. Defining the terms of retributive justice is part of a process of national reconciliation necessary to keep the wounds inflicted under military rule from festering. The experience of the countries of the Southern Cone, however, provides some sobering lessons.

Two weeks before the election that brought a return to civilian rule, the Argentine junta issued a Law of National Reconciliation that created a blanket amnesty for all offenses connected with the "war against subversion." In his first week as president, however, Raúl Alfonsin delivered on his campaign promise that all nine members of the three military juntas that had run Argentina from 1976 to 1982 would be prosecuted. No less significant was Alfonsin's decision to create the CONADEP, which would conduct an official investigation of the Dirty War. CONADEP's September 1984 report contained over 50,000 pages of documentation and provided an extensive, official, public accounting of the Dirty War. The summary, published under the title *Nunca Más* (Never again)—a phrase that first attained wide political currency in the aftermath of the Holocaust—became an instant best-seller.[23]

Where so much of the violence was clandestine, to know the nature of the crime was the essential first step to overcoming its legacies. *Nunca Más*, at minimum, finally recognized and publicly memorialized the victims, whose very existence had for so long been officially denied. Truth, however, is only a first step. Punishment or pardon usually follows, and preventing future abuses must be a high priority.

Argentina made several changes in domestic law and ratified several international human rights treaties. The military command structure was reorganized. Military spending declined from 4.3 percent of gross domestic product in 1983 to 2.3 percent in 1987. And in April 1988, a new Law of Defense defined the role of the armed forces as protection from external aggression, effectively renouncing the national security doctrine.

Punishment was pursued through the courts, but a defense of obedience to orders was permitted. Ordinary soldiers and lower-ranking officers were thus effectively pardoned. In addition, the Supreme Council of the Armed Forces was given initial jurisdiction to allow the military the dignity of dealing with its own through the system of military justice. But when the supreme council could find nothing illegal in any of the actions of the military government, the civilian Federal Court of Appeals took over the cases.

On December 9, 1985, the day before the second anniversary of the return of civilian government, the court handed down its sentence. Five of the 9 commanders received prison sentences ranging from four and one-half years to life sentences for General Videla, the leader of the first junta, and Admiral Massera, the commander most intimately associated with the Dirty War. In addition, the court left open the possibility of additional trials against more than 650 members of the armed forces.

Under extreme pressure from the military and its supporters, Alfonsin in December 1986 pushed through the *Ley de Punto Final*—literally, the Law of Full Stop (period), more loosely, the "final deadline." No new prosecutions could be filed after sixty days. The hope was that the legendary slowness of the Argentine judicial bureaucracy would leave most officers untouched. *Punto Final*, however, actually spurred monumental efforts by human rights groups and the courts. Judges even canceled their summer vacations to meet the deadline. Some 400 new indictments were registered against over 100 officers.

On April 15, 1987, rebellious soldiers occupied several garrisons throughout the country and forced Alfonsin to push through a Law of Due Obedience, which limited prosecutions to chiefs of military areas. Even this, however, was not enough for the hard-liners. In January and December 1988, new (but much less effective) revolts broke out, suggesting a precarious balance of power between hard-liners and moderates in the military and between the armed forces and the government. A fourth military rebellion took place in Buenos Aires in December 1990, killing as many as twenty people, including some innocent civilians.

The new civilian government of Carlos Menem, despite Menem's strong public opposition to *Punto Final*, pardoned thirty-nine senior military officials in October 1989, effectively halting ongoing investigations of high leaders such as General Galtieri, the leader of the last junta. In addition, hundreds of those involved in the first three military uprisings were also pardoned. And the entire process was concluded when another eight senior officers, including General Videla, were pardoned at the end of December 1990. This was met by popular protests and the resignation of Julio Strassera, who had prosecuted Videla, from his position as Argentina's representative to the UN Commission on Human Rights.[24] General Videla, however, publicly indicated that even this gesture was not enough, asking instead for a full vindication of the military. Although the government refused to grant it, this call for a public declaration that the Dirty War was, at worst, an honest mistake suggests that the military rejected not only punishment but even the need for pardon.

Uruguay's new civilian government, when it took power in 1985, faced the even more difficult task of dealing with a military that had not been humiliated on the battlefield. It is thus not surprising that President Sanguinetti chose to accept the military's self-amnesty. In December 1986 Uruguay adopted the Law of Limitations, which protected the military against prosecution for crimes committed while it ruled the country.

The reaction against what critics called *impunidad* (impunity) for the military—there had not been a single prosecution, or even an official investigation—was dramatic.[25] In February 1987, a campaign was launched to hold a national referendum. By Christmas Eve, the organizers had gathered 634,702 signatures, from a total population of about 3 million people. This was equivalent to obtaining nearly 50 million signatures in the United States.

In the April 16, 1989, plebiscite, however, a majority chose to let the amnesty stand. Despite heavy rain, voter turnout was over 80 percent. Fifty-three percent voted "yellow," to let the amnesty stand. Forty-one percent voted "green," to overturn it. The example of Argentina seems to have been the deciding factor—especially after public statements by highly placed members of the military suggested that they would not allow the amnesty to be overturned.

Nonetheless, although it was not an entirely free choice, Uruguayans had the opportunity to choose to pardon, or at least not punish, the military. Many victimized nations have not had even that much. For example, in Guatemala the military declared an amnesty just before leaving office in 1986. And to remind everyone where real power still resided, five dozen mutilated bodies appeared in various places in the country in the first three weeks of civilian rule. There was no plebiscite, nor was there even an investigation of the tens of thousands of disappearances and arbitrary executions.

Chile, following the lead of Uruguay and the lesson of Argentina, chose to forgo prosecutions, which the military had made clear it would not permit. In April 1990, however, President Aylwin created the Commission for Truth and Reconciliation (CVR, the Rettig Commission). Its report, which was released in March 1991, documents close to one thousand disappearances that resulted in death. (The commission's mandate did not include other violations, including tens of thousands of cases of torture.) In addition, the Aylwin government has pressed the limits set by the military. In particular, it has refused to halt investigations of corruption during the period of military rule. Serious consideration is also being given to extraditing those responsible for the 1976 assassination of Chilean exile Orlando Letelier in Washington, D.C.

The outcome of such efforts will be determined by a complex interplay among the political will and skill of the government, its popular support, and the tolerance or intransigence of the military. These efforts do suggest, however, that even where punishment is impossible, it may prove possible to deny the guilty complete impunity.

"Men are unable to forgive what they cannot punish."[26] These words of Hannah Arendt, which have often been cited by those in the Southern Cone working on the problem of military impunity, nicely capture the central problem with military-imposed amnesties. To pardon is an act of charity and compassion. To punish is an act of justice (and a deterrent to future injustice). Civilian regimes that succeed grossly repressive regimes often are unable to punish because the guilty retain considerable political power. The pardons thus received by torturers and murders may have legal effect, but they are profoundly defective. This corruption of both punishment and pardon by power also makes preventing future abuses more difficult.

The task of prevention, however, is likely to be greatly aided by the truth, which can sometimes be a partial substitute for punishment or pardon. A public declaration of the crimes of the guilty may help to put the past behind and focus a country's energy and attention on preventing future abuses. At the very least, a nation unable even to acknowledge its past is unlikely to be able to prevent the continuation of human rights violations.

The official name of Chile's Rettig Commission was thus particularly well chosen: Commission for Truth and Reconciliation. Especially where suffering has been denied, truth may permit mourning and provide a public solace that may help to make reconciliation possible. There may even be a punishment of sorts in being forced to face a public demonstration of one's crimes.

Truth alone is never enough. Sometimes, though, it may make inroads against power. In any case, the task of human rights advocacy is to speak truth to power, in the name of past and present victims and in the hope of preventing future victims.

> accuracy is essential
> we must not be wrong
> even by a single one
>
> we are despite everything
> the guardians of our brothers
>
> ignorance about those who have disappeared
> undermines the reality of the world.[27]

Nunca Más. Never again. Never *this* horror again. Ultimately, this is the meaning of the struggle against systematic violations of human rights.

FOUR

□ □ □

The Multilateral Politics
of Human Rights

The following two chapters are the heart of this book. Chapter 4 examines multilateral human rights policies, that is, those carried out within the framework of international and regional organizations. Chapter 5 considers human rights in bilateral foreign policy.

At several points I will use the concept of international regimes. An **international regime** is typically defined as a set of principles, norms, rules, and decision-making procedures that are accepted by states (and other international actors) as binding within a particular issue area.[1] In Chapters 1 and 2 we in effect reviewed the principles and norms that govern international human rights regimes, as outlined in the International Bill of Human Rights (the Universal Declaration of Human Rights and the International Human Rights Covenants). In this chapter we consider international and regional decision-making and implementation procedures. We will review the activities of the United Nations Commission on Human Rights, the Human Rights Committee, the International Labor Organization, special committees created under international human rights treaties on racial discrimination, women's rights, and torture, the international campaign against apartheid, regional human rights regimes in Europe, the Americas, and Africa, and the human rights provisions of the Conference on Security and Cooperation in Europe.

THE UNITED NATIONS COMMISSION ON HUMAN RIGHTS

The United Nations is the world's most prominent multilateral political forum.[2] It is not, however, a world government. It is an intergovernmental organization, a "club" whose members are sovereign states. Few UN decisions create binding international legal obligations, and even fewer can be effectively enforced. Nonetheless, when the United Nations acts on the basis of consensus, it may reasonably be said to speak for the society of states (see Chapter 2). Therefore, we can call the resulting international human rights norms and procedures the global human rights regime.

The UN Commission on Human Rights, a permanent subsidiary body of the Economic and Social Council (ECOSOC), is the center of the global human rights regime. During its first several years, the commission devoted its principal efforts to work on the Universal Declaration of Human Rights and the International Human Rights Covenants. The elaboration of international human rights norms remains one of the commission's most important activities. But through the early 1960s the Commission on Human Rights undertook no serious monitoring or enforcement activities.

This narrow focus began with a 1947 decision by the commission not to act on the thousands of complaints of human rights violations that the UN was receiving annually. ECOSOC Resolution 75, later that year, denied the commission even the right to see details of those complaints. The UN Secretariat recorded and acknowledged their receipt and then filed them away. Nothing else was done. This limited range of commission activities reflected a very strong conception of sovereignty, that is, a narrow reading of the range of international human rights activities permitted by the principle of nonintervention. It also reflected the ambiguous position of intergovernmental human rights bodies.

The principal subjects of international human rights obligations, and the principal violators of international human rights, are the same sovereign states that are the members of the United Nations. They are thus unlikely to grant the UN significant enforcement powers. Furthermore, the members of the Commission on Human Rights are representatives of and directed by states, not independent experts. The commission's initial decision not to act on human rights complaints was thus both legally justifiable and politically understandable—although understandably disappointing to those who desired a more active and aggressive approach. From this perspective, the most notable fact about the Commission on Human Rights may be that it was created at all. As we saw in Chapter 1, the very existence of such a body was unprecedented.

In 1967, however, ECOSOC Resolution 1235 authorized the commission to discuss publicly human rights violations in particular countries. Public discussions and even resolutions are hardly forceful international action. Nonetheless, states at least began to talk about specific human rights violations in the UN rather than maintain a complicitous silence.

And in 1970, ECOSOC Resolution 1503 authorized the commission to conduct confidential investigations of "communications" (complaints) that suggested "a consistent pattern of gross and reliably attested violations of human rights and fundamental freedoms."

Although administratively cumbersome—there are three levels of scrutiny before a situation reaches the full commission—this "1503 Procedure" often operates with considerable impartiality. A large part of the explanation lies in the fact that the members of the subcommission where the process begins serve as independent experts, not state representatives. In practice, of course, many subcommission members have been neither independent nor particularly expert. Nevertheless, initial screening of communications is relatively impartial. As a result, referral of a case to the commission is usually taken as very strong evidence of serious violations.

The 1503 Procedure, however, is strictly confidential. The hope is that states will be encouraged to cooperate and to reform their practices before they are forced into a corner by adverse publicity, or to avoid such publicity. In return, however, the UN renounces the use of publicity, its most powerful weapon in the struggle for human rights.

Few states fear the immediate political power of the UN. Its findings, however, have a certain authority, even though they are not legally binding. Domestic human rights NGOs and other opposition groups may be able to draw support from UN reports and resolutions. International human rights NGOs and foreign governments may also use the findings of the Commission on Human Rights and other respected international organizations. The confidentiality of the 1503 Procedure thus represents a major concession on the part of the UN. Whether this is compensated by an increased willingness of states to cooperate with the commission is hard to assess, in part because of the very confidentiality of the procedure.

The problem of confidentiality has been partially circumvented by an annual announcement by the commission chair of the countries that have been considered under the 1503 procedure that year. This "black list" is certainly better than no publicity. It is also the most that states are willing to allow. Its weakness, however, is evident.

A second serious problem is the slow pace of the 1503 procedure. For example, in November 1974 the UN received its first important complaint against Macias Nguema's regime in Equatorial Guinea, a former Spanish colony in West Africa. Macias Nguema was one of the most vicious dictators of the past half century. In addition to more standard forms of brutality, he forcibly rounded up thousands of innocent civilians to work as virtual slave laborers on an offshore island. The case, however, was not forwarded to the commission until 1977. When he was removed from power in 1979, the investigation still had not been completed.

Because the subcommission and the commission each meet just once a year, the 1503 procedure cannot be brought fully into play in less than two or three years after complaints are received (which may be quite some time after serious violations began). A state can almost always add a year to the process by pretending to be willing to cooperate, as, for example, Argentina did in 1979 and 1980. And political considerations often stretch a case out much longer. For example, Paraguay's genocidal massacres of its Indian population remained under 1503 scrutiny for nine years without any substantial action. A decision on Uruguay, after seven years of scrutiny, came only after the guilty government had been removed from office. Indonesia remained under scrutiny for four years without any action.

The 1503 procedure's restriction to "situations" rather than individual cases presents a third problem. This constraint does focus the commission's attention on systematic violations where the government is obviously culpable. In addition, it was originally possible to obtain sufficient political support for the procedure only by guaranteeing that states would not be subject to embarrassing scrutiny for isolated violations. However, it leaves individual victims without redress and restricts the commission to deterring further human rights violations in countries that have already suffered severe systematic abuses. The 1503 procedure has little or no value as a preventive or early warning device.

Finally, the 1503 procedure is simply weak. The strongest "enforcement" action possible is to make the evidence that has been acquired, along with the commission's views on it, publicly available. This is better than nothing. But rather than real international enforcement, this involves at most a certain degree of semi-independent international monitoring (see Figure 4.1). And in practice, the commission has never fully exercised even these weak procedures.

Nonetheless, we should not ignore the value of publicizing violations and trying to shame states into better compliance with international human rights norms. Even vicious governments may care about their international reputation. Furthermore, publicity often helps at least a few of the more prominent victims of repression. We should also note that in the 1970s human rights violations in approximately twenty countries were examined under the 1503 procedure. In the 1980s, roughly thirty cases were considered. Given that until 1971 the commission could not even read the complaints received at the UN, it is at least moving in the right direction.

The increase in 1503 cases in the 1980s illustrates a general growth in the range and intensity of commission activities. This in turn reflects political changes that began in the late 1970s.

FIGURE 4.1 Leah Levin, *Human Rights: Questions & Answers* (Paris: UNESCO, 1981). Reprinted by permission of UNESCO Publishing.

In the late 1940s and 1950s, a unified Western bloc (itself dominated by the United States) controlled the commission. By 1967, the commission, like the rest of the UN, was largely under the control of the Third World (Nonaligned Movement), with substantial Soviet bloc support. Those states used the UN to focus international attention on apartheid in South Africa, Israeli practices in the Occupied Territories, and issues of self-determination. But the same states strongly opposed general human rights–monitoring procedures.

By 1979 or 1980, however, some Third World countries, such as Costa Rica and Senegal, were ready to consider stronger and broader international human rights initiatives. A revitalized Western bloc, led by countries such as Canada and the Netherlands, also emerged as a major force in the commission. For the first time in its history, the commission was not under the control of a single political bloc. This allowed the development of a coalition that favored more-aggressive commission activity.

To reduce political constraints, a decision was made to consider human rights violations on a "global" or "thematic" basis. Rather than examine the full range of abuses in individual countries, the commission addressed particular types of violations globally, wherever they occurred.

In 1980, the commission created a Working Group on Enforced or Involuntary Disappearances. Its principal goal has been to assist families and friends in determining the whereabouts of disappeared persons. After receiving and examining written communications offering details of a disappearance, the working group transmits the case to the government in question. If necessary, reminders are sent, at least once a year. Over 19,000 cases were handled in the group's first decade of work. In roughly one case in ten, government responses have established the whereabouts or fate of the individual. There are also urgent-action procedures for disappearances within the past three months. This is when most victims suffer torture or execution, but also when they are most likely to reappear. Urgent inquiries have resolved about one case in five.

Ironically, the first urgent inquiries concerned Mohamed al-Jabiri, Iraq's representative to the commission. He had been crucial in establishing the working group and was slated to be its first chair. But he apparently ran afoul of Iraqi dictator Saddam Hussein and was recalled to Baghdad. When even his wife was unable to locate him, Theo van Boven, director of the Division of Human Rights, began diplomatic inquiries and threatened to publicize the case. About a week later, van Boven received a handwritten note from al-Jabiri saying that he had decided to retire.

It is uncertain what al-Jabiri's fate would have been had there not been immediate UN intervention. His case does suggest, though, that aggressive international procedures can help at least a few victims. Furthermore, the working group's annual inquiries about unresolved cases, even when they are ignored, are at least a reminder that someone still cares.

A special rapporteur on summary or arbitrary executions was appointed in 1982. S. Amos Wako, a Kenyan national and secretary-general of the Inter-African Union of Lawyers, has aggressively pursued his mandate. Wako's first report identified thirty-seven governments alleged to practice summary or arbitrary executions. The 1990 report noted over 1,500 alleged cases in forty-eight countries. Once more, the chosen instrument is publicity, with the aim of helping at least a few victims or potential victims of a widespread and particularly reprehensible type of human rights violation.

In 1985, Peter Kooijmans, the Dutch delegate and outgoing chair of the commission, was appointed special rapporteur on torture. In addition to approaching governments with information on alleged torture in their countries—thirty-three in the first year alone—Kooijmans has developed urgent-action procedures similar to those of the working group on disappearances. He has made also official visits to several countries, including Guatemala, South Korea, Peru, Turkey, and Zaire.

In addition to these thematic monitoring initiatives,[3] the commission in the 1980s undertook important new normative work, including the 1984 convention against torture, a 1986 Declaration on the Right to Development, and the 1989 Convention on the Rights of the Child. A Second Optional Protocol to the International Covenant on Civil and Political Rights, outlawing the death penalty, was also completed in 1989. New initiatives were also introduced on human rights defenders, minorities, and indigenous peoples.

There were also efforts at revitalizing public information and advisory services. Training courses were held on implementing human rights conventions. Experts sent to advise new civilian governments in Bolivia, Equatorial Guinea, Guatemala, Haiti, and Uganda, however, seem to have had little or no impact. Regional seminars held in Asia seem to have had no real influence on developing a regional human rights regime.

There are still substantial political constraints on the commission's activities. For example, during the 1990 session, an almost embarrassingly mild resolution on human rights violations in the PRC, which did not even explicitly condemn the 1989 Tienanmen massacres but only asked for clemency for convicted dissidents, welcomed the lifting of martial law and the release of prisoners, and urged further future positive steps, was defeated. Nonetheless, the Commission on Human Rights is likely to remain an active, and occasionally even effective, part of the global human rights regime. And it remains the primary international body that, in principle at least, may examine human rights violations anywhere in the world.

THE GENERAL ASSEMBLY
AND THE HUMAN RIGHTS COMMITTEE

The two other principal institutions of the global (UN) human rights regime are the UN General Assembly (GA), the formal center of the UN system, and the Human Rights Committee, a body of independent experts that supervises implementation of the International Covenant on Civil and Political Rights.

The General Assembly, in which each member of the United Nations has one vote, must give final UN approval to any proposed human rights treaty. On occasion it has even made important drafting decisions. For example, the final compromises on the 1984 convention against torture were worked out at the last minute in the General Assembly. The GA also sets guidelines for the entire organization, both through formal resolutions and through cues provided by its discussions and its well-known political dynamics. The GA has also been a major actor in the international struggle against racism and colonialism and has even taken a leading role in the public condemnation of human rights violations in selected countries.

Here, however, we come face-to-face with the problem of political bias in the UN system, for until recently, public action was largely limited to the pariah regimes of South Africa, Israel, and Chile. Although all three countries richly merited international condemnation, comparable violations elsewhere have not received comparable—or in some cases any— scrutiny or action.

In both South Africa and the Occupied Territories, human rights violations of special concern to the Third World have been linked to regional political struggles. The resulting politics is thus easily understood. But the case of the third pariah, Chile, did not even raise issues of racism or colonialism.[4] Furthermore, comparable violations in neighboring Argentina and Uruguay went unaddressed. And barbaric regimes in Africa and Asia, such as that of Pol Pot in Cambodia, the Amin and (second) Obote governments in Uganda, and the Mengistu regime in Ethiopia, were never even the subject of a GA human rights resolution.

Political bias did decline a bit in the General Assembly in the 1980s, with the passage of repeated human rights resolutions on El Salvador, Guatemala, and Iran. Nonetheless, the omissions still are more striking than the inclusions. Although no country with a good human rights record has been the subject of UN action, politics has largely determined which repressive regimes have been condemned in the General Assembly and which have not.

The United Nations is a political body, used by sovereign states to further their own national interests. Rarely do states define their national interest to include strong and impartial international monitoring and enforcement of human rights. The decision of all but one of the Latin American members of the Commission on Human Rights to abstain on the 1990 resolution on the PRC reminds us that even newly democratic regimes do not necessarily support strong international human rights initiatives. Nonetheless, an increasing number of states have begun to accept the idea of more or less nonpartisan international monitoring of at least some rights, in a growing number of particular countries.

The Human Rights Committee is a body of eighteen experts that supervises implementation of the International Covenant on Civil and Political Rights. Although not a permanent organ of the United Nations, it does report annually to the UN. Its principal activity is to review reports on compliance submitted by parties to the covenant.

The questions posed by members of the committee often are penetrating and critical. Sometimes the responses are serious and thoughtful. In such cases, the result is a genuine exchange of information that provides a real element of international monitoring. The representative of the reporting state, however, need not answer any question, let alone provide an answer that satisfies the questioner. And many reports contain little more than extracts from laws and the constitution or obviously evasive claims of compliance. Furthermore, whatever the quality of the report, once it has been reviewed, the monitoring process typically ends until the next report is due, in five years. The committee may ask for, but cannot demand, supplemental material, and it has chosen not to ask for interim or ad hoc reports. It cannot even assure timely submission of reports. Zaire presents an extreme example: its initial report, due in 1978, was not submitted until 1987. And the entire process applies only to the (currently 114) parties to the covenant.

Despite these weaknesses, the Human Rights Committee can draw some public attention to a country's record. This may occasionally embarrass a state into altering its practices. The need to report to a relatively impartial international body may even be a minor check on certain contemplated violations. Perhaps the greatest contribution of this or any other reporting process, however, is the review of national practices required to conscientiously prepare a report. Where there is a commitment to improved performance, international reporting can help to highlight areas where change is needed or possible. This may be particularly valuable in newly democratic countries.

The Human Rights Committee may also consider complaints from individuals in states that are parties to the covenant's (first) optional protocol.[5] Although there are only 66 parties and democratic countries are disproportionately represented, the optional protocol provides a strong system of international monitoring.

The committee is authorized not only to gather information and ask questions but also to state its "views" on the substance of the case; that is, to make a public declaration of violations. Through July 1992, 514 communications concerning individual victims in twenty-nine states were registered, and the committee had made a substantive determination on the merits of 138 cases, finding violations in 106. And in response, several states have altered their behavior or provided redress to the victim. For example, Canada has altered its legislation concerning the rights of Indians living off their tribal lands, Mauritius has altered legislation concerning women's rights, and the Netherlands has altered social security legislation that the committee found discriminatory.

Table 4.1 lists the final actions taken by the Human Rights Committee under the optional protocol during a representative three-year period, from mid-1986 to mid-1989. Although the list of countries on which action was taken is hardly representative of the world's major human rights violators, there is some geographical diversity.[6] Furthermore, complaints are pursued relatively aggressively. This is perhaps clearest in the committee's innovative decision to treat a state's failure to respond as an admission of culpability.

The limitations of the procedure, however, are no less noteworthy. Most major human rights violators, not surprisingly, have elected not to be covered. This is the overriding problem of treaty-based enforcement mechanisms. Obligations apply only to parties to the treaty, and states are free to choose not to accept these obligations. The stronger the monitoring and implementation procedures, the fewer the states that are willing to be covered. The optional protocol thus presents a striking example of the typical trade-off between the scope and the strength of international procedures.

The small number of cases considered under the optional protocol is another major shortcoming. This is an inherent limitation of a process that deals only with individual cases rather than groups of cases or broader situations. The focus on individual cases, however, gives the process a valuable specificity and concreteness. Because violations are personalized and detailed evidence of individual violations is provided, it is much more difficult for states to deny responsibility. The 1503 procedure and the optional protocol thus have roughly opposite strengths.

Nonetheless, the Human Rights Committee, along with the parallel Committee on Economic, Social, and Cultural Rights,[7] provides a substantial degree of independent international monitoring. And because it may examine violations that are not severe enough to merit scrutiny by the Commission on Human Rights, the Human Rights Committee plays an important and distinctive role in the global human rights regime.

SINGLE-ISSUE
HUMAN RIGHTS REGIMES

We now turn to five narrower, single-issue, or "functional," regimes, dealing with workers' rights, racial discrimination, apartheid, women's rights, and torture.[8] These single-issue regimes provide both elaborations of international human rights norms and additional procedures for monitoring and supervising their implementation.

TABLE 4.1   Decisions Under the Optional Protocol, 1986–1989

Final Verdicts

Bolivia: torture and denial of a fair trial
Colombia: torture and the right to life
Dominican Republic: arbitrary arrest and inhuman treatment
Ecuador: right to a timely trial
Finland: due process in a case of military discipline
France: right to a fair hearing; discrimination in the awarding of military pensions
Jamaica: special procedural guarantees to assure a fair trial in capital cases
Netherlands: gender discrimination in social security benefits; discrimination against
    cohabiting couples in social security benefits; family rights (visitation rights of divorced
    parents)
Peru: right to a fair hearing; right of a married woman to litigate
Sweden: educational discrimination; cultural rights of ethnic minorities
Uruguay: torture and right to a fair trial (under the military regime); preferential access to
    public employment for persons dismissed during military rule
Zaire: torture and right to life

Complaints Declared Inadmissible[a]

Canada: three cases, dealing with discrimination, fair trial, and the rights of aliens
Costa Rica: one case concerning the rights of aliens
Finland: two cases of due process in drug trials
France: five language-discrimination cases
Italy: two cases, dealing with double jeopardy and the rights of detainees
Jamaica: six death penalty cases
Netherlands: eight cases, most dealing with discrimination of various types
Sweden: one case concerning religious freedom
Trinidad and Tobago: two cases of freedom of the press

[a]Most were declared inadmissible because the parties had failed to exhaust local remedies or
because the complaints were unsubstantiated or did not deal with rights covered in the
Covenant.

Workers' Rights

The first international human rights regime of any sort was the work-ers' rights regime developed in the International Labor Organization (ILO) after World War I. Important ILO conventions (treaties) have dealt with freedom of association, the right to organize and bargain collectively, forced labor, migrant workers, and indigenous peoples, as well as with a variety of technical issues concerning working conditions and workplace safety. Even ILO recommendations are widely respected and provide an important international point of reference for national standards and practices.

ILO monitoring procedures, which date back to 1926, have been the model for other international human rights reporting systems. The Committee of Experts meets annually to review periodic reports submit-ted by states on their implementation of ratified conventions. If apparent problems are uncovered, the committee may issue a "direct request" for information or for changes in policy. Over the past two decades, more than a thousand such requests have brought changes in national policies. If the problem remains unresolved, the committee may make "observations," that is, authoritative determinations of violations of the convention in question.

The Conference Committee, which is made up of ILO delegates rather than independent experts, provides an additional level of scrutiny. Each year, it selects cases from the report of the Committee of Experts for further review. Government representatives are called upon to provide additional information and explanation. Special complaint procedures also exist for violations of the right to freedom of association and for discrimination in employment.

No less important than these inquisitorial or adversarial procedures is the institution of "direct contacts." Since 1969, the ILO has engaged in an extensive program of consultations and advice, often initiated by a government concerned about improving its performance with respect to a particular convention. The ILO is a leader in this method of cooperative resolution of problems *before* they reach international monitoring bodies.

Part of the ILO's success can be attributed to its unique tripartite structure. Virtually all other intergovernmental organizations are made up entirely of state representatives. NGOs often participate in deliberations but have no decision-making powers. In the ILO, however, workers' and employers' representatives from each member state are full voting members of the organization. It is therefore much more difficult for states to hide behind the curtain of sovereignty.

The transideological appeal of workers' rights has also been important to the ILO's success. In addition, the Committee of Experts, the ILO's central monitoring body, deals principally with technical issues such as hours of work, minimum working age, radiation protection, exposure to benzene, and identity documents for seamen. In monitoring implementation of these conventions, the committee develops and confirms expectations of neutrality. This relatively depoliticized institutional environment often helps to moderate controversy when more contentious "political" issues do arise.

The ILO is, however, an international organization and thus not entirely immune from political pressures and biases. For example, ILO criticisms of Israel for labor practices that went uncriticized in many other countries led the United States to withdraw temporarily in the late 1970s. Nonetheless, the ILO has been unusually active, effective, and impartial in its human rights work and a model for other international monitoring bodies.

Racial Discrimination

The central document of the racial discrimination regime is the 1965 International Convention on the Elimination of All Forms of Racial Discrimination, which entered into force in 1969 and had 132 parties at the end of 1992. Other important documents include the 1960 UNESCO Convention Against Discrimination in Education, and ILO Convention No. 111 Concerning Discrimination in Respect of Employment and Occupation.

The racial discrimination convention establishes an eighteen-member Committee on the Elimination of Racial Discrimination (CERD) and a reporting system that was the direct model for that of the Human Rights Committee, discussed above. The provision for complaints by one state against another (Article 11), however, has never been used. And only fourteen states have authorized the committee to receive complaints from individual citizens, rendering the procedure effectively useless.

CERD's principal activity has been to review state reports. It has discharged this task with seriousness and relative impartiality, although its review has often been less penetrating than that of the Human Rights Committee. The procedure provides a mandatory international exchange of information, with the hope that publicity may shame at least some current or potential violators into better performance. Like other supervisory bodies, however, CERD has often had difficulties assuring that reports are submitted. More than 10 percent of the reports due during the entire life of the convention have not been received, some despite a dozen reminders over nearly a decade.

We should also note that the regime deals only with *racial* discrimination. Discrimination on the basis of (nonracial) ethnicity is not covered. In fact, ethnic discrimination is not a high priority in international human rights forums, although (or, perhaps, because) it is a more widespread problem.

Apartheid

South Africa has become virtually synonymous with **apartheid**—literally, separateness; more loosely, racial separation—a distinctive style of unusually wide-ranging systematic racial domination. Although apartheid was officially abolished in 1991 and the decision confirmed in a whites-only referendum in April 1992, it had been government policy for over four decades and a major international human rights issue for thirty years.

A System of Racial Domination. Racism and racial discrimination go back to the initial Dutch colonization of South Africa in 1652. Local hunting peoples (San, often called by the pejorative term *Bushmen*) were largely killed off or pushed out, whereas local herding peoples (Khoikhoi, "Hottentots") were forced off their grazing lands. Slaves began to be imported in 1658. Blacks have been discriminated against in voting from the very beginning (and they lost the formal right to vote in 1936) and legally excluded from many jobs since 1911. And so forth.

The electoral victory of the conservative Nationalist party in 1948, however, marked a major qualitative change. Old policies that had not always been fully or consistently enforced were tightened, extended, certified and coordinated. Racial distinctions became the basis for regulating all aspects of life in post-1948 South Africa. Moreover, the white government created an essentially totalitarian bureaucracy to enforce racism in all aspects of social, economic, and political life. The official rationale was racial and cultural preservation—separation and separate development—rather than inequality. In practice, though, apartheid meant white privilege and domination. Perhaps the easiest way to see this is to consider population and income figures in Table 4.2.

The Population Registration Act of 1950 was the cornerstone of apartheid, requiring the racial registration of each person at birth (usually on the basis of the race of the parents). The fundamental divide in South African society is between white and nonwhite (although there are important social and political differences between the Afrikaner community, descended principally from Dutch colonists of the seventeenth and eighteenth centuries, and the English-speaking community, descended primarily from British colonists of the nineteenth century). Nonwhites are further divided officially into three groups. The descendants of the non-Bantu indigenous peoples of central and western South Africa (and of intermarriages and interbreeding) are known as "Coloureds." Africans (or Bantus) are descended from the other indigenous peoples (largely from eastern South Africa). "Asians" are primarily of Indian descent, having been imported as laborers in considerable numbers between 1860 and 1911.

The Group Areas Act of 1950 (amended in 1957) consolidated and extended earlier laws designating land by race, and the 1954 Natives Resettlement Act provided for forced removals of blacks from white-designated land.[9] Controls on the movement of nonwhites begun by the 1945 Urban Areas Act culminated in a series of pass laws and regulations that made it illegal for most blacks to be in urban areas for more than seventy-two hours without special permission from the authorities. The result has been the creation of black "townships" on the outskirts of (white) cities, often two hours away from the (white) areas where blacks worked. Even ignoring the inferior housing, education, and social services of the townships, distance alone created an intolerable burden on those legally in the area.

TABLE 4.2   South African Population and Income, 1980

Ethnic Group	Population (%)	Income (%)
White	15.4	64.9
African	73.0	24.9
Coloured	8.9	7.2
Asian	2.7	3.0

Source: Francis Wilson and Mamphela Ramphele, Uprooting Poverty: The South African Challenge. Report of the Second Carnegie Inquiry into Poverty and Development in Southern Africa. New York: W. W. Norton, 1989, Figure 1.04.

Because of the absurdities of the system of restrictions on movement, the ordinary nonwhite was subject to the constant threat of prosecution. Pass law prosecutions averaged about 320,000 per year in the 1950s, 470,000 per year in the 1960s, and well over one-half million per year in the 1970s. With a black and Coloured population of under 24 million in 1980, this meant that the average nonwhite South African had a better than one in fifty chance of being prosecuted on pass law violations each year. More than one-fifth of the population could expect to be prosecuted within a ten-year period. This is a staggering level of legal intrusion on the basis of just one set of rules. And because those violations often led to expulsion from the area and the loss of one's only source of income, the pass law was an extraordinarily powerful instrument of social control.

The policy of geographical separation was taken to its logical culmination in the 1959 Promotion of Bantu Self-Government Act, which redefined black areas of the country as "Bantustans," purported "Homelands" for South Africa's various black ethnic groups. The Black Homelands Citizenship Act of 1970 went one step further, providing for the eventual independence of these Homelands from South Africa. From the white government's point of view, this had the tactical advantage of defining large numbers of black South Africans as aliens, who enjoyed even fewer legal protections. More than one-third of the black population was legally redefined as aliens, guest workers in their own country.

There was little connection to reality in the Homelands system. According to the official census of 1980, 48 percent of all blacks were living in white areas (a figure that does not include illegal residents). And it was a good thing, for the land defined as Homelands was largely barren and completely unable to support the population.[10] To get all the people where they "belonged" would have involved moving about 40 percent of the total population of the country. And the result would have been mass starvation for blacks and the collapse of white standards of living and the white economy, which were built around ready access to cheap (black) labor.

This so-called grand apartheid was fully supported by an elaborate system of "petty apartheid" laws and regulations. The 1927 Immorality Act had made extramarital sexual relations between whites and Africans punishable by up to seven years in jail. The 1949 Prohibition of Mixed Marriages Act extended the ban to legal unions. The 1953 Reservation of Separate Amenities Act removed the formal legal requirement that racially segregated facilities be equal. The 1957 State-Aided Institutions Act gave the government the authority to determine who could visit a library or any place of entertainment. The Native Laws Amendment Act of 1957 prohibited holding classes, church services, or any meeting by Africans in designated white areas. The euphemistically named Extension of University Education Act of 1959 effectively removed nonwhites from most existing universities and established new, and decidedly inferior, ethnic universities. And so forth.

Increasingly repressive internal-security laws were passed to prevent political opposition. The 1950 Suppression of Communism Act banned the Communist party and allowed the minister of justice to declare kindred groups illegal. This cast a very wide net, because the act defined communism as in effect any doctrine seeking to change the basic structure of South African society, economy, or political system. By 1967, there were essentially no legal safeguards left for those suspected of political offenses. At least 100 people have died while being detained by the police or security forces, usually after having been tortured. The best-known victim was black-consciousness activist Steve Biko.

Many who were not formally detained were brought in by the authorities for questioning, often as a not-so-subtle warning. Any organization could be banned (that is, outlawed), and the printing or dissemination of any publication prohibited. South Africa also "banned" individuals, restricting their movements, limiting whom they might see (sometimes only their immediate family), and prohibiting them from speaking publicly or being quoted in the media. The basic strategy was to question, detain, or ban anyone showing any signs of dissidence. This effectively forced all nonparliamentary opposition underground.

This does not mean that there was no resistance. The African National Congress (ANC), the leading black political group in contemporary South Africa, was founded in 1912. The 1952–1953 Pass Law Demonstrations marked the beginning of modern organized resistance to apartheid. Resistance, however, took on new forms after the police opened fire on a group of peaceful demonstrators on March 21, 1960, killing nearly 70 people and wounding about 200 others in what has come to be known as the Sharpeville Massacre.

When the ANC and several other groups were banned, a number of leading activists of the 1950s, including Nelson Mandela, concluded that peaceful protest alone could not be successful. Umkhonto we Sizwe (The Spear of the Resistance) was formed by ANC and Communist party activists to carry out a sabotage campaign. They caused little damage, however, and had no discernible political effect, except perhaps to increase the intensity of official repression. Mandela and several other leaders were arrested in Rivonia in 1963 and in 1964 convicted and sentenced to life imprisonment. The ANC was forced into exile. The mass protests and riots of 1976 and 1977 were more damaging, but the government weathered the storm through a combination of force, new restrictions, and minor concessions.

Peaceful opposition also continued, despite the best efforts of the government to make it illegal. South African churches were particularly important in this regard, since almost all overtly political opposition organizations were banned. The awarding of the Nobel Peace Prize in 1984 to Bishop Desmond Tutu symbolized this struggle. Black trade union activity also increased, and became an important political force with the formation of the Congress of South African Trade Unions (COSATU) at the end of 1985.

New and unusually violent uprisings in the townships, however, broke out in the fall of 1984 and lasted for nearly two years. A state of emergency was declared in July 1985. A new, even harsher, state of emergency was declared in June 1986. Torture and abuse of those detained increased dramatically, and doctors and clinics who treated torture victims became subjects of official and unofficial harassment. Official violence against those not detained also increased. Symbolic was the widely seen video footage of armed security force personnel popping up from their hiding place inside a passing vehicle and opening fire on unarmed children. Another symbol was the massacre of about twenty unarmed marchers on the road between Langa and Uitenhage in March 1985. According to the official inquiry, at least fifteen were shot in the back, as were most of those who were wounded. In addition, and even more ominous, violence by police-sponsored vigilante groups increased dramatically.[11]

Direct repression was accompanied by no less severe social and economic exploitation and degradation. As one can calculate from the figures in Table 4.2, the average white has an income more than twelve times that of the average black. Infant mortality, a widely used measure of health care, also shows a striking difference: a black child is eight to ten times likelier to die before the age of one than a white child (see Table 4.3). In 1980, the doctor-to-patient ratio was 1:330 for whites and 1:19,000 for blacks. More than half of all urban dwellers, and an even higher percentage of rural dwellers, lived in extreme poverty. White illiteracy was less than 2 percent, black illiteracy 29 percent. Other standard statistical measures paint a similar picture.

TABLE 4.3   South African Infant Mortality, 1981–1985 (per 1,000 live births)

	White	Asian	Coloured	African
National	12	18	52	94–124
Ten major urban areas	12	17	26	39
Rural and peri-urban	12	20	66	100–135

Excludes four "independent" Homelands and thus probably understates levels.

Source: Francis Wilson and Mamphela Ramphele, *Uprooting Poverty: The South African Challenge. Report of the Second Carnegie Inquiry into Poverty and Development in Southern Africa.* New York: W. W. Norton, 1989, Table 5.02b.

Apartheid has ended officially, and negotiations are under way to institute a political system based on universal suffrage and majority rule. The legacy of apartheid remains, however, in the economy, psyche, and very geography of South Africa. It is always dangerous to predict the future, but it seems clear that from a human rights point of view the end of apartheid merely opens a new chapter in the struggle for human rights in South Africa. It is by no means a solution in itself. South Africa, like most of the other cases considered in this volume, reminds us of the difference between ending old forms of human rights violations and establishing new rights-protective regimes, a problem to which we will return in Chapter 6.

The International Campaign Against Apartheid. The United Nations has addressed racial discrimination in South Africa since 1946, but it was a relatively low-priority issue until the 1960 Sharpeville Massacre. In the subsequent thirty years, however, a flood of resolutions sought to mobilize international support for the national and international struggle against apartheid.

In 1962, the UN General Assembly called on states to break diplomatic relations and boycott all trade with South Africa. The decisions of the General Assembly, however, are only recommendations, and until the 1980s they were largely ignored by most powerful states. The Security Council, which does have the authority to impose mandatory sanctions, established only a voluntary arms embargo in December 1963. A mandatory arms embargo was not approved until November 1977, after the death of Steve Biko while in police custody and the ensuing repression in Soweto. Not only nationally but internationally as well the death of the charismatic Biko, the subject of books, films, and popular songs, was a crucial turning point in South African history. Although efforts over the following decade failed to establish a more comprehensive trade embargo, several states undertook a variety of actions to reduce or eliminate their diplomatic, cultural, and commercial relations with South Africa, as we will see in Chapter 5.

The United Nations has developed a complex web of procedures and forums for mobilizing pressure on South Africa. The Special Committee on Apartheid, created in 1962, has played a central role in promoting a broad international campaign against apartheid. Over the years, the committee's activities have become quite extensive and sophisticated. National support committees have been formed, and opinion leaders in several countries have been specially targeted. In 1975 a Trust Fund for Publicity Against Apartheid was established.

Material assistance has also been provided to victims. The United Nations Educational and Training Program for Southern Africa, established in 1964, has made over 20,000 grants to South Africans studying abroad. The United Nations Trust Fund for South Africa, established in 1965, has provided over $30 million in legal, educational, and humanitarian assistance to the victims of apartheid, including refugees.

The 1973 International Convention on the Suppression and Punishment of the Crime of Apartheid came into force in 1976 and had ninety-four parties at the end of 1992. Although the convention attempts to establish international criminal liability, no prosecutions have occurred in any of the parties to the convention. Furthermore, the "Group of Three," which receives reports on and make recommendations with respect to the implementation of the convention, has had no discernible impact. The apartheid convention is thus largely a symbolic normative document.

Reiteration of antiapartheid norms and associated condemnations of South Africa have become a regular feature of most international organizations. For example, the ILO has paid considerable attention to questions of workers' rights in South Africa. Other specialized agencies, such as the World Health Organization, have also given particularly close scrutiny to South African policies in their areas of special competence. Others have adopted the alternative strategy of excluding South Africa, beginning with the International Telecommunications Union in 1965. The South African government has been prevented from taking its seat in the United Nations General Assembly since 1970.

The norm of isolation was applied with particular force in sports, culminating in the 1985 International Convention Against Apartheid in Sports. South Africa was unable to participate in the Olympics from 1964 until 1992. The Special Committee on Apartheid also kept and publicized a list of sporting contacts with South Africa, in an attempt to pressure national sporting federations to join the boycott. Less systematic efforts were also made to monitor, deter, and give adverse publicity to cultural contacts.

The principal positive influence of the apartheid regime probably was the support, encouragement, and justification it provided for individuals and national and international NGOs trying to alter the foreign policies of individual states. Difficult as it may be to specify, Stultz suggested that "simple reiteration of regime norms" may have been not only a real, but also the most important, contribution of the apartheid regime.[12]

Its concrete achievements, however, are more questionable. Changing the foreign policies of other states has not been, and could not be, in itself, a solution to the problem of apartheid. The persistence of white rule in South Africa after the dismantling of formal apartheid in 1991 underscores the ultimate weakness of even extensive and relatively strong international human rights regimes in the face of a truly recalcitrant human rights violator. And even these changes have come about only after thirty years of just about the strongest actions available to the United Nations. Nonetheless, international pressure certainly played a role in the process of reform that led to the March 1992 decision of the white electorate to abolish a race-based social and political system in South Africa.

Women's Rights

The 1979 Convention on the Elimination of Discrimination Against Women, which entered into force in 1981 and had 120 parties by the end of 1992, significantly extends the women's rights provisions of the International Bill of Human Rights.[13] In addition, it establishes a twenty-three-member expert body, the Committee on the Elimination of Discrimination Against Women (CEDAW). CEDAW operates very much like the Human Rights Committee in its review of reports but is not authorized to receive individual communications.

The other major supervisory body is the Commission on the Status of Women, a permanent functional commission of ECOSOC. Although authorized to study individual communications, it does not have the authority to study or comment on conditions in individual countries. Furthermore, it meets only biennially, with little publicity and little discernable impact.

Throughout the UN system, women's rights issues have been subject to a variety of subtle, and sometimes not so subtle, denigrations. For example, women's rights are not usually handled in the Commission on Human Rights but rather in the separate—and definitely not equal—Commission on the Status of Women. Moreover, CEDAW does not meet in Geneva or New York, like the other human rights bodies, but in Vienna. And whereas twenty-two of the twenty-three members of CEDAW in 1988 were women, only one of eighteen members of the Committee on the Elimination of Racial Discrimination (CERD), and two of eighteen in each of the committees supervising the International Human Rights Covenants were female. Women's rights seem to be of little interest to men in international organizations, and other human rights would seem to be "too important" to be handled by women.

A major treaty on gender discrimination was not negotiated until 1979, fourteen years after the racial discrimination convention. CEDAW meets for only two weeks a year, while the Committee on the Elimination of Racial Discrimination typically meets for *three* two-week sessions. Such a difference simply cannot be justified by differences in the nature of the groups' work or the pervasiveness of the problems they address. If anything, the amount of time would be reversed, were it based on the number of victims or the severity of violations. Furthermore, until 1989 the members of CEDAW were not even authorized to meet in a working group before the annual session to prepare for the review of reports. "The Committee lacks the meeting time and the resources to carry out even its most basic functions properly."[14]

None of these problems is irremediable. Nonetheless, without substantial changes, the supervisory mechanisms of the women's rights regime will remain significantly weaker than those of other international human rights regimes (which, as we have seen above, are not terribly strong).

Torture

Torture is the final major single-issue human rights regime. We saw above that the Commission on Human Rights established a special rapporteur on torture in 1985, just months after the 1984 Convention Against Torture and Other Cruel, Inhuman, or Degrading Treatment or Punishment was opened for signature. In addition, a UN Voluntary Fund for Torture Victims has operated since 1981, providing financial assistance for victims, support groups, and research on strategies to help torture victims and their families.

There has been unusually close and fruitful cooperation among states, NGOs, and intergovernmental organizations on the issue of torture. For example, both the convention and the special rapporteur owe much to the intensive lobbying and public information activities of Amnesty International over more than a decade. In a very different vein, Copenhagen is the home of an international Rehabilitation and Research Center for Torture Victims, a location that reflects the leading role of Denmark in international action against torture. Similar centers operate in Canada, Norway, and other countries (see Figure 4.2).

The provisions of the convention against torture, which entered into force in 1987 and had seventy parties by the end of 1992, are unusually strong. "No exceptional circumstances whatsoever, whether a state of war or threat of war, internal political instability or any other public emergency, may be invoked as a justification of torture" (Article 2[2]). Orders from superiors are explicitly excluded as a defense. In addition, the convention imposes special obligations concerning the training of law enforcement personnel and the periodic review of interrogation regula-

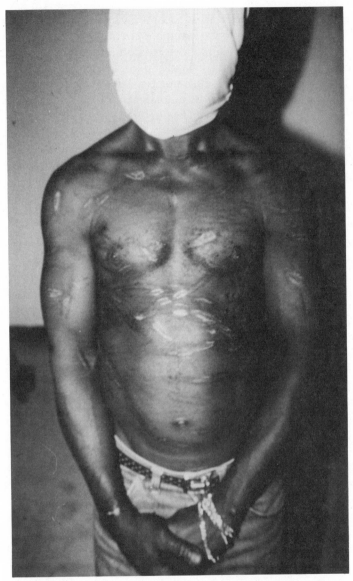

FIGURE 4.2 Torture in Kuwait: Thirty-five-year-old Sudanese man arrested in March 1991 and later examined by Amnesty International's pathologist. He had been beaten with electric cables and burned with cigarettes. Amnesty International photo.

tions and methods. To reduce police incentives to resort to torture, statements obtained through torture must be made inadmissible in all legal proceedings. The convention also requires that wherever the alleged torture occurred, and whatever the nationality of the torturer and the victim, parties must either prosecute the alleged torturers or extradite them to a country that will.

As in other treaty-based implementation schemes, the principal function of the ten-member Committee Against Torture (CAT) is to receive and review periodic reports, which must be submitted by parties every four years. Article 19 authorizes the committee to "make such general comments on the report as it may consider appropriate." In addition, almost half the parties to the convention have accepted the authority of the committee to consider individual communications.

CAT is also authorized to investigate communications concerning *situations* where torture is systematically practiced. These powers, which are similar to the 1503 procedure in the Commission on Human Rights, are unique for a treaty-based supervisory body. Four-fifths of the parties have agreed to be covered by this procedure.

On the basis of the convention and the early work of the CAT, the torture regime would seem to be perhaps the strongest of all international human rights regimes. It deals with only one right, in about one-third of the countries of the world, all of which have voluntarily agreed to this international monitoring. It is, however, a significant achievement.

There are also regional conventions against torture in Europe and the Americas. In addition, there has been growing international attention to the broader issue of the rights of detainees. For example, in December 1988 the UN General Assembly adopted a "Body of Principles for the Protection of All Persons Under Any Form of Detention or Imprisonment." This is the first major international legal document in this area since the 1955 Standard Minimum Rules for the Treatment of Prisoners. And in 1991 the Commission on Human Rights established a Working Group on Arbitrary Detention, a practice that is often associated with torture.

ASSESSING INTERNATIONAL HUMAN RIGHTS REPORTING SYSTEMS

As we have seen, member states' reporting is the central implementation mechanism of most international human rights regimes. Although the weakness of such an "enforcement" mechanism hardly needs to be emphasized, we should be careful not to think of international reporting systems in overly adversarial terms. Reporting procedures cannot force recalcitrant states to alter their practices. Those procedures can, however, provide additional incentives for states seeking to improve or safeguard their human rights record.

Preparing a report requires a national review of law and practice. If the review is thorough and conscientious, it can uncover areas where improvement may be needed or possible. In any case, it provides a concrete periodic reminder to officials of their international legal obligations and assures that there will be at least one international body periodically reviewing the actions of those responsible for implementing internationally recognized human rights. The reports of some countries may even provide ideas and models for other countries, as may the comments of the supervisory committee.

Reporting as an implementation technique thus functions primarily through the goodwill and good intentions of reporting states. The obvious limitations of such a process simply reflect the basic problem of international action on behalf of human rights in a world of sovereign states. Each state has almost exclusive responsibility for implementing human rights in its own territory. The human rights practices of all states are (in principle) subject to scrutiny in the Commission on Human Rights. Many states have accepted additional scrutiny by becoming parties to the Covenants and other human rights treaties. But actual implementation is up to states. Supervisory bodies must thus struggle to make the most of the opportunities for influence available during the review of reports.

This sometimes means attempting to chastise or embarrass a state into better compliance. A more productive course, however, may be to try to establish a constructive dialogue between the state and the supervisory body and to exert pressure through that dialogue not just once but over time. "Weaker" and less adversarial techniques thus may in some cases actually have a greater positive effect.

Initiatives directed toward states with less bad, or even relatively good, records are thus a particularly promising place for international action. States that are not severe violators have, by their behavior, given concrete evidence of relatively good intentions. They are thus likely to be more open to international suggestions and more concerned about their international human rights reputation. If monitoring committees can make the reporting process a more valuable exercise for such states, through a combination of constructive guidance and selective pressure, the reporting process itself may contribute to improvements in national human rights practices.

There is thus a paradox at the root of international monitoring procedures. They are likely to be most effective in improving national human rights practices where they are in some sense least needed; that is, where human rights records are relatively good (or less bad). Recalcitrant states usually can violate human rights with impunity. But the fact that international reporting schemes are unlikely to have much impact in such cases does not make them worthless. A country with a relatively good (or less bad) record may still violate human rights. A victim of human rights violations in such a country is likely to receive little solace from knowing that there are people who are treated worse elsewhere. Any victim who is helped is a victory for international action, wherever that person resides.

The proliferation of international human rights reporting systems, however, may be creating a problem even for well-intentioned states. All committees face a problem with seriously late reports. For example, in 1991 twelve parties to the International Covenant on Economic, Social, and Cultural Rights (one-eighth of the total) had been parties for ten years or more but still had not submitted their *first* report. Although much of the explanation is state indifference, we should not overlook the administrative burden of reporting, especially in small or poor states.

If a state lacks the skills or the resources required for a conscientious review of its practices, reporting is an empty formality, even if the government is well intentioned. The impact of reporting systems thus could be significantly improved by linking them to a system of technical and financial support. Although many states would not avail themselves of such help, at least some would. (Countries that have recently undergone a change of government would be particularly promising candidates.) But given the financial problems of the UN system and the tendency not to support human rights projects through traditional channels of development assistance, such changes are unlikely. Substantially less than 1 percent of the UN budget is devoted to human rights work.

Another way to help to ease the reporting burden would be to standardize reporting systems. It is still too early, however, to determine what impact efforts at standardization that began in 1987 will have. The UN has also recently attempted to set standards and procedures for the development of new human rights treaties (General Assembly Resolution 41/120). The goal here is to control the excessive proliferation of single-issue regimes and the reporting burden they involve.

There has also been an increased interest in alternatives to treaty reporting systems. It seems unlikely, though, that real international monitoring can be achieved through any politically acceptable alternative. For example, special rapporteurs and working groups, which gather their own information from a variety of sources, seem to have fallen into disfavor among most Third World states, largely because of their relative independence from political control. Likewise, proposals for a high commissioner for human rights, which have surfaced periodically for more than a quarter century, have received only limited support. For all their drawbacks, reporting schemes seem to be the best that is politically possible.

REGIONAL HUMAN RIGHTS REGIMES

Single-issue regimes seek to supplement and extend the global human rights regime by elaborating norms and developing new procedures covering a single human right or a relatively narrow set of rights. Regional human rights regimes, by contrast, address a wide range of rights in a smaller and more homogeneous group of states.

Europe

A very strong regional human rights regime exists for the twenty-three (primarily Western European) members of the Council of Europe. Article 3 of the council's Statute requires each member to "accept the principles of the rule of law and of the enjoyment by all persons within its jurisdiction of human rights and fundamental freedoms." Such provisions were treated seriously enough to prevent Spanish membership until after the death of fascist dictator Francisco Franco in 1975 and the establishment of a democratic government. In addition, Greece (in 1969) and Turkey (in 1981) were suspended for their human rights practices. Currently, they set standards that must be met by the newly democratic states of Central and Eastern Europe if they wish to be fully incorporated into "Europe."

Whether we consider scope, depth, or impact, the European human rights regime is unprecedented. The European Commission of Human Rights, based in Strasbourg, France, is the central enforcement body of the regime established under the 1950 (European) Convention for the Protection of Human Rights and Fundamental Freedoms. The commission's principal function is to receive, review, and evaluate "applications" (complaints) from individuals. In recent years, the commission has received roughly 4,000 communications a year. About four-fifths of these inquiries, though, are dropped by the individual after an initial exchange of letters, and most of the rest are clearly inadmissible. The fact that the commission has in the end registered only about 40 new cases annually is largely a testament to relatively good regional human rights records. Once a case is accepted, the commission pursues it vigorously, and a majority end with a decision against the state. Furthermore, the decisions of the commission, although not technically binding, are usually accepted as authoritative.

Even more striking is the authority of the European Court of Human Rights to take legally binding decisions on cases initially decided by the commission. It has dealt with over 150 cases on a great variety of issues, including such sensitive questions as public emergencies and the treatment of prisoners in Northern Ireland. The European convention also permits complaints by one state against another. Although similar procedures in other human rights regimes have almost never been used, there have been eighteen interstate applications involving six different situations, including British interrogation practices in Northern Ireland and torture in Greece and in Turkey.

The decisions of the European commission and court, and the general guidance provided by the European convention, have had a considerable impact on law and practice in a number of states. For example, detention practices have been altered in Belgium, Germany, Greece, and Italy. The treatment of aliens has been changed in the Netherlands and Switzerland. Press freedom legislation was altered in Britain. Wiretapping regulations have been changed in Switzerland. Legal aid practices have been revised in Italy and Denmark. Procedures to speed trials have been implemented in Italy, the Netherlands, and Sweden.

Economic and social rights are specified in a separate European Social Charter and are supervised through somewhat weaker procedures. Despite the absence of the individual complaint and legal enforcement machinery of the commission and the court, the review of reports by a Committee of Independent Experts has produced significant changes in social policy in a number of member states.

Special procedures also exist under the 1987 European Convention for the Prevention of Torture and Inhuman or Degrading Treatment or Punishment, which has been signed by all members of the Council of Europe and already had fifteen parties by the start of 1990. The (European) Committee for the Prevention of Torture is authorized to visit *any* place within the territory of a party to the convention where even a single individual might be detained, either legally or illegally, even by military authorities. Such on-site inspections, at the discretion of an independent monitoring committee, are unprecedented.

The Council of Europe system also includes a European Committee for Equality Between Women and Men, a Human Rights Documentation Center, and a Steering Committee for Human Rights (with three expert committees, dealing with the further development of human rights norms, improving procedures, and promotion, education, and information). There are also well-developed procedures for NGO participation. For example, Amnesty International and the International Commission of Jurists are observers in the Steering Committee for Human Rights. NGOs even participate in some of the activities of the European court.

There is also a human rights dimension to the activities of the twelve-member European Community (EC), whose principal component is the European Economic Community (EEC, the "Common Market"). Economic integration in recent years has been accompanied by efforts to harmonize social policy. This has often had a positive impact on economic and social rights because policies tend to be standardized not according to the lowest common denominator but on the basis of the better performers.

The EC has also incorporated human rights concerns into its external relations. For example, from 1967 until 1974 the special agreement between Greece and the EEC was suspended, at significant economic cost to Greece, in protest against military rule and human rights violations. Weak human rights provisions have also been included in the Lomé Conventions, which over the past two decades have provided special foreign aid to more than fifty African, Caribbean, and Pacific countries that were former colonies of community members. In 1986, the foreign ministers of the twelve community states issued a Declaration on Human Rights. In addition, the community has engaged in "quiet diplomacy" on behalf of human rights and individual victims in a number of countries.

The European Parliament, a largely advisory body selected by direct popular election, has shown considerable interest in human rights issues over the past decade. In 1989, it even issued a Declaration on Fundamental Rights and Freedoms, in an attempt to further increase the importance of human rights within the program of the community. The European Parliament has also tried to increase the emphasis on human rights in relations with countries outside Europe. For example, it adopts an annual or biennial resolution on Human Rights in the World and Community Policy on Human Rights, based largely on the extensive reports of its human rights rapporteur.

A cynic might argue that the unusual breadth and strength of the European human rights regime simply illustrate the paradox of international action on behalf of human rights: strong procedures exist precisely where they are least needed. Strong procedures can only be established with the permission of the states concerned, which is likely only when a state has both a high interest and a good record.

"Least needed," however, does not mean "unneeded." Even committed governments with good records can fall short of their best intentions. For example, Germany, Italy, and the UK have been criticized in Amnesty International reports on torture. The enforcement procedures of the European regime are available to victims when slips occur. They also provide an additional incentive to states to minimize the frequency and severity of such slips, and they maintain subtle but constant pressures on states to meet the highest standards of behavior. Furthermore, Turkey, although a member of the Council of Europe, is not a liberal democratic regime in the standard Western European sense of that term.

No less important than these adversarial remedial procedures has been the impact of the European human rights regime on national political reforms. For example, the new constitutions in Greece, Portugal, and Spain after they escaped military rule were explicitly written with the Europe convention in mind. In addition, decisions of the commission and the court have led to constitutional revisions in Sweden and the Netherlands. On a day-to-day basis as well, an additional level of regional scrutiny may subtly influence national political processes. In fact, in most countries the convention has had a significant impact on the formulation of new legislation. For example, Italy's revision of its privacy laws in 1974 was very heavily influenced by the European convention.

Furthermore, regional human rights standards are constantly evolving. For example, the European Court of Human Rights applies the principle of "evolutive interpretation," by which the European convention is interpreted not according to the conditions and understandings that existed in 1950 when it was formulated but in light of the dominant current practices of the states of Europe. Important cases have dealt with corporal punishment in schools in the UK and discrimination against unmarried mothers and children born outside of marriage in Belgium. Especially where individual states lag significantly behind European norms, this principle can contribute to national changes.

The Americas

As in Europe, the Inter-American human rights regime's procedures revolve around a commission and a court. The Inter-American Court of Human Rights, which sits in San José, Costa Rica, may take binding enforcement action with respect to the (currently eleven) parties that have recognized its jurisdiction. Since it began operating in 1980, however, it has decided only two contentious cases, one dealing with a disappearance in Honduras and the other, a military attack on two journalists in Peru. (It has also issued a number of advisory opinions, but in the most important of these cases, the government of Costa Rica chose not to follow the advice of the court concerning restrictive legislation directed against journalists.)

The real heart of the regime is the seven-member Inter-American Commission of Human Rights. Established in 1959 as a part of the Organization of American States (OAS), its authority does not rest on a separate human rights treaty (although there is a 1948 American Declaration of the Rights of Man and a 1969 American Convention on Human Rights). As with the UN Commission on Human Rights, all states that are members of the organization may in principle come under its scrutiny. And the Inter-American commission has aggressively exploited its charge to promote and develop awareness of human rights, make recommendations, prepare studies and reports, handle individual complaints, and conduct on-site investigations of human rights questions throughout the Western Hemisphere.

The commission receives about 500 communications each year. Like the European commission, it begins by seeking additional information and attempting to facilitate a friendly settlement between the state and the complaining individual. Ultimately, the Inter-American commission can take a decision on the merits of the case. Its decisions, however, have usually been ignored, in sharp contrast to those of its European counterpart.

The primary reason for this is the very different domestic human rights environment in the two regions. Almost all the countries in the European regime have excellent human rights records and a strong desire to maintain them. Communications thus typically deal with narrow or isolated violations, which are inherently unthreatening to the government. Even when there are serious, systematic violations, as during the period of military rule in Greece, the government involved is seen as aberrant and, if the behavior persists, is treated as a pariah.

Most countries in the Americas, by contrast, have suffered repressive military rule within the past generation. In fact, until recently, at any given time several OAS member states typically were ruled by dictatorial governments. As a result, many communications have concerned systematic human rights violations that represented an important element in the government's strategy to keep itself in power. In such circumstances, it is hardly surprising that the findings of the commission have usually been ignored.

Therefore, a more important activity of the Inter-American commission has been its studies and reports on human rights situations in over twenty countries. These reports have often been an important element in international efforts to publicize violations. For example, during a two-week visit to Argentina in 1979, the commission interviewed a number of high officials, including the president, members of the military junta, and the president of the Supreme Court; all the living former presidents of Argentina; representatives of major religious and human rights groups, trade unions, professional associations, political parties, and business groups; prominent individuals, such as Jacobo Timerman and Ernesto Sábato; and members of the public who came forward in four cities. About 5,000 complaints were received. And in response to the commission's report, the military government in Argentina seemed to have modified some of its practices concerning arrests, disappearances, and conditions of detention.

The strengths and weaknesses of this process can be illustrated by a detailed look at the work of the Inter-American commission in response to military rule in Chile.[15] Within a week of the September 11, 1973, coup, the commission sent a cable to Chile expressing its concern and asking for information. In October, its executive secretary, Luis Reque, visited Chile.

His report advised a formal on-site visit by the Inter-American commission, which finally took place July 22 through August 2, 1974. Although this was nearly a year after the coup, the Inter-American commission's response was both rapid and aggressive compared to most of the other procedures we have considered.

During its visit, the commission interviewed government authorities and met with representatives of the International Red Cross and the UN high commissioner for refugees. The commission received 575 new communications and took statements from witnesses to support previously submitted communications. Commission members also observed military tribunals, studied the records of trials in both military and ordinary courts, and gathered information on the junta's legislation. One of their most important activities was to visit detention centers. This not only led to some minor changes but also helped to identify the facilities where systematic torture was being practiced.

The Inter-American commission's report concluded that the government of Chile was guilty of a wide range of human rights violations, including systematic violations of the rights to life, liberty, personal security, due process, and a number of civil liberties. In October 1974, this was hardly news. Nonetheless, the report was thorough and tough. Furthermore, it provided authoritative international support for most of the charges that had been made against the Chilean junta. For example, it was a standard source of information in congressional hearings in the United States. The Inter-American commission's report also made it more difficult for foreign governments sympathetic to the junta to dismiss the charges of exiles and human rights activists as partisan or unsubstantiated. It was thus a significant event in the mobilization of international public opinion.

Over the next two years, the commission's work on Chile focused on individual communications, which it received in great number. In 1975 alone it considered over 600 cases of torture and 160 disappearances. The government of Chile, however, was uncooperative. Furthermore, the systematic nature of these violations indicated that investigation of individual communications, which are best suited to occasional and unsystematic abuses, was not the optimum way to proceed.

The commission's second report on Chile, in 1976, applied new pressure on the Pinochet government. Although noting that the number of certain violations had declined, it documented continuing gross and systematic violations of human rights and explicitly concluded that government actions and policies continued to be an impediment to the restoration of respect for human rights in Chile. This helped to undercut arguments made by and on behalf of Chile that the situation was returning to normal.

The rest of the OAS, however, proved extraordinarily reluctant to follow the commission's lead. The first report on Chile had provoked only an exceedingly innocuous resolution that did little more than ask for additional information from Chile. In fact, the OAS was so little moved that in 1975, by a vote of seventeen to two, with five abstentions, it accepted Chile's offer to be the host of the next session of the OAS General Assembly. In 1976, following the commission's second report, Chile was merely asked to cooperate with the Inter-American commission and "to continue adopting and implementing the necessary procedures and measures for effectively preserving and ensuring full respect for human rights in Chile." By implying more progress than was in fact occurring, this resolution was in many ways worse than nothing. And after the third report, in March 1977, the OAS General Assembly did not ask for an additional report, as it had following the second.

This icy reception underscores the limits of even an aggressive and independent monitoring body when it is part of a political organization that has little concern for human rights. Nonetheless, the commission persevered. Its annual reports for 1977, 1978, and 1979–1980 included special sections on Chile. The 1980–1981, 1981–1982, and 1982–1983 annual reports, in a concession to the generally hostile organizational environment, contained no separate discussions of particular countries. In the 1983–1984 annual report, however, the commission began to return to a tougher stand, with the addition of a chapter on violations in several states, including Chile. And in May 1984, in response to the worsening situation in Chile, the commission began work on a new country report, which was issued in 1985.

At the OAS General Assembly meeting of December 1985, the First Committee, which deals with human rights, adopted a resolution that criticized both Chile and Suriname by name. In the full General Assembly, however, the reference to Chile was deleted.[16] Although this was a major setback, the Inter-American commission had at least again increased regional political pressure on Chile. And it continued to do what it could to further increase that pressure, until the final fall of the Pinochet regime.

What can we conclude from all this? A cynic can point to "the bottom line," namely, the persistence of military dictatorship in Chile. This is a striking example of the ultimate impotence of international human rights regimes in the face of concerted national resistance. If a state is willing to accept the costs to its international reputation—costs that rarely exceed strained relations and a reduction in aid—it almost always can ignore the decisions of international human rights regimes.

But to expect international human rights regimes to force recalcitrant states to mend their ways is unrealistic. In the Inter-American system there simply are not any enforcement powers, except for the rare cases handled by the Inter-American court. The Inter-American commission must rely principally on the power of publicity. It can help to promote the regional implementation of human rights norms. It can monitor and publicize the practice of states. But it cannot force a state to do anything that state is set against doing. In the end, sovereignty remains the overriding norm in the Inter-American human rights regime—as in all other international regimes as well (with the exception of Europe).

Nonetheless, we should not dismiss the importance of publicity. In summarizing the commission's work on Chile, Cecilia Medina argued that

> in a situation of gross, systematic violations, the constant attention of the international community is of the highest importance; it serves as a support and encouragement for those suffering and opposing repression within the country, and at the same time prompts, and serves as a basis for, further international action by other governmental and nongovernmental international organizations.[17]

This is particularly true when a state is subject to scrutiny in multiple intergovernmental organizations and by several international NGOs.

Perhaps the strongest evidence for the importance of international publicity is the diplomatic effort states exert to avoid it. In the late 1970s and early 1980s, both Argentina and Chile devoted much of their diplomacy, in both the United Nations and the Organization of American States, to avoiding public criticism.[18] If states guilty of violations take international condemnation seriously enough to struggle to avoid it, this condemnation is unlikely to be an entirely pointless exercise.

We must remember also that "the bottom line" includes individuals who are helped, even if the overall situation in the country remains repressive. States often respond to adverse international human rights publicity by releasing or improving the treatment of prominent victims. These may be small victories for international action, but they are victories nonetheless—and of immense significance to the individuals involved.

In rare cases, there may be a more systematic impact. Nicaragua provides a good example. The commission's 1978 report substantially increased the pressure on the dictatorial Somoza government. Furthermore, the OAS call for Somoza to resign in June 1979 clearly shook his political confidence and seems to have hastened his departure from Nicaragua.[19]

In the end, though, the reports of the Inter-American commission are just that: reports. And its decisions on individual cases are only nonbinding resolutions. Reports and resolutions require additional action by states to have any real impact. This is an inherent shortcoming of all international human rights regimes, except the European regional regime.

Comparison with Europe, however, is not entirely fair, because of the immense differences in the regional political environments. The Inter-American commission has aggressively exploited its powers, to at least some effect in a number of countries. Its activities have undoubtedly improved the treatment of many thousands of victims of human rights violations over the past three decades. If we compare it to the global regime or the single-issue regimes discussed above, it stands in a relatively good light.

Africa, Asia, and the Middle East

A third regional human rights regime exists within the Organization of African Unity (OAU) under the 1981 African Charter on Human and Peoples' Rights. The African charter—or Banjul charter, as it is often called, after the site of its adoption (Banjul, The Gambia)—entered into force in 1986 and had forty-nine parties at the end of 1992. Although most other international human rights treaties largely follow the substance of the International Bill of Human Rights, the Banjul charter gives unusual emphasis to collective or peoples' rights and individual duties (Articles 19–24 and 27–29).

The International Human Rights Covenants recognize the right of peoples to self-determination. The apartheid convention also includes important references to peoples' rights. The Banjul charter, however, recognizes not only the equality of all peoples and their right to self-determination but also the rights of all peoples to development and to peace. The significance of such peoples' rights, however, is a matter of controversy.

One standard dictionary definition of a people is "the persons belonging to a place or forming a group, the subjects or citizens of a state." This is usually the relevant sense in regional and international organizations, with the emphasis on citizens of an already established state. In the African context in particular, "people" most definitely does not mean "the persons composing a community or tribe or race or nation," another standard definition of the term. For example, Nigerians would be considered a people entitled to self-determination, peace, and development. Nigeria, however, contains a number of ethnic communities, such as the Yoruba and the Ibo. Although these are also "peoples" in the other sense of the term, they are most definitely not subjects of the "peoples' rights" enumerated in the African charter. The Ibo were forcefully reincorporated into Nigeria, with the full support of the OAU, when they attempted to secede (as Biafra) in 1967.

Focusing on the rights of peoples/states directs our attention to the external, international threats to human rights, to the threats posed by powerful foreign governments, international markets, and multinational corporations. Although these external impediments to the implementation and enjoyment of human rights are real and important, the great majority of human rights violations, in Africa as elsewhere, are perpetrated by states against their own nationals.

Peoples' rights also focus attention on the collective dimension of human rights and the connection between the collective goods of peace and development and more traditional individual human rights (which are also recognized in the African charter). But neither peace nor development, in the ordinary senses of those terms, will guarantee the enjoyment of internationally recognized human rights. For example, the citizens of the Soviet Union enjoyed peace but not human rights for four decades. In numerous countries, a small elite has obtained most of the benefits of national economic development.

The African charter's emphasis on individual duties is similarly problematic. The effective operation of a system of rights is possible only if individuals attend to their reciprocal duties. Although commonplace, this is well worth repeating. Yet one may ask whether the real human rights problem in Africa (or elsewhere) is that people have too few duties to the state and society. I would suggest instead that far too many states are all too aware of the duties of individuals but insufficiently attentive to their own duties and the rights of their citizens. Thus a provision such as the duty of the individual "to serve his national community by placing his physical and intellectual abilities at its service" (Article 29[2]) may seem either innocuous or ominous.

Much the same can be said of the "clawback" clauses of the Banjul charter. For example, Article 6 recognizes "the right to liberty and to the security of the person" but then goes on to state that "no one may be deprived of his freedom except for reasons and conditions previously laid down by law." Because there are no restrictions on such reasons and conditions—the European convention, by contrast, explicitly restricts permissible grounds—this effectively allows the state free rein. A person has freedom of association "provided he abides by the law," freedom of conscience "subject to law and order," and freedom of speech "within the law." So long as a state bothers to pass a law eliminating free speech, it has not violated the provisions of the charter. Freedom of assembly may be restricted not only in the interest of national security but also out of concern for "the safety, health, ethics and rights and freedoms of others." In effect, any assembly that may offend anyone else (the ethics of others) may be banned. In good circumstances, this may not be a problem. But human rights are supposed to protect individuals above all in bad times.

Fears raised by the language in which the norms of the Banjul charter are specified would seem to be confirmed by its relatively weak implementation provisions. The eleven-member African Commission on Human and Peoples' Rights, in addition to reviewing reports, may consider communications. Only situations, however, may be discussed, not individual cases. And an in-depth study of a situation requires permission from the OAU's Assembly of Heads of State and Government. This is by far the most politicized regional or international human rights complaint procedure.

The commission held its first meeting in November 1987 and its eleventh, and most recent, in March 1992. Its initial reviews of state reports have not been promising, and the reports themselves have had little substance. Through late 1990, 105 communications had been received, but no public action had been taken on any of them. Nonetheless, the African commission does seem to be approaching its task with seriousness and energy. It has not merely permitted but actually encouraged NGO participation. And something may yet come out of the consideration of communications. Recall, for example, the lethargic pace of the UN Commission on Human Rights' 1503 Procedure.

Whatever the ultimate fate of this African regional human rights regime, though, it is already much further advanced than those in the Arab world or in Asia and the Pacific. The League of Arab States established a Permanent Arab Commission on Human Rights in 1968, but the commission has been notably inactive, except for occasional efforts to publicize human rights violations in Israeli-occupied territory. There are not even authoritative regional norms.

Asia and the Pacific is not really a region in any functioning social or political sense. Not surprisingly, then, the only substantial result of a 1982 UN-sponsored seminar in Colombo, Sri Lanka, was a decision to abandon a broad regional approach in favor of either the global institutions discussed above or subregional groupings. But the relatively low level of Asian-state ratifications of the International Human Rights Covenants (the lowest percentage of any geographical region) suggests that more than size and diversity stand in the way of even subregional human rights regimes in Asia.

The Pacific Island subregion shows perhaps the greatest promise. Lawasia, an association of Asian and Pacific lawyers, based in Australia, organized a series of meetings between 1985 and 1989 attended by delegates from a dozen countries. These led to a draft Pacific Island Human Rights Charter, formulated using the African charter as an initial working document. The draft has been sent to all governments in the region, but the success of this initiative is very uncertain.

The role of NGOs such as Lawasia reminds us that even without intergovernmental organizations, there may still be important transnational action on behalf of human rights. For example, more than one thousand NGOs are listed in Human Rights Internet's recent *Human Rights Directory: Asia and the Pacific*. Most of these groups operate only domestically. Nonetheless, they and their transnational colleagues play an important role, especially in countries with relatively good human rights records. Even in extremely repressive countries, international human rights NGOs, such as New York–based Asia Watch, engage in considerable, and occasionally successful, efforts to assure that human rights violations are not ignored by the international community.

In the Middle East as well, NGO initiatives have tried to compensate for the absence of a functioning regional regime. For example, the Arab Organization for Human Rights (AOHR), founded in 1983, issues annual reports on human rights conditions in the countries of the Arab world. In 1988 the Mauritanian Human Rights League organized the first Maghreb Conference on Human Rights. And in 1989—through a joint initiative of the Arab Lawyers Union, AOHR, and the Tunisian League for Human Rights,[20] with the support of the UN Center for Human Rights—an Arab Institute for Human Rights was established in Tunis to provide information on human rights conditions and training for both government and nongovernmental personnel.

The general environment in the Arab world, however, is unusually hostile to even NGO activities. For example, AOHR operates out of Geneva, rather than an Arab country. As its president recently noted, "Most Arab governments initially adopted a hostile attitude towards it."[21] The general hostility of governments, however, only increases the importance of the activities of national and transnational human rights NGOs. They can help to keep the idea alive and at least on the fringes of the political debate. NGOs also are likely to be important in probing the limits of political tolerance and attempting to take advantage of what limited political space exists for action on behalf of internationally recognized human rights.

The Helsinki Process

A hybrid—not exactly regional—human rights regime exists within the Conference on Security and Cooperation in Europe (CSCE), an organization made up of European countries (with the breakup of the Soviet Union and Yugoslavia, there are fifty-two now), plus the United States and Canada. The **Helsinki process** is an informal description of the human rights activities of the CSCE. The best-known product of this regime is the Helsinki Final Act of 1975.

The principal Soviet objective in the initial CSCE negotiations was recognition of the postwar territorial and ideological division of Europe. The Soviets also wanted to use political detente to improve their access to Western technology and trade. Only very reluctantly did they agree to include human rights on the agenda. The Western Europeans, however, insisted on incorporating human rights provisions, under the notion of domestic security for citizens.

The resulting document is a marvel of diplomatic compromise. Three very different "baskets"—dealing with political and military issues (particularly the inviolability of frontiers and the principle of nonintervention), economic relations, and humanitarian relations—are held together in a delicate political balance. Our concern here will be solely with Principle VII ("Respect for human rights and fundamental freedoms, including the freedom of thought, conscience, religion or belief") and the human rights provisions of "Basket III" ("Co-operation in Humanitarian and Other Fields"), which are the provisions of the Final Act that have received the most publicity and had the greatest political impact.

Basket III deals solely with human contacts (especially family contacts and reunification), the free flow of information, and cultural and educational cooperation. Principle VII, however, includes a general agreement to "promote and encourage the effective exercise of civil, political, economic, social, cultural and other rights and freedoms." Much of the history of the Helsinki process can be seen as a struggle over the relative priorities of these two provisions. The Soviet bloc states attempted to stick to the narrow focus of Basket III (and even that only reluctantly). Western states and human rights NGOs in both East and West stressed the broad language of Principle VII.

Follow-up meetings in Belgrade (1977–1978), Madrid (1980–1983), and Vienna (1986–1989) provided the principal diplomatic arena for this struggle. The Belgrade and Madrid meetings deadlocked and produced little beyond harsh words. The Vienna meeting, however, was more productive. Its Concluding Document included extensive new language on freedom of religion and the treatment of detainees and established new CSCE procedures for state-to-state consultations over alleged human rights violations. This was a move toward regularizing diplomatic discussions of human rights violations and was also an initial step toward institutionalizing the Helsinki process between follow-up meetings. In addition, a separate Conference on the Human Dimension of the CSCE was established.

In hindsight, the Helsinki process can be seen as a chronicle of the gradual demise of the cold war and Soviet-style communism in the face of increasing national and international demands to implement internationally recognized human rights. The Helsinki follow-up meetings provided a forum for the West to place continued international pressure on the Soviet bloc regimes. Even more important, however, was the legitimation that the Helsinki Final Act gave to the activities of dissident groups in the Soviet bloc.

The Final Act recognized the "right of the individual to know and act upon his rights and duties," and Basket III included provisions relating to the free flow of information. In May 1976, physicist Yuri Orlov and ten others, including Yelena Bonner, Aleksandr Ginzburg, and Anatoly Scharansky, attempted to take the Helsinki Final Act at its word. They founded the Public Group to Assist the Implementation of the Helsinki Accords in the USSR, which soon came to be known as the Moscow Helsinki Group. Its stated purpose was "to inform the governments that signed the Final Act in Helsinki, as well as the publics of those countries, of cases of direct violations of the humanitarian articles of the Final Act in the Soviet Union."[22]

In six years of work, the Moscow Helsinki Group prepared more than 150 reports on a great variety of human rights issues. These reports were an important subject of discussion at the Belgrade and Madrid follow-up meetings. The Moscow Helsinki Group also issued numerous statements, letters, and appeals. Local Helsinki-monitoring groups were formed in four other Soviet republics (Armenia, Georgia, Lithuania, and the Ukraine). A number of affiliated groups, such as the Working Commission to Investigate the Abuse of Psychiatry for Political Purposes and the Christian Committee to Defend Believers' Rights, cooperated more or less closely with the Moscow group.

Over 100 individuals publicly joined the Soviet Helsinki groups, at great personal risk. All were harassed, and most were legally punished, often under the charge of anti-Soviet agitation and propaganda. This was a serious offense in Soviet law, and one could be found guilty even if all the facts that one was accused of disseminating were true, as was the case with the information in the Moscow group's reports. From the very outset, members were intimidated into leaving the group or accepting an exit visa from the Soviet Union. In February and March 1977, Soviet authorities arrested Ginzburg, Orlov, and Scharansky. By 1980, the group's principal activity had become monitoring the cases of their colleagues. By August 1981 only three remained at liberty in the country. In September 1982, the group was finally forced to disband.

In Czechoslovakia, the coming of the Belgrade follow-up meeting helped to spur Charter 77, a manifesto signed in January 1977 by 242 people, including Vaclav Havel, who in 1990 became the first elected president of newly democratic Czechoslovakia. During the succeeding decade, Charter 77 became a powerful local human rights group with over 1,300 public adherents.

As in the Soviet Union, official harassment began immediately. In fact, a car containing Havel and two others was stopped by the security forces while they were on their way to deliver the signed document to the government and the media. Members were physically attacked, fired from their jobs, blacklisted, and in some cases arrested. Telephones were cut off, apartments taken away, driving licenses and passports revoked, and individuals detained without charge for up to forty-eight hours to prevent them from engaging in group activities. Some were convicted of political crimes. Children and other family members of activists were also harassed and discriminated against in employment, residence, and schooling.

On the one hand, the Moscow Helsinki Group and Charter 77 may be seen as stories of failure. Of the twenty-two members of the Moscow Helsinki Group, only Naum Meiman managed to remain active, in the country, and unpunished, although he too was regularly harassed and forced into early retirement. Furthermore, once the more public figures had been neutralized, Soviet authorities continued to arrest and harass less prominent activists and even those only peripherally involved in the human rights movement. Persecution of Charter 77 members was less thorough and often less harsh, but very real and costly. In other countries, the situation was no better—and often worse. The Polish Helsinki Committee was forced underground during martial law. In some countries, such as Bulgaria and Romania, repression was so effective that monitoring groups could not even be formed.[23]

On the other hand, the immense international publicity accorded the activities of the Moscow Helsinki Group both embarrassed the authorities and helped to mobilize private and public political pressure in the West. The formal Helsinki meetings also provided a regular, well-publicized forum for airing human rights grievances. And in Czechoslovakia, Charter 77 provided much of the leadership for the Velvet Revolution of 1989 that overthrew forty years of Communist rule.

The Helsinki process also had an impact on international human rights activities outside the Soviet bloc. In the United States, Helsinki Watch was founded in 1979. This then became the model for the creation of new regional watch committees, Americas Watch, Asia Watch, Africa Watch, and, most recently, Middle East Watch. Operating out of New York under the general umbrella of Human Rights Watch, they have become an important source of information and a major human rights lobby in the United States.

In other countries as well, local and transnational NGO monitoring activities have been greatly spurred by the Helsinki Final Act and the model of the Moscow Helsinki Group. And the various national Helsinki groups have developed cooperative relations within the framework of the International Helsinki Federation for Human Rights. The federation helped new groups to learn from the experience of more-established groups in other countries. It also provided a source of international support for new groups, which were particularly vulnerable to state repression.

Repressive governments can almost always ignore the pressure such NGOs bring to bear. They may even choose to apply the power of the state to weaken or eliminate human rights NGOs. Nonetheless, there may be international costs to such behavior, especially if the victims are prominent or have developed good international contacts. There may also be domestic political costs.

Rarely will the consideration of such costs be politically decisive. In some cases, however, we know that they have made at least some human rights violations less burdensome to their victims. As we are coming to see, this is the most that usually can be realistically hoped for from international action on behalf of human rights. Whatever its shortcomings—and they are very real—modest amelioration of human rights conditions is much better than nothing, and well worth the effort.

The revolutions of 1989 in Eastern Europe certainly cannot be attributed to either the formal Helsinki proceedings or the activities of national and international Helsinki monitors. Nonetheless, the combined pressures from above and below helped to open political space for some of the forces that ultimately overthrew Communist rule. Perhaps the greatest testimony to the value of the process is the fact that the new governments of Eastern Europe seem committed to using CSCE to help to consolidate and extend their achievements. This is clearly illustrated by the June 1990 meeting of the Conference on the Human Dimension of the CSCE in Copenhagen, the first attended by democratic governments from Central and Eastern Europe.

The first part of the Document of the Copenhagen Meeting deals extensively with the rule of law and free elections. This is followed by a broad list of human rights and fundamental freedoms, including a right to property. The third part deals with democratic values and institutions, largely as they have been understood in Western liberal democratic states. And "The Charter of Paris for a New Europe," adopted at the Paris Summit of Heads of State or Government of the CSCE in November 1990, forcefully reaffirms the centrality of human rights in the new Europe.

These remain essentially statements of principles. Nonetheless, one of the lessons of the Helsinki process would seem to be that even principles can have a certain political power in the hands of dedicated human rights advocates. As the Charter of Paris puts it, "The courage of men and women, the strength of the will of the peoples and the power of the ideas of the Helsinki Final Act have opened a new era of democracy, peace and unity in Europe." The Helsinki process thus seems not to have been rendered obsolete by recent political changes. In the Europe of the 1990s, CSCE remains well situated to bring public and private pressure to bear on states that violate international human rights norms.

FIVE

□ □ □

Human Rights
and Foreign Policy

The preceding chapter dealt with international organizations and the multilateral politics of international human rights. This chapter considers national foreign policy, the bilateral politics of international human rights. The first four sections are devoted to the United States. The international human rights policies of a number of other Western countries are discussed in much less detail in the final two sections.

CENTRAL ISSUES IN U.S.
INTERNATIONAL HUMAN RIGHTS POLICY

Chapter 1 provided a brief overview of some of the major events in postwar international human rights policies. For the United States, we can distinguish four phases.

□ 1945–1948: initial enthusiasm, culminating in the adoption of the Universal Declaration of Human Rights
□ 1949–1973: human rights concerns subordinated to anticommunism and cold war rivalry with the Soviet Union
□ 1974–1980: human rights emerge as a prominent element in the public diplomacy of the United States, first in the Congress and then during the Carter presidency
□ 1981–1988: the (ultimately unsuccessful) Reagan attempt to subordinate human rights once more to the (new) cold war[1]

As 1992 came to a close, we seemed to be well into a fifth, more difficult to characterize, stage. This arose from the greater moderation of the Bush administration (even where it pursued the same objectives as its predecessor), the global trend of liberalization and democratization, and, most important, the altered international environment created by the collapse of the Soviet Union. This chapter, however, will focus on the 1970s and 1980s, leaving the 1990s to Chapter 6. And because we have already looked at international human rights policies chronologically, our approach here will be thematic and topical.

Anticommunism and American Exceptionalism

U.S. foreign policy from 1945 through the end of the 1980s was dominated by anticommunism. Even during the "liberal" Democratic presidencies of Truman, Kennedy, Johnson, and Carter, fear of communism was an overriding concern. The Korean War began under Truman. U.S. advisers and then troops were committed to Vietnam under Kennedy and Johnson. Carter's Central American policy was strongly shaped by the desire to avoid "another Cuba." Individual presidents certainly disagreed on the best way to defeat communism, but from Truman through Reagan, anticommunism was given the highest priority in the foreign policy of every postwar U.S. administration. As a result, the United States usually supported avowedly anticommunist governments. Whether this was good foreign policy or bad, its human rights consequences were disastrous.

Totalitarian, Soviet-style communism, which today persists only in isolated enclaves such as the PRC and Cuba, certainly did rest on the systematic violation of most internationally recognized civil and political rights. But anticommunist regimes have often been guilty of serious, and in some instances no less severe, violations. Nonetheless, the United States regularly equated anticommunism with the pursuit of human rights. In country after country—Bolivia, Chile, the Dominican Republic, Guatemala, Haiti, Iran, Liberia, Pakistan, Paraguay, Somalia, South Africa, Sudan, South Vietnam, South Korea, and Zaire, to name just a few—the United States supported repressive military dictatorships and narrow civilian oligarchies (along with U.S. economic and geopolitical interests) in the name of democracy.

This confusion of anticommunism with human rights has been strengthened by what students of domestic politics in the United States call **American exceptionalism,** the belief that the United States is different from (and generally superior to) most other countries, in large part because of its domestic commitment to individual rights. The isolationist variant of American exceptionalism, expressed with particular clarity in George Washington's Farewell Address, has seen the country as a beacon of hope for an oppressed world—but only an example, not an active participant in the struggle for freedom overseas. No less powerful, however, has been interventionist exceptionalism, which stresses an active American mission to spread its values through direct foreign policy action, even military force.

This interventionist strand has often led to identifying the international interests of the United States with human rights or, as Americans usually put it, "democracy." The logic typically has run something as follows: Communism is (inherently) opposed to human rights. The United States is (almost by definition) in favor of human rights. Therefore, U.S. action against international communism is equivalent to action on behalf of human rights.

Even where it has not led to intervention, American exceptionalism has often been associated with a narrow and self-serving definition of human rights. Americans typically act as if human rights problems exist only in places that must be reached by crossing large bodies of salt water. Other countries have human rights problems. The United States, however, is said to suffer from, for example, police brutality, civil rights problems, or a health care crisis, which are spoken of as if they are qualitatively different from torture, racial discrimination, or denial of the right to health care. Although strictly speaking beyond the scope of this book, which is about international human rights, this systematic failure of Americans to look at themselves through the lens of internationally recognized human rights cannot be ignored.[2]

This is particularly true because the interaction of exceptionalism and anticommunism has contributed to an American tendency to denigrate economic and social rights. Only civil and political rights (plus certain elements of the right to property) are constitutionally guaranteed in the United States. Because most Americans think first of constitutional rights when they hear the term *human rights*, there has been a strong tendency to view economic and social rights as at best much less important.[3] For example, homelessness or lack of access to medical care is rarely presented as a human rights problem. The fact that Communist regimes emphasized economic and social rights bestowed on those rights a sort of guilt by association (see Figure 5.1).

Internationally, this perspective has often led Americans to misinterpret events, especially in the Third World. U.S. foreign policy has generally reacted suspiciously to action on behalf of economic and social rights (other than the right to private property), especially when it has involved the redistribution of wealth. By labeling economic and social reformers "Communists" and "subversives," right-wing rulers generally have been able to retain U.S. support for the use of systematic repression to protect their own wealth, power, and privilege. In fact, they have often been able

FIGURE 5.1 Copyright 1992 by *The Miami Herald*. Reprinted with permission.

to do so under an American banner of "democracy" (read, "anticommunism").

The human rights consequences have been devastating. In addition, such a policy has frequently prevented the achievement of professed U.S. goals. For example, repressive military dictatorships often have eliminated not only the Far Left but also the political moderates that the United States has claimed to support, for example, in Central America (see below). There is more than a touch of irony in the fact that in all of Central America, only in "Marxist" Nicaragua has a democratic opposition been allowed not merely to survive and compete in elections but also to acquire power through peaceful political means.

American exceptionalism also manifests itself in an unflinching commitment to elections, regardless of historical and political context. Because elections are perceived to solve political problems in the United States, Americans seem to believe that they must be the definitive political solution in other countries as well. Unfortunately, even where a government has won an open, competitive election, it may hold office, but not power. For example, in the 1980s the Duarte government in El Salvador and the Cerezo government in Guatemala were (more or less) freely elected but simply did not rule their countries. In addition, many elections of U.S.-supported anticommunist governments have been shams because of restrictions on political participation, intimidation of voters, or outright fraud.

The United States regularly, and rightly, criticized one-party elections in Communist countries. But the mere fact of voting in "friendly" (anticommunist) countries usually has been accepted as evidence of the ruling regime's democratic character. And when the United States has been dissatisfied with free and fair elections that have brought (real or alleged) Communists to power, it has used subversion and even military force to remove an elected government. Sponsorship of the 1954 military coup in Guatemala, covert support for the military prior to the 1973 coup in Chile, and continued support for the Nicaraguan contras after the 1984 election are striking examples of U.S. efforts to overthrow freely elected governments.

Such inconsistencies typically were "reconciled" by an appeal to anticommunism. Elections that brought (alleged) Communists to power were bad and had to be overturned. When force or fraud brought anticommunists to power, that was an acceptable price to pay to keep Communists out of power and on the run. And the United States, the leader of the "Free World," appointed itself the judge of what counted as "democratic" credentials, and who had them.

The Problem of Trade-offs

The preceding discussion has focused entirely on the international human rights dimension of U.S. foreign policy. One might accept this description of U.S. foreign policy but argue that the policy was nonetheless entirely justified. The standard version of this argument has been that the struggle against communism or the military and political power of the Soviet Union was until recently an appropriate overriding priority for U.S. foreign policy. This raises the issue of the place of human rights concerns in a country's overall foreign policy.

In a world of sovereign states, foreign policy is principally concerned with the pursuit of the national interest, as that country sees it. The national interest may include respect for human rights in other countries because it is good in itself or for instrumental reasons (such as the belief that governments that respect human rights are more likely to be dependable friends in international relations). But in no country can the national interest be reduced to international human rights alone.

The obvious question, then, is *what* place human rights occupy. To find out, we must look at what happens when there is a conflict of objectives. Talk about human rights is cheap—often not entirely without cost, but in general relatively cheap. The decisive issue is what costs a country is willing to bear in pursuit of its international human rights objectives and what other objectives it is willing to sacrifice or subordinate.

In a well-designed foreign policy, means are chosen by matching the cost associated with their use to the value of the goal being pursued. The three principal means used by the United States (and other countries) on behalf of international human rights have been **quiet diplomacy** (private discussions with foreign governments), public statements, and granting or withholding foreign aid. This consistent use of only weak instruments of foreign policy is clear evidence of the low value placed on human rights.

Consider, for example, the Reagan administration's insistence on quiet diplomacy as the principal, and in most cases the sole, appropriate means to pursue human rights goals in foreign policy—at least with "friendly" (anticommunist) governments. Governments rarely engage in the sorts of human rights violations that provoke serious diplomatic concern unless they feel that something very important is at stake. Therefore, it is implausible to imagine that quiet diplomacy alone, without at least the threat of more forceful public action, will produce anything more than symbolic gestures.

Even symbolic gestures, however, may improve the lot of prominent individual victims. Quiet diplomacy, under both Carter and Reagan, helped free hundreds of political prisoners, and it ameliorated the conditions of detention of many more. But in no case has it had a major impact on the general human rights situation of a country.

The strongest means typically used in international human rights policies has been the conditioning of aid on human rights practices. Although Congress has required that bilateral economic assistance, bilateral security assistance, and U.S. participation in multilateral financial institutions take into consideration the human rights records of potential recipients, such linkages have had little systematic impact. Aid decisions have been altered in a number of individual cases, but studies have found little statistically significant relationship between either economic or security assistance and the human rights practices of recipient states.[4]

The United States, like most other states, has been willing to pay very little to achieve its international human rights objectives. The Carter, Reagan, and Bush administrations all took steps ranging from private diplomatic expressions of concern to the suspension of foreign aid. But almost never has the United States been willing to go further than a suspension of aid. It is only a small exaggeration to say that when human rights conflict with even minor security, political, economic, or ideological objectives, human rights usually lose out. Human rights have consistently had a place in U.S. foreign policy since the mid-1970s. Their place, however, has been largely peripheral, as we can see by looking in some detail at the cases of Central America, the Southern Cone, and South Africa.

CENTRAL AMERICA
AND U.S. HUMAN RIGHTS POLICY

Central America is the geographical area that lies between North America (Canada, the United States, and Mexico) and South America. It became a major international human rights concern in the 1980s largely as a result of U.S. support for the conservative government of El Salvador and parallel U.S. efforts to overthrow the leftist government of Nicaragua.

Human Rights in El Salvador and Nicaragua

Salvadoran independence from Spain in the 1820s was in many ways less significant than the economic reforms in the second half of the nineteenth century that transferred about one-third of the country's land to a small coffee oligarchy. For the following half century, protests by dispossessed Salvadoran peasants were ruthlessly suppressed. In the most dramatic example, the military systematically killed at least 10,000 people, and perhaps as many as 30,000, in the *matanza* (massacre) of 1932.

In the decades after World War II, the Salvadoran economy grew considerably, but the benefits of growth were distributed extremely unequally. In the mid-1970s, more than two-thirds of the children under five suffered from malnutrition. Three-quarters of rural families (who made up about two-thirds of the total population) were landless, and less than 40 percent had access to piped water. Half lacked the income necessary to purchase a minimum healthy diet. Urban poverty was only somewhat less extreme.[5] Distributing the benefits of growth to the mass of the population simply was not a goal of Salvadoran governments. In fact, the ruling oligarchy regularly used force to repress those seeking a more egalitarian society, especially in rural areas.

Elections were held regularly, but the official military-backed party used patronage, threats, and, when necessary, blatant fraud to assure victory for its candidates. As disillusionment grew, workers, peasants, students, and neighborhoods formed "popular organizations" to engage in direct nonviolent action—sit-ins, strikes, demonstrations, civil disobedience—on behalf of their rights and interests. A few opponents of the dictatorship also turned to armed insurrection, but in the mid-1970s they were of negligible political significance.

The security forces and their paramilitary supporters responded to peaceful protest and guerrilla activity alike with violence (see Figure 5.2).

FIGURE 5.2 A Salvadoran army vehicle with a sticker that reads "I love killing Communists." Amnesty International photo.

The government of General Carlos Humberto Romero, installed after the fraudulent elections of 1977, imposed total press censorship, outlawed not only strikes but also public meetings of all sorts, and suspended judicial due process. Death squads, which worked closely with both ORDEN (Nationalist Democratic Organization), the paramilitary arm of the official party, and the Salvadoran national security agency, became a regular part of the Romero regime's repressive apparatus. This state terrorism helped to radicalize the opposition. People were forced to choose exile, acquiescence to brutal dictatorship, or violent resistance.

In an attempt to head off civil war, a group of junior military officers staged a reformist coup in October 1979. In January 1980, however, all the civilian members of the cabinet resigned over the government's failure to gain control over the security forces. For example, military sharpshooters opened fire from the top of the National Palace on a peaceful demonstration commemorating of the *matanza* of 1932, killing between twenty and fifty people. A second junta collapsed in March, again because of the unwillingness of the military to permit civilian political control. This was vividly illustrated by the assassination on March 24, 1980, of Archbishop Oscar Arnulfo Romero, a crime that helped to focus international attention on human rights in El Salvador. In response to steadily growing opposition, the government declared a state of siege, which completed the establishment of a police state in El Salvador.

Although the intensification of repression led all other civilian political parties to refuse to participate, the conservative wing of the Christian Democrats, led by José Napoleon Duarte, joined the third junta. Political deaths jumped from under 2,000 in 1979 to roughly 12,000 in 1980. In November 1980, six leaders of the FDR (Democratic Revolutionary Front), a party made up principally of Social Democrats and the left wing of the (centrist) Christian Democrats, were dragged from a meeting and brutally murdered. After this, most of the remaining leaders of the nonviolent opposition went underground or into exile. Duarte, however, remained in the fourth junta, while the security forces (along with their paramilitary and death squad allies) instituted a reign of terror. Americas Watch estimated that, out of a total population of less than 5 million, there were over 30,000 government-sponsored murders in 1980–1983 alone (roughly equivalent to the death of 1.25 million Americans).

Duarte's election as president in 1984 (largely as a result of U.S. pressure) helped reduce the level of violence, but the human rights situation remained dismal. Death squad activity continued. The government estimated that death squads were killing "only" about thirty people a month in 1985.[6] Torture continued. And the number of political prisoners actually increased, apparently because of the decline in political murders.

El Salvador thus settled into a sad routine of reduced, but still widespread and systematic, human rights violations. By the late 1980s, most civil and political rights still were regularly violated. A bad economic situation was, at best, not much worse than it had been a decade earlier (and that only because of massive U.S. aid). The guerrillas, whose strength grew along with the repression in the early and mid-1980s, continued to operate, but with no real success. And peaceful political opposition, or even economic organization on the part of workers and peasants, remained dangerous.

The peaceful transfer of power between civilian governments in March 1989 was a notable event in Salvadoran political history. But under Alfredo Cristiani's right-wing National Republican Alliance (ARENA) government, political space in El Salvador actually contracted in 1989. At least seventy human rights activists were arrested, labor activists came under increased attack, the offices of COMADRES (Committee of Mothers of Political Prisoners, Disappeared, and Assassinated in El Salvador) were bombed, and six Jesuit priests and two lay women were murdered by the military.

A UN-mediated end to the civil war was agreed upon at the end of 1991, and UN monitors were stationed in the country in 1992. The end of the civil war, however, will not in itself address the broader human rights questions raised by the continued rule of a civilian-military oligarchy in El Salvador. It may ameliorate the situation, but it cannot address the root causes of human rights violations in El Salvador, a country that for nearly its entire history has known little but the systematic violation of human rights.

Nicaragua's early political history was not much different from that of El Salvador.[7] In 1936, however, Anastasio Somoza García seized power and initiated what was to be more than forty years of authoritarian rule, based on control of the Nicaraguan National Guard. When Somoza was assassinated in 1956, power passed first to his son Luis Somoza Debayle and then to his younger son, Anastasio Somoza Debayle, who ruled until overthrown in 1979.

The Somozas retained the forms of democracy, but elections were rigged and civil and political rights were regularly violated. (Large-scale systematic killings, though, were not part of their repertoire.) Economic, social, and cultural rights were also systematically infringed, both through the predatory accumulation of immense personal wealth by the Somozas and their cronies and through disregard of social services. For example, in the early 1970s the Nicaraguan government spent three times as much on defense as on health care, while its neighbors typically spent about equal amounts.

Massive corruption in the cleanup and recovery effort following the 1972 earthquake in the capital city of Managua, which left perhaps 10,000 dead and hundreds of thousands homeless, exacerbated and highlighted the endemic problems of inequality. Two years later, Somoza was re-elected in a contest that even by Nicaraguan standards was farcical. In January 1978, the pace of disaffection accelerated after the assassination of Pedro Joaquin Chamorro, the leader of the moderate opposition. Even the business community turned against Somoza, under whom it had profited in the preceding decades, organizing a successful general strike to protest Chamorro's death. Eighteen months later, Somoza was forced into exile.

The revolution that swept Somoza from power was a mass popular revolt incorporating many different social and political groups. Its military forces were led by the Sandinista National Liberation Front (FSLN), established in 1961 as a radical breakaway from the Soviet-oriented Nicaraguan Socialist party. But during his final two years in power, Somoza was opposed even by Nicaragua's extremely traditional and conservative Catholic church, as well as by the United States, the Somozas' traditional patron.

The revolution, although widely supported, had immense human and economic costs. Aerial bombardments of civilian targets helped to create perhaps 500,000 refugees, out of a total population of about 2.5 million. Casualties included 40,000 to 50,000 people, mostly civilians, killed, 150,000 wounded, and perhaps 40,000 orphaned. The war also disrupted agricultural production and most other sectors of the economy. Real gross domestic product fell by a quarter in 1979 and by another fifth in 1980. Direct economic losses from the revolution were about $2 billion, roughly Nicaragua's annual gross domestic product.

Human rights conditions generally improved in revolutionary Nicaragua, especially in the early years. The Sandinista government greatly increased spending on social programs, especially health care, and redirected spending for education toward mass literacy. Personal and legal rights were fairly widely respected. Internationally recognized civil liberties were extensively implemented for the first time in Nicaraguan history. Mass political participation was actively fostered, and the 1984 election was generally considered by outside observers to have been relatively open and fairly run.

The government itself admitted serious human rights violations during the forced relocation of Indian populations on the Atlantic Coast. Significant restrictions on freedom of the press, freedom of association, and legal due process were imposed at various times. Sandinista-organized mass popular organizations and the government-controlled media received preferential treatment. Nonetheless, political opponents operated under fewer constraints, and with less fear of retaliation, than most of Somoza's opponents had (let alone members of opposition groups in neighboring Guatemala and El Salvador). Independent monitoring groups such as Americas Watch consistently judged the overall human rights situation to be significantly better than in neighboring El Salvador and Guatemala.

This record, although acceptable only in relative terms, was noteworthy because the Sandinista government was under intense attack from U.S.-financed counterrevolutionaries. The "contras" (a shortened form of the Spanish for counterrevolutionaries), had their origin in the Nicaraguan Democratic Forces (FDN), a group of former Somoza national guardsmen led by colonel Enrique Bermúdez. In 1981, the U.S. Central Intelligence Agency (CIA) began to provide the contras financial and logistical support. By 1983 the United States had provided $100 million to a force that had grown to more than 10,000 guerrillas.

Contra strategy emphasized economic and political terrorism, including attacks on farms, schools, and health clinics, indiscriminate attacks on civilian economic targets, and kidnappings and assassinations (see Figure 5.3). Nonetheless, the rights to life and security of the person were consistently respected by the Nicaraguan government. This was in sharp contrast to U.S.-supported governments in neighboring Guatemala and El Salvador, which typically justified state terrorism by the need to combat guerrilla violence.

With the winding down of the contra war in 1988 and 1989, respect for civil and political rights again improved. Peaceful political opposition

FIGURE 5.3 A rural school destroyed in a contra attack in 1987. Amnesty International photo.

was generally tolerated during the 1989–1990 election campaign. And in national elections in February 1990, the Sandinistas were voted out of power. This was particularly noteworthy because it involved not merely a change in government, as in neighboring El Salvador and Guatemala, but a change in social and political philosophy.

President Violetta Chamorro has tried to set aside ideological and political disputes in the name of national reunification. The army remained under Humberto Ortega, one of the more radical Sandinista officials, and Sandinista trade unions and popular organizations have not been significantly repressed. In fact, in January 1991 the Sandinistas supported Chamorro's faction of the ruling coalition in the election for the leadership of the National Assembly.[8] Questions continue to be raised about the long-run loyalty of both the Sandinistas and the contras. Nonetheless, after two years in office, the Chamorro record on civil and political rights remained relatively good, although the economic situation in Nicaragua, as in the rest of the region, is grim.

U.S. Human Rights Policy in Central America

Early in this century, U.S. policy in Central America was directed toward establishing military, economic, and political hegemony. Central America was strategically significant for its proximity to the United

States, the Panama Canal, and vital sea-lanes in the Caribbean. U.S. pressure and intervention were also regularly used to further the interests of U.S. banks and corporations. By the 1920s, Central America had become a special U.S. sphere of influence, "our backyard," as it is still often put.

Since World War II, however, the role of economic concerns in U.S. policy has declined dramatically. In 1954, the U.S.-backed overthrow of the freely elected government of Jacobo Arbenz in Guatemala did reflect the interests of the United Fruit Company, which had special influence in both the State Department and the CIA. Even then, though, anticommunism was probably a stronger motivating force. By the 1980s, when Central America reemerged as a central issue in U.S. foreign policy, economic interests were largely irrelevant. For example, U.S. exports to Nicaragua averaged just under $200 million per year for 1976 to 1978. Total U.S. direct foreign investment was under $60 million (which was less than one-tenth of total U.S. investment in Mexico and Central America).

Human rights concerns, however, have not taken the place of economic interests. As Lars Schoultz argued, "Human rights is a residual category in United States policy toward Latin America; it (along with economic development) is what policy emphasizes when there is no security problem on the horizon."[9] U.S. policy has instead been driven by the fear of domestic instability and the inroads it might provide for local Communists and their Soviet (and Cuban) supporters. As a result, U.S. policy in Central America has oscillated between neglect during periods of domestic calm and active, sometimes frantic, intervention during times of domestic instability. In both modes, though, U.S. policy has usually supported or strengthened the military and traditional civilian elites, to the detriment of the human rights of most Central Americans.

Consider Nicaragua. In 1912, U.S. troops were sent to prevent a liberal political revolution. They remained until 1933, except for eighteen months between 1925 and 1927. Furthermore, the United States was the leading force behind the creation of the National Guard, the principal base of power of the Somoza family. Economic interests and strategic concerns (especially concern over a potential second canal through Nicaragua) explain the initial U.S. involvement. After World War II, though, the Somozas' support of U.S. cold war policies, such as the overthrow of Arbenz in Guatemala and efforts to isolate Cuba in the 1960s, became their major asset. The (probably apocryphal) assessment of the senior Somoza attributed to Franklin Roosevelt aptly summarized the relationship: "He's a son of a bitch, but he's *our* son of a bitch." Even when the United States was not actively backing the Somozas, its toleration of their dictatorial rule was widely seen, with some justice, as tacit support.

In Guatemala and El Salvador as well, the United States consistently supported repressive dictatorships. In the decades after the overthrow of Arbenz in 1954, the United States supported a series of vicious Guatemalan military governments. And in El Salvador, although dictatorship was established with little U.S. involvement, the United States supported a series of military-dominated governments.

The postwar U.S. record on economic, social, and cultural rights in Central America was somewhat more mixed. In 1961, the United States launched the Alliance for Progress, a major foreign aid program for Latin America. Central America received a substantial increase in U.S. aid, which seems to have contributed to relatively rapid economic growth in the region in the 1960s and early 1970s. U.S. aid also helped to improve life expectancy and literacy. The benefits of growth in Central America, however, were distributed extremely unequally. In fact, the gap between rich and poor actually grew in the 1960s and 1970s. And in El Salvador, Guatemala, and Nicaragua alike, U.S.-backed governments regularly used their power against political parties, trade unions, peasant organizations, and most other groups that tried to foster more rapid reforms or structural changes in society or the economy.

There were signs of U.S. uneasiness. For example, after martial law was imposed in Nicaragua in 1974, the Ford administration moved to distance itself from Somoza (although not so far as to support any alternative). Nonetheless, the logic of anticommunism dominated U.S. policy in Central America in the first three decades after World War II.

The Carter administration entered office in 1977 intent on giving human rights at least equal place in its policy. In Central America, the administration took a significant step in that direction. Early in 1977, Guatemala's military government announced that it would not accept U.S. aid if it was contingent on public U.S. reporting of Guatemalan human rights practices. Neither Congress nor Carter, however, was willing to leave it at that. Military assistance credits to Guatemala were banned in 1978 and the United States refused to support multilateral loans to Guatemala in 1979 and 1980. The United States also carried out an active program of public diplomacy, including a well-publicized visit by Assistant Secretary of State William Bowdler. Likewise, in the summer of 1977, the Carter administration announced that it would not support new military aid to Nicaragua until the human rights situation improved.

Notable as such changes were, their limits must also be recognized. In Guatemala, although new military aid was cut off, already committed ("pipeline") aid was continued, and Israel emerged an alternate source of supply. Furthermore, the United States simply did not press for major structural reforms. For example, when Somoza lifted censorship regulations and the state of siege, the United States largely dropped the issue of human rights.

When Nicaragua did emerge as a major concern of U.S. foreign policy, in the fall of 1978, the United States was worried principally about internal turmoil in Nicaragua, not human rights. The Carter administration's goal was to remove Somoza without yielding power to the Sandinistas, who were seen as too closely tied to Cuba and the Soviet Union. In fact, the desire to avoid "another Cuba" dominated the consideration of policy options. The United States tried to strengthen the political center, but the centrist opposition was suffering under political and financial retaliation by Somoza, and the assassination of Pedro Joaquin Chamorro earlier that year had deprived the opposition of its most respected and effective leader. After four frustrating months of U.S. mediation, Somoza simply refused to leave.

Carter responded with wide-ranging sanctions: military and economic aid was terminated, the Peace Corps was withdrawn, and the size of the U.S. Embassy in Managua was reduced by more than one-half. But when these sanctions failed to convince Somoza to step down, there was little that could be done short of the use of force, which for reasons of principle and policy alike the Carter administration refused to consider.

In June 1979, when the Sandinistas (FSLN) launched their "final offensive," the United States once more tried to promote a centrist "third force." The pace of events, however, combined with the moderate opposition's lack of organization and foresight, frustrated this effort. When Somoza was forced into exile in July, power passed to a provisional coalition government that was dominated by its most astute and best-organized faction, the FSLN.

The Carter administration, however, attempted to set aside its suspicions. Food and medical supplies were sent almost immediately. By the time Carter left office in January 1981, eighteen months after Somoza's fall, the United States had provided $118 million in aid to Nicaragua. This was more than the United States gave to any other Central American country in the same period, and it was by far the largest amount provided to Nicaragua by any Western government. In addition, the United States supported $262 million in loans from the World Bank and the Inter-American Development Bank.

In El Salvador, because of human rights concerns, the United States backed the October 1979 coup led by reformist military officers. But when most of the civilians in the junta resigned in January 1980, to protest the government's inability to control the military or halt human rights violations, the Carter administration remained supportive (although it still did not restore military aid). Even after Colonel Majano, the leader of the reformist faction in the military, was forced out of the junta in December

1980, the Carter administration continued to characterize the Salvadoran government as reformist, despite massive and mounting violations of civil and political rights and the failure to make any progress on land reform or other programs to improve the enjoyment of economic and social rights.

It is also important to note that even Carter's limited efforts on behalf of human rights in Central America met with substantial domestic opposition. For example, in June 1979 more than a hundred members of Congress signed a full page ad in support of Somoza that ran in the *New York Times* under the headline "Congress Asks: Please, Mr. President, Not Another Cuba!" Within the Carter administration as well there were high officials—most prominently National Security Adviser Zbigniew Brzezinski—who remained fundamentally opposed to the Sandinistas. As these elements increasingly came to dominate the policy-making process, the Carter administration began moving the United States toward what would become Reagan's new approach.

The Reagan administration's approach to Central America (as well as to the rest of the world) started from radical anticommunism. Although Soviet power prevented efforts to "roll back" communism in Central and Eastern Europe, there did appear to be opportunities in the Third World. Along with Afghanistan, Central America became a test case for Reagan's new global political strategy.

In April 1981, the Reagan administration announced that U.S. aid to Nicaragua, which had been temporarily suspended in January, would not be resumed, despite the fact that U.S. intelligence confirmed that the Sandinistas had stopped their aid to the Salvadoran guerrillas. By the summer, the Central Intelligence Agency began to help to organize an external counterrevolutionary (contra) military opposition. On March 14, 1982, two bridges were destroyed by former members of the National Guard who had been trained by the CIA.

The "Kirkpatrick Doctrine" provided the human rights rationale for this new approach. In an influential article that helped to earn her a position as U.S. ambassador to the United Nations, Jeane Kirkpatrick argued that Carter had failed to understand that the most serious threats to human rights were posed not by authoritarian dictatorships such as Somoza but by totalitarian Communist regimes. Furthermore, because many authoritarian dictatorships were U.S. allies, Carter's policy hurt U.S. friends at the same time that it gave insufficient attention to communism, the most serious threat to human rights.[10] As one conservative group summed up the Carter approach, "Faced with the choice of an occasionally deplorable ally and a consistently deplorable enemy, since 1977 the United States has aided its adversary and alienated its ally."[11] For the Reagan administration, global strategic rivalry with the Soviet Union *was* a struggle for human rights, whatever the actual human rights practices of the governments in question.

Many in Congress, however, had a more complex vision of Central America, and they were supported by a wide range of liberal interest groups. The Reagan administration thus faced constant, but only sporadically successful, resistance to its requests for aid to the contras. Although aid was suspended in July 1983, "humanitarian" assistance resumed in June 1985 and military aid was approved the following summer. Not until February 1988, in Reagan's last year of office, was military aid again stopped. In addition, the administration blocked loans to Nicaragua in the World Bank and the Inter-American Development Bank, cut the import of Nicaraguan sugar by 90 percent in 1983, and imposed a complete trade embargo in May 1985.

The United States orchestrated a massive assault on Nicaragua, using the full range of resources short of the direct use of U.S. troops—but including the illegal mining of Nicaraguan harbors in 1984. Moreover, it is now known that funds were illegally diverted toward this operation and those responsible lied under oath to Congress. This campaign of military and economic aggression had devastating human consequences. As many as 40,000 were killed and at least 250,000 displaced. Food production declined by at least one-quarter. Advances in health care and social services were halted or reversed, often by terrorist attacks on clinics and social service offices. By 1988, the Nicaraguan economy had been destroyed, with inflation raging at 31,000 percent.

All of this must be contrasted with strong U.S. support for the government of El Salvador. The human rights situation in El Salvador in the late 1970s and early 1980s was far worse than in Nicaragua under either Somoza or the Sandinistas. Salvadoran security forces regularly used indiscriminate violence against civilians. Clandestine paramilitary death squads, with links to the security forces and right-wing political parties, operated with impunity, kidnapping and killing politicians, labor leaders, peasant activists, intellectuals, church activists, and other civilians that the death squads believed to sympathize with the guerrillas.[12] And in addition to the tens of thousands of Salvadorans killed, Americans were also victims. In December 1980, four American churchwomen were abducted, raped, and murdered, and in March 1981 two officials of the American Institute for Free Labor Development were assassinated by government forces in the San Salvador Sheraton Hotel. Yet U.S. aid continued, in huge amounts—about $500 million a year in 1984 and 1985 (compared to less than $100 million in 1979 and 1980 combined) and about $4 billion total for the decade of the 1980s.

In order to release this aid, Congress required the president to certify that the government of El Salvador was respecting internationally recognized human rights and that it had gained control over the armed forces. The Reagan administration, however, cynically manipulated this procedure. The first certification came in January 1982, after a year in which the Salvadoran government and allied paramilitary forces had murdered well over 10,000 civilians. Although the numbers of victims did decline to a few thousand a year, and then several hundred, torture remained commonplace and most civil and political rights were systematically restricted or violated. Nonetheless, President Reagan certified the human rights performance of the Salvadoran government as acceptable four separate times, and at the end of 1983 he vetoed new legislation requiring further certifications.

The human rights situation in neighboring Nicaragua was hardly ideal. For example, Americas Watch's 1984–1985 annual report noted "prior censorship of the press, political jailings, the denial of due process of law by special tribunals, the mistreatment of prisoners by incommunicado detention, and forced relocation."[13] But torture and extrajudicial executions, which were commonplace in El Salvador, were quite rare in Nicaragua. Nonetheless, the United States helped to launch and aggressively supported a guerrilla war of terrorism against Nicaragua. As Americas Watch put it, "So consistent is this double standard that it can be fairly said [that] the Reagan administration has no true human rights policy."[14]

The Kirkpatrick Doctrine did suggest that the cause of human rights would be furthered in the long term by the success of a geopolitical struggle against the Soviet Union and its client states. Human rights as an independent and immediate concern, however, had virtually no place in the Reagan administration's Central America policy. Criticisms of the human rights practices of leftist regimes and the defense of the human rights practices of "friendly" governments were simply a continuation of the ideological and geopolitical struggle with the Soviet Union by other means.

The differences between Carter and Reagan policy toward Central America, however, were not as great as the rhetoric of either side suggested. Although Carter spoke of human rights as the "heart" of U.S. foreign policy, in Central America they were only a secondary goal. And Reagan's attempts to relegate human rights to the bottom of the list of U.S. foreign policy objectives were at least partially defeated by Congress. Carter did significantly elevate the place of human rights in U.S. policy toward Central America, but they never reached the top. And Reagan did force human rights further back down the list, but they never reached the bottom.[15]

The Bush administration's Central America policy, both in word and in deed, lay somewhere between those of its predecessors. It was generally supportive of the existing governments in Guatemala and El Salvador, despite their lack of control over the military. Bush acted to attempt to prevent a further deterioration in the situation, for example, by suspending military aid to Guatemala in late 1990 after an upsurge in political violence. Even in Nicaragua he pursued a somewhat less belligerent strategy of opposition to the Sandinistas. And Vice President Dan Quayle was sent to El Salvador twice in 1989 to express the administration's concerns. But Bush also strongly opposed congressional efforts to cut military aid to El Salvador after the November 1989 murder of six Jesuits. In fact, in January 1991 he fully restored the aid that Congress had cut in half just two months earlier, despite the continuing violation of human rights and the failure of the government to prosecute successfully anyone for these (or any other) violations.

Human rights again seemed to have a foot in the door of U.S. foreign policy in Central America. Concrete actions, however, were limited to mildly opposing only the most blatant violence. Systematic and structural impediments to the realization of civil and political and economic, social, and cultural rights alike in Central America remained almost entirely ignored.

THE UNITED STATES
AND THE SOUTHERN CONE

As we saw in Chapter 3, Argentina, Chile, and Uruguay suffered under particularly brutal military regimes in the 1970s and 1980s. What Argentineans call the Dirty War was a concerted campaign of torture and violence directed against the political Left, trade unions, intellectuals, mainstream autonomous social organizations, and dissidents of all sorts, as well as numerous ordinary, apolitical citizens who were forced into or became accidentally enmeshed in the politics of torture and disappearances.

The United States played a significant supporting role in the rise to power of the Chilean military. The Nixon administration saw the 1970 election of Salvador Allende, an avowed Marxist, as an intolerable intrusion of communism in Latin America, despite Allende's fair and free election, strong democratic socialist background, and independence from Soviet and Cuban influence. Henry Kissinger, national security adviser and later secretary of state, crafted a campaign of economic sabotage that helped to weaken popular support for Allende. In addition, the United States provided support for and encouragement to dissident military officers (although the 1973 coup was largely a local Chilean initiative). The United States played a smaller role in the rise of military rule in Uruguay and Argentina. In all three countries, however, U.S. diplomacy was generally supportive of the coups and the new military regimes.

Congress attempted to distance the United States from the junta in Chile, initially by asking that the issue of human rights violations be raised diplomatically and then by placing a ceiling on economic aid and a ban on new military assistance. Kissinger, however, did his best to ignore the desires of Congress. For example, in 1976 he publicly reprimanded the U.S. ambassador to Chile for even raising the issue of human rights in private discussions. In Argentina and Uruguay as well, torture, disappearances, and the suppression of the full range of internationally recognized human rights were considered an acceptable price to pay to eliminate the leftist "threat" in the Southern Cone. Even when diplomatic initiatives on behalf of human rights were undertaken, as in Argentina in 1976, they were low-key, entirely private, and accompanied by public support for the military.

The Carter administration sharply reversed U.S. policy in the region. President Carter, Secretary of State Cyrus Vance, and Assistant Secretary of State for Human Rights Patricia Derian all drew public attention to human rights violations in the Southern Cone. No head of a Southern Cone military regime was invited for a state visit to Washington. By contrast, human rights activists and major figures in the political opposition were publicly received at the State Department and had considerable access to local U.S. embassies.

A month after entering office, Carter reduced military aid to Argentina and Uruguay by two-thirds. In fact, during Carter's term all military aid to Southern Cone countries was halted (although Congress deserves much of the credit for this). The Carter administration voted against or abstained on twenty-three loans by international development banks to Argentina, eleven to Uruguay, and five to Chile (although the fact that all of these loans ultimately were approved suggests that the votes were largely symbolic). At both the UN and the OAS, the Carter administration supported activities directed against Chile, Argentina, and Uruguay.

These policies led to the release of a number of political prisoners, including prominent opposition journalist Jacobo Timerman and human rights activist (and future Nobel Peace Prize recipient) Adolfo Pérez Esquivel. Conditions of detention were eased for many others. The Carter administration also claimed some credit for reductions in disappearances and in the number of political prisoners, although a much more important factor probably was the success of earlier efforts at terror and repression.

The Carter policies, however, did not end military rule. And relations with Chile, Uruguay, and especially Argentina were strained. One may debate whether the achievements were sufficiently great or the costs sufficiently low to justify the policy. It is clear, though, that the Carter approach to the Southern Cone represented a major shift in U.S. policy. And unlike the case of Central America, this new approach was sustained through the full four years of the Carter presidency.

In 1981, the Reagan administration, no less dramatically and no less abruptly, returned to the policies of Nixon, Kissinger, and Ford. In fact, Argentina and Chile were two of the principal examples Jeane Kirkpatrick had in mind when she argued that the Carter administration had foolishly sacrificed more important U.S. interests to the quixotic pursuit of human rights.

Although in 1981 Congress had explicitly prohibited economic or military aid to Chile, the Reagan administration did everything it could to foster cordial relations with the Pinochet government. In August 1981, Ambassador Kirkpatrick paid a formal visit to Chile and called for the full normalization of U.S.-Chilean relations. At the UN Commission on Human Rights, the United States voted against the continuation of the special rapporteur on Chile. Joint military exercises were reinstituted, and loans from the Inter-American Development Bank to Chile jumped from zero in 1980 to over $180 million in 1981 and 1982. In 1983 alone, Chile received $690 million in multilateral loans from international financial institutions, more than three times the total during the entire Carter administration.

For Argentina, the Reagan administration successfully sought repeal of the 1978 Humphrey-Kennedy amendment that had banned U.S. military sales and security assistance. General Viola, the newly designated leader of Argentina's second junta, was invited for a state visit in March 1981. U.S. representatives to the World Bank and other international financial institutions were instructed to cease abstaining on loan applications, despite a clear legal requirement that they do so. And Ambassador Kirkpatrick did not even reply to a letter from the Mothers of the Plaza de Mayo asking for a meeting during her August 1981 visit to Buenos Aires.

These events were interpreted in Santiago and Buenos Aires as a signal of renewed U.S. support. Immediately after Kirkpatrick's visit, Chile expelled several political leaders, including some centrist Christian Democrats, and arrested and tortured a number of human rights activists. The United States made no public statement. Yet more brazen was the incommunicado detention of seven of Argentina's leading human rights activists immediately prior to General Viola's visit to Washington, apparently to keep them from saying anything that might cloud the reception Viola received. Although the Reagan administration did engage in private efforts to obtain their release, it made no public protest and provided an extremely cordial welcome to Viola.

More generally as well, although the Reagan administration did engage in quiet diplomacy on behalf of individual victims of human rights violations in the Southern Cone, human rights violations in the Southern Cone were treated solely as a matter for private discussions between friends. The overriding priority was to maintain close relations. Other interests were considered far more important than the pervasive human rights violations of the military regimes of the Southern Cone.

Even after Argentina's Falklands disaster, the Reagan administration did not publicly raise human rights concerns in Argentina or press for democratization. Although the new civilian government was embraced in Washington, the United States had nothing to do with its creation. In Uruguay as well, civilian rule returned despite, rather than because of, U.S. policy.

In Chile, however, the Reagan administration did speak out against the second wave of intensified repression that led to the reimposition of martial law in 1984. Assistant Secretary of State for Human Rights Elliott Abrams, who had earlier been a vocal supporter of the Chilean regime, publicly criticized the Pinochet government. Moreover, the United States abstained on some multilateral loans to Chile in February and March 1985. But the Reagan administration's actions were weak and inconsistent. Soon after the state of siege had been formally lifted in June 1985, the United States supported Chilean requests for $345 million in multilateral development bank loans, despite the fact that the human rights situation had not significantly improved. And in December 1985, the United States cast the decisive vote in the OAS General Assembly that removed reference to Chile in a resolution on human rights violations. Even after Pinochet lost the 1988 plebiscite for another eight-year term as president, U.S. criticism of military rule in Chile remained low-key. As in the rest of the region, democracy returned to Chile almost entirely in spite of U.S. policy.

U.S. POLICY
TOWARD SOUTH AFRICA

The human rights situation in South Africa was discussed in Chapter 4. Prior to the Sharpeville Massacre in 1960, which left nearly seventy peaceful protesters dead and led to a state of emergency in much of the country, U.S. policy toward South Africa had been focused on containing Soviet influence in the region. Apartheid had been treated largely as an internal South African matter. Sharpeville, however, raised the specter of revolution, mobilized U.S. fear of Communist influence, and led to U.S. willingness to admit apartheid as a matter of international concern. For example, the Eisenhower administration agreed to put apartheid permanently on the agenda of the United Nations Security Council.

The new Kennedy administration initiated a major policy review in 1961 (which dragged on until 1964). Kennedy also imposed a selective arms embargo even before the Security Council finally called for a voluntary embargo at the end of 1963. As the crisis receded, however, so did U.S. attention. Sanctions remained in effect, but they were modest and had no discernible impact.

When Henry Kissinger took over as national security adviser to President Nixon in 1969, he instituted a series of policy reviews for all areas of the world. The resulting document on South Africa, National Security Memorandum 39 (NSM 39), proposed closer association with South Africa in order to put the United States in a better position to exert influence over the government of South Africa to reform its policies. In effect, the policy of detente, which would come to shape U.S.-Soviet relations during the Nixon-Kissinger era, was to be applied to South Africa as well.

The Nixon-Kissinger policy did not involve full normalization of relations. The arms embargo was loosened but not eliminated. The goal was to combine negative sanctions with more positive inducements to change and to use areas of mutual interest, such as regional security, as a wedge to open South Africa to U.S. pressure on apartheid. This approach, however, had no more impact than the Kennedy-Johnson strategy of dissociation had.

Part of the problem was weak and inconsistent implementation. For example, patently false certifications of the nonmilitary nature of certain arms were accepted. As a result, a 1978 U.S. Department of Justice study found that 178 of South Africa's 578 military aircraft had been purchased from the United States after 1963.[16] In fact, U.S. concessions seem not to have been tied to any particular demands on South Africa. In other words, there was no real *policy* on South Africa. NSM 39 was adopted, but never seriously implemented.

There were also major conceptual flaws in both the Kennedy-Johnson and the Nixon-Kissinger approaches. The United States asked for changes that the white government in South Africa simply was not willing to make. Many white South Africans felt that their survival was at stake. Neither the negative sanctions nor the positive inducements from the United States were anywhere close to sufficient to achieve U.S. goals, given such a perception of the stakes. Although willing to ease certain elements of "petty apartheid" (for example, by desegregating some public facilities in large cities), the government was not willing to end racial separation—which is all that the Nixon administration ever asked for—let alone move to democratic majority rule.

The other conceptual error in U.S. policy was an excessive reliance on economic change and private enterprise. Liberals and conservatives alike believed that apartheid could not weather the social changes associated with economic development, which was progressing rapidly in South Africa. South Africa's atavistic racial policies, it was widely believed, would inevitably be eroded by the irresistible, if difficult to specify, attitudinal changes that accompany economic modernization. Trade and investment thus appeared as instruments for change rather than as support for apartheid. In fact, although the reforms required by economic necessity were made, they were actively prevented from spilling over into social and political changes. South Africa's immense bureaucracy, which intervened with totalitarian thoroughness in all aspects of life, largely prevented unplanned changes in the fundamental character of apartheid from going unnoticed or unchecked.

Furthermore, after the Portuguese coup in April 1974, which led to the rapid decolonization of Angola and Mozambique, these modest U.S. efforts were largely abandoned in favor of a focus on "regional security"; that is, containing expanding Soviet influence. South Africa now appeared as an important, pro-Western regional power. Kissinger even agreed to meet Prime Minister Vorster twice in 1976, the first high-level meeting between U.S. and South African government officials in thirty years.

The Soweto riots of 1976 returned apartheid to the center of international attention. Soon afterward, the election of Jimmy Carter changed the U.S. approach. The arms embargo was restored to its pre-Nixon status. Outstanding Export-Import Bank credits to South Africa were cut in half during the first three years of the Carter administration. The United States even responded to the October 1977 clampdown on the nonviolent opposition in South Africa by supporting a Security Council call for a mandatory arms embargo.

These actions, however, were largely symbolic. Furthermore, there were tensions in the Carter policy from the outset. National Security Adviser Zbigniew Brzezinski favored something much more like the Kissinger emphasis on regional security. As Brzezinski surpassed Secretary of State Cyrus Vance as the leading voice on U.S. foreign policy in the second half of the Carter term, U.S. policy took on an increasingly cold war tone, stressing the Cuban presence in Angola and the Soviet naval threat in the South Atlantic and Indian Ocean. Even more dramatically than in Central America, the end of the Carter administration prepared the way for Reagan.

Reagan's policy of "constructive engagement" represented a return to the Nixon-era strategy of pursuing closer and more-cordial relations in an attempt to increase U.S. leverage. Assistant Secretary of State Chester Crocker, the principal architect of the policy, had been a staff member on Kissinger's National Security Council. In the 1980s, he tried to turn the idea behind NSM 39 into an effective policy. Although some in the Reagan administration gave the appearance of being active friends of South Africa, Crocker was sufficiently critical for Senator Jesse Helms to block his appointment as assistant secretary for nine months, and on Crocker's first visit to South Africa the prime minister refused to meet with him.

Despite growing national and international demands for additional sanctions, the Reagan administration not only refused to support new sanctions but also eased many existing ones. New Export-Import Bank credits began to be approved in 1981, and efforts to discourage private bank loans were terminated. Restrictions on the sale of aircraft and computers with dual military and civilian uses were eased. South Africa became the second largest purchaser of U.S. dual-use nuclear-related equipment in 1981–1982. By the early 1980s, the United States had become South Africa's largest trading partner, and U.S. direct foreign investment and bank loans to South Africa totaled about $10 billion. In 1982, the Reagan administration supported a $1 billion International Monetary Fund (IMF) credit to South Africa, the largest ever made through the fund's Compensatory Financing Facility.

The justification for constructive engagement was a belief that the government of P. W. Botha was pragmatic and committed to managing an ongoing transition from apartheid. The U.S. role, therefore, was to foster change through enlightened private enterprise and through support for moderate forces of social change, such as trade unions and improved black education. But as during the Nixon administration, there was an immense gap between verbal policy and actual practice. The United States in fact devoted almost no resources to education or support for trade unions, and the reforms introduced by U.S. corporations, although they helped a few relatively privileged black employees, had no systematic impact on apartheid. Furthermore, as in the early 1970s, the United States asked almost nothing (except on regional security issues) in return for improved relations.

The central problem with constructive engagement, however, was a misjudgment of South Africa's intentions. The Botha government was willing to modernize apartheid. It was not willing to eliminate it. And the Reagan administration's support for the 1983 constitution, which completely excluded blacks from direct political participation, suggested that the United States was willing to settle for that.

Once more, however, events in South Africa forced a reevaluation of U.S. policy. The Reagan administration had argued that despite the exclusion of blacks from the national electorate, local councils allowed meaningful black political participation. By 1984, however, most black political activists in South Africa saw the councils as an example of indirect rule and white domination. In fact, the local councils were increasingly unable to exercise physical control over the townships. Violence erupted in August in protest over elections held under the new constitution, and repression once more tightened rather than eased. Constructive engagement was effectively dead as a defensible policy.

The decisive changes in U.S. policy, however, came from Congress. In July 1985, a House-Senate conference committee agreed to a compromise sanctions bill, which was finally tabled in September when Reagan issued an executive order imposing similar economic sanctions. Reagan, however, continued to support a nonpunitive approach. For example, in a speech on July 26, 1986, he argued, "We and our allies cannot dictate to the government of a sovereign nation—nor should we try." Critics dismissed this as a political double standard, noting that Reagan had for years been funding a war against Nicaragua and had imposed sanctions against Cuba, Libya, Nicaragua, and Poland. And soon afterward, Congress overrode a presidential veto of a new sanctions bill.

Part of the explanation for this change must be traced to the Republican leadership in the Senate, especially Senator Richard Lugar, chair of the Foreign Relations Committee, and Senator Nancy Kassebaum, chair of the African Affairs Subcommittee. Although they had earlier supported constructive engagement, in November 1984 they sent a letter to the president asking him to review the administration's South Africa policy. The following month, thirty-five conservative members of the House, including Newt Gingrich, also called for abandoning constructive engagement, citing it as an embarrassment and a political liability to the Republican party. Sanctions, which had long been supported by the Democrats in Congress, finally achieved bipartisan support.

These changes in Congress, however, mirrored changes in the electorate that had been prepared by extensive NGO activities. U.S. NGO activity on South Africa goes back to at least 1912, when the National Association for the Advancement of Colored People (NAACP) was involved in the initial formation of South Africa's African National Congress (ANC). The American Committee on Africa (ACOA) was formed in 1953 in response to the pass law demonstrations. And in the late 1970s and 1980s groups like TransAfrica and the Washington Office on Africa focused their efforts on apartheid. Other NGOs, such as the American Friends Service Committee, the Interfaith Council on Corporate Responsibility, and the Lawyers' Committee for Civil Rights Under Law made South Africa a major priority in their activities. In addition, churches, state and local governments, colleges and universities, student organizations, unions, and black organizations divested assets in corporations that did business in South Africa.

These activities brought home to a local audience the concerns and activities of the international antiapartheid regime (see Chapter 4). Some of these U.S. NGO activities were even loosely coordinated with divestment campaigns in other countries, international antiapartheid groups such as the International Defense and Aid Fund, and other international NGOs such as the World Council of Churches and the Lutheran World Fund. They were also greatly facilitated by Bishop Tutu's Nobel Peace Prize and the publicity he received during his visit to the United States at the end of 1984.

It is important not to overestimate the impact of U.S. sanctions. The 1985 executive order was limited to loans and a few products, such as Krugerrands, and was full of loopholes. Bishop Tutu described it dismissively as "not even a flea bite." The 1986 sanctions were also limited and partial. Nonetheless, South Africa was losing access to international capital (although in the short run more from lender fear caused by the 1984–1986 township riots than from sanctions).[17] And the loss of U.S. support, even if the Reagan administration never actively opposed the white government, created concern among many of South Africa's less-conservative leaders and citizens, particularly in light of the growing internal crisis.

Apartheid ultimately collapsed because of the inability of the white government either to modernize apartheid or to keep the lid on opposition through increasing repression. Nonetheless, the change in U.S. policy, particularly in the context of the global antiapartheid campaign, played at least a small part in shaping the political context in which apartheid was legislatively dismantled. And even if the sanctions were primarily symbolic—as was the support provided by constructive engagement—it was a very different sort of symbolism than had been typical of U.S. policy in the preceding years.

OTHER WESTERN APPROACHES
TO INTERNATIONAL HUMAN RIGHTS

As we saw in Chapter 1, the United States played a major role in the 1970s in introducing human rights into the mainstream of bilateral diplomacy. A number of other countries, however, have also made human rights an important part of their foreign policies. Particularly notable have been the efforts of the **like-minded countries,** a dozen small and medium-size Western countries that since the mid-1970s have attempted to act together in international diplomacy as intermediaries between the larger Western countries, with which they are formally or informally aligned, and the countries of the Third World, for whose aspirations they have considerable sympathy. In this section we will look in particular at the activities of Norway, the Netherlands, and Canada, three countries that have especially emphasized human rights in their foreign policy, going as far as having issued White Papers on the subject in 1977, 1979, and 1987 respectively.

Even more than in the United States, foreign aid has been a central instrument in the international human rights policies of the like-minded countries. Their approach to the linkage of human rights and development assistance, however, is somewhat different. The United States tends to make initial decisions on allocating foreign aid on the basis of a combination of political and humanitarian concerns. At a later stage, allocations may be modified marginally on the basis of human rights performance, typically by reducing or eliminating aid to gross violators (where political considerations do not override human rights concerns). In the like-minded countries, by contrast, overall human rights performance, in civil and political as well as in economic, social, and cultural rights, is a central part of the initial selection of priority countries.

In addition, development assistance policies in the like-minded countries tend to be very important elements of their foreign policies and matters of considerable consensus among the major political parties. In fact, in the Netherlands there is a separate minister for development cooperation within the Foreign Ministry.[18] By contrast, in the United States, foreign aid is a relatively peripheral part of foreign policy and yet a subject of considerable political controversy.[19]

None of the like-minded countries have the resources to engage in a massive, global foreign aid program such as that of the United States. They therefore target their development assistance funds at a small set of countries, variously referred to as "core," "program," or "priority" countries, with which they seek to develop relatively intensive, long-term aid relations. The Dutch and the Norwegians in particular have emphasized human rights, both civil and political rights and economic, social, and cultural rights, in the selection of their program countries over the past two decades.

As early as 1973, the Dutch officially emphasized a "close relationship between peace, a just distribution of wealth, international legal order and respect for human rights."[20] Since the late 1970s, especially after the 1979 White Paper, the Dutch have stressed a desire to cooperate with countries that emphasize civil and political as well as economic, social, and cultural rights in their domestic politics and development strategies. In Norway, criteria developed in 1972 for the selection of program countries stressed a strong preference for countries in which "the authorities of the country concerned [are] following a development-oriented and socially just policy in the best interests of all sections of the community." In 1976 the Norwegian Storting (parliament) reiterated its special desire to cooperate with countries pursuing a "socially just policy" and committed to the implementation of the economic, social, and cultural rights laid out in the Universal Declaration and the Covenants.[21] And in 1984, a center-right coalition government, using language characteristic of those who would be considered extreme liberals in the United States, declared that "development assistance is an extension to the international level of the efforts to create social justice, characteristic of the Norwegian welfare state" and that "all have the right to have their basic needs for food, water, clothing, education, and housing satisfied."[22] This concern with social justice is in addition to, and given roughly equal priority with, the concern with civil and political rights.

In practice, the selection of priority countries only partially meets these noble statements of intent. For example, in 1974 the program countries of the Netherlands were Indonesia, India, Pakistan, Bangladesh, Sri Lanka, North Yemen, Nigeria, Tunisia, Kenya, Tanzania, Upper Volta, Zambia, Sudan, Egypt, Colombia, Suriname, Netherlands Antilles, Peru, Cuba, Jamaica, and Turkey. By 1984, Nigeria, Turkey, Tunisia, Peru, Cuba, Colombia, and Jamaica had been deleted, the programs in Upper Volta and Zambia had been expanded to broader regional programs for the Sahel and Southern Africa, and a Central American regional program, with special emphasis on Nicaragua, had been introduced. Historical (that is, colonial) ties explain the inclusion of Indonesia, Suriname, and the Netherlands Antilles. Pakistan provides geopolitical balance to India, and Kenya provides an ideological balance to Tanzania, which was selected on social justice and human rights criteria. Nonetheless, the overall human rights records of these countries compare favorably with international averages, and very favorably with a comparable list of countries supported by the United States.

Even more striking than the selection of priority countries has been the relatively rapid response of the like-minded countries to changes in human rights conditions. For example, Norway broke its aid relationship with Uganda in 1972, the year that Idi Amin overthrew the government of Milton Obote and embarked on a dictatorial career that made him one of the most notorious human rights violators of the decade. The Netherlands dropped Uganda from its list of program countries in 1974. The United States, by contrast, was Uganda's largest trading partner until October 1978, when a trade embargo was imposed, less than a year before Amin was finally overthrown.

Sweden stopped all assistance to Chile shortly after Pinochet's coup and then became a significant international supporter of the work of the Vicaría. Canada also emerged as a vocal critic of military rule in Chile and the rest of the Southern Cone. In the 1980s, as ethnic violence escalated in Sri Lanka, a country with which Norway had developed especially close ties in the 1970s, the Norwegians dramatically downgraded their relationship. Canada, the Netherlands, and the Nordic countries all significantly increased their aid to Nicaragua in the 1980s, reflecting a radically different understanding of human rights from that of the Reagan administration. In fact, when Reagan imposed a U.S. economic embargo on Nicaragua in 1985, the Europeans provided an additional $200 million in aid in an effort to offset some of its effects.

The Dutch response to the deteriorating human rights situation in their former colony of Suriname is especially revealing. They strongly condemned the 1980 military coup. Following the execution of fifteen political opponents of the government in 1982, the Netherlands not only suspended all aid but also refused to provide new aid for the remainder of the decade. And the Dutch led the effort to apply international pressure on Suriname, regularly raising the issue in annual UN discussions of human rights violations in particular countries. The contrast to U.S. behavior during the same period toward its Caribbean Basin clients in Guatemala and El Salvador, who were guilty of violations comparable in severity and much greater in number, is striking.

The like-minded countries also adopted an approach to South Africa very different from that of the United States in the 1970s and 1980s. Starting in 1969, Sweden and Norway provided both political support and development assistance funds to liberation movements in Southern Africa, especially the ANC during its exile from South Africa and the South-West Africa People's Organization (SWAPO) in Namibia. The Dutch adopted a similar policy in 1973. And in the 1980s these efforts were expanded by the Nordic countries and the Netherlands alike into broad, high-priority regional programs for Southern Africa. These countries also played a leading role in the international movement for sanctions against South Africa.

We should be careful not to romanticize the policies of the like-minded countries. Considerations other than human rights are indeed central to their foreign policies and at times override human rights concerns. For example, although the Netherlands reduced its aid to Indonesia from 1974 to 1978, aid increased again in the following years, despite the absence of significant human rights improvements. Economic considerations clearly played a major role. Canada has also pursued close relations with Indonesia for commercial reasons. Likewise, economic interests in South Africa seriously delayed Canada's decision to adopt sanctions. Economic interests also explain the Norwegian decision to exclude shipping from its sanctions against South Africa. Nonetheless, the overall international human rights record of the like-minded countries is clearly superior to that of the United States, both in avoiding associations with severe human rights violators and in responding forcefully to severe violations in countries with which they do have special relations.[23]

EXPLAINING DIFFERENCES IN
INTERNATIONAL HUMAN RIGHTS POLICIES

A number of factors might account for these differences in policies. For example, Jan Egeland, in comparing Norwegian and U. S. international human rights policy, argued that "small and big nations are differently disposed to undertaking coherent rights-oriented foreign policies." In fact, Egeland argued that the relatively meager international human rights accomplishments of the United States are "because of, rather than in spite of, her superpower status."[24]

Small countries are not so much "better," according to Egeland, as less constrained than large states. "The frequency and intensity of the conflict between self-interest and [international human rights] norms seems, in short, proportional to a nation's economic and military power, as well as to its foreign policy ambitions."[25] Large states have multiple interests and responsibilities that preclude the consistent pursuit of international human rights objectives. Small states, by contrast, rarely face a situation where they are forced to choose between international human rights and other foreign policy goals.

This explanation focuses on the structure of the international system. States with considerable power have many more competing foreign policy objectives than states with little power—or at least more places in which they must face a conflict between human rights and other goals. In addition, large states are more likely to pursue bilateral policies because such states are more likely to have the power to achieve their aims through unilateral action. Small states, however, are likely to prefer working through international organizations because multilateral processes allow them greater opportunities to exert international influence. The importance of size would also seem to be underscored by the fact that larger powers such as Britain, France, Germany, and Japan have international human rights policies much closer to that of the United States.

Size alone, however, is not a full explanation even for differences that clearly are influenced by differences in relative power. For example, as U.S. power declines, the United States remains reluctant to operate through multilateral channels (unless it can control the organization). Britain has tended to pursue a much more unilateral foreign policy than France, Germany, or Japan. And as German and Japanese power grows, those countries continue to exercise it principally through multilateral organizations. As for small states, Sweden, Finland, Austria, and especially Switzerland have emphasized a generally neutralist foreign policy, whereas Canada, Belgium, and the Netherlands have been much more committed to a strong Western orientation in their foreign policies. Size or power at most inclines states in certain directions.

Furthermore, we should not overlook factors that have little or nothing to do with size. Why did the United States emphasize international human rights in the 1970s while other large powers did not, and Japan still does not? Why did the United States so often actively intervene on behalf of anticommunist governments, with such deadly human rights consequences, whereas the British and French did so in their own spheres of influence much less frequently? Why are human rights a far more controversial foreign policy issue in the United States than in all other Western countries? We can offer answers to such questions only if we take into account considerations of political culture.

Throughout the cold war era, the United States viewed the world in East-West terms. All foreign policy issues tended to be reduced to U.S.-Soviet rivalry. Radical reformers and their programs usually were simply assumed to be Soviet backed, inspired, or influenced. Some part of this can be attributed to the size of the United States. But the cold war was not just any kind of bipolar political rivalry. It was a rivalry that placed immense emphasis on ideology. Without the ideological element, many actual or attempted political changes in the Third World would not have seemed a threat to the United States and thus would not have produced the same sort of conflict with human rights objectives. Ideology, however, has nothing to do with size. Many small states, especially in Latin America, were at least as anticommunist as the United States. And it is historically rather rare for a large state to define its interests in ideological terms.

Much the same can be said of the tendency of the Nordic states and Canada to view international conflicts more in North-South than in East-West terms. These countries have tended to see the principal lines of international cleavage as those between rich and poor, not liberal democratic and Communist, states. For example, in March 1982, Mark MacGuigan, the Canadian secretary of state for external affairs, in attempting to specify the nature of Canada's disagreement with U.S. policy in Central America, argued that "instability in Central America ... is not a product of East-West rivalry. It is a product of poverty, the unfair distribution of wealth, and social injustice. Instability feeds poverty and injustice. East-West rivalries flow in its wake."[26] The Dutch and the Nordic countries share this view.

Some part of this might be related to size. For example, a country like Canada that fears being overwhelmed by the United States may be more likely to be sympathetic to a perspective that sees differences in power as no less important than differences in ideology. But size alone cannot explain the difference in ideological perspective.

We can see this even in Egeland's own analysis. In trying to account for the relative success of Norwegian international human rights policies, he argued that "strong moral impact may be seen as a product of the following criteria, which are by and large positively related to Norway and the other small, Western, industrial countries, and negatively related to the USA and other powers": (1) no legacy of imperialism and intervention, (2) a good domestic human rights record, (3) a high level of foreign aid and support for changes in the world economy to favor Third World countries, and (4) consistent support for decolonization and national liberation movements.[27] The first of these four factors is indeed related to size (although Belgium and the Netherlands did have significant colonial holdings). But the other three factors, which certainly do help to explain why Norwegian human rights initiatives have been relatively well received, simply have nothing to do with size. They are more characteristic of the fact that Norway is a liberal (even social democratic), Western, industrialized democracy than that it is small. Likewise, the inferior U.S. domestic human rights record and its low levels of foreign aid have very little to do with its being large.

Much the same can be said of the role of consensus in Norwegian international human rights policy (and foreign policy more generally). Consensus on long-term foreign policy objectives has indeed facilitated Norwegian initiatives. Likewise, the changeable nature of U.S. foreign policy and its frequent shifts in interest and attention have impeded U.S. initiatives. But foreign policy consensus is hardly characteristic of small states, as the reality in numerous Third World countries indicates. In the Nordic countries it is more a function of a parliamentary system, in which there is no sharp division between executive and legislative branches, a strong reliance on a professional foreign and civil service (in contrast to the extensive use of political appointees in the U.S. bureaucracy), and a political tradition that assures direct representation and special consideration for all major social groups.[28] Conversely, although the multiple interests and large size of the U.S. bureaucracy do create more arenas for foreign policy conflict, the lack of consensus is at least as much a function of a presidential (rather than a parliamentary) system and the turnover of the leadership of most bureaucratic agencies with every election.

Size tells us little or nothing about whether or why a country will choose to emphasize human rights in its foreign policy. Certainly it is not size that explains why Norway and the Netherlands have had an active international human rights policy while Austria, Belgium, and Greece have not. Likewise, size certainly cannot explain either the active (if inconsistent) international human rights policy of the United States or the lack of an active international human rights policy in Japan, let alone the PRC.

How a country defines its interests usually will be constrained by its power and its position in the international system. But most of the impediments to strong international human rights policies lie in the relatively free decisions of states to give greater weight to other foreign policy objectives. Likewise, most of the factors that contribute to efforts to pursue international human rights aggressively in a country's foreign policy have much more to do with its national political culture than with its international political position. The simple fact is that countries such as Norway and the Netherlands place a high value on international human rights and are willing to accept some costs in an attempt to realize them.

The importance of national political culture is especially striking when we consider the contrast between Canada, Norway, and the Netherlands on the one hand and the United States on the other with respect to economic, social, and cultural rights. The United States has used foreign aid as an instrument in its international human rights policies, but almost exclusively in the pursuit of civil and political rights objectives. In the United States, foreign aid and human rights are seen as two fundamentally separate issues that have been tactically linked, reflecting the deep American suspicion of economic, social, and cultural rights. By contrast, development assistance is central to international human rights policies of the like-minded countries, and they strongly emphasize the intrinsic importance of economic, social, and cultural rights and the linkage of civil and political and economic, social, and cultural rights.

Size, power, and the structure of the international system are by no means irrelevant to international human rights policies. They are, however, of only secondary significance. States have considerable latitude in choosing their international human rights policies. The differing policies of the United States and the like-minded countries are largely matters of choice, of differing understandings of and priorities attached to internationally recognized human rights.

SIX

□   □   □

International Human Rights
in a Post–Cold War World

The collapse of the Soviet empire, culminating in the dissolution of the Soviet Union at the end of 1991, marks a decisive turning point in modern international relations. Combined with a decade of democratization in Latin America and rapidly accelerating liberalization in Africa, these changes have led to much talk of a new world order. Their impact on *international* human rights policy, though, is likely to be rather modest. Ours may be "a new world of hope," as George Bush put it.[1] In the field of international human rights, however, many of those hopes are unlikely to be realized.

At the national level, many recent changes have not penetrated very deeply. Although some newly democratic countries are likely to consolidate recent progress, many others will fall back into dictatorship. The military coups in Haiti, Togo, Algeria, Peru, and Thailand in the latter half of 1991 and the first half of 1992 were but early instances of what is certain to be a long series of human rights setbacks.

Internationally, the end of the cold war has eliminated the principal U.S. rationale for supporting repressive regimes. The demise of the Soviet Union has eliminated the postwar world's other major supporter of rights-abusive regimes. But a variety of rationales for antihumanitarian intervention[2] remains. Furthermore, there is no necessary connection between a decline in foreign policy actions that harm human rights abroad and the development of positive international human rights policies. For all the changes of recent years, international human rights policies in the

133

1990s, especially in their positive dimensions, are likely to look very much like those of the late 1970s and 1980s.[3]

IDEOLOGY AND INTERVENTION

In recent years, both bipolarity and ideological struggle, defining features of the cold war international order, have (for very different reasons) largely disappeared. Although their absence is undoubtedly beneficial for human rights, the limits of this progress are substantial.

In the postwar (or cold war) era, both superpowers intervened militarily to reverse impending or ongoing human rights improvements. In addition, both superpowers regularly supported (more or less autonomous) domestic forces of oppression in order to maintain political influence or exclude those (alleged to be) sympathetic to "the other side." Marcos in the Philippines, Duvalier in Haiti, Park in South Korea, the Shah in Iran, Stroessner in Paraguay, Pinochet in Chile, and Mobutu in Zaire were but a few of the dictatorial beneficiaries of U.S. support. The Soviet record was comparably appalling. In addition to the well-known examples of Central and Eastern Europe and Afghanistan, the Soviets backed the Mengistu regime in Ethiopia, arguably the most brutal Third World regime of the past fifteen years.

Economic decline and internal political change have largely eliminated Soviet (or Russian) incentives and capabilities for such behavior. The U.S. capability still persists, as the Gulf War vividly illustrates. The end of the cold war, however, has eliminated a central part of the U.S. justification for such antihumanitarian interventions.

Almost all U.S. antihumanitarian interventions since 1945 have had a substantial element of anticommunism, and few could have been sold to Congress and the public without it. During the cold war, most unsavory dictators could acquire, or at least maintain, U.S. support by playing on anticommunism. This is no longer the case. As a result, the post–cold war environment for human rights should be significantly improved.

U.S. intervention in the Third World, of course, predates the cold war and will continue in the future. Strategic and economic rationales will persist, and new justifications, such as the fight against drugs, will emerge. Nonetheless, without the overarching appeal to anticommunism, U.S. administrations will find it much more difficult to muster domestic support for repressive foreign regimes.

We should not underestimate the remaining problem. For example, U.S. pressure on the Andean countries to militarize their war on drugs may create disaffection in the military or an exalted sense of power, either of which may lead the military to reassert a predominant role in politics. The attempted coup in 1984 by Bolivia's Leopards, an elite antidrug squad created, funded, and trained by the United States, is only the most dramatic example of a broader U.S.-created threat to human rights in the Andean region. In addition, "elections" and "free markets" may be emerging as new ideological bases for policies destructive of human rights.

Nonetheless, the antidrug rationale for intervention has relatively limited application. Elections and markets are somewhat narrower and rather less emotional issues than anticommunism. That relatively few countries are of real strategic significance is becoming increasingly clear as ideological fervor subsides. And economic interests, other than oil, have played a minor role in U.S. foreign policy toward the Third World since the mid-1970s. Less support for repression overseas does not mean none. It is, however, a sign of genuine progress attributable to the demise of the cold war.

Consider military tolerance, under some U.S. pressure, of civilian governments and negotiations with the guerrillas in Guatemala and El Salvador. Even if the human rights situation remains far from good and elected civilian leaders do not fully control the armed forces in these countries, the end of the cold war has forced the military to eliminate—or at least reduce—some of the worst human rights violations. The Bush administration's reduction of aid to Kenya, the most favored African country during the Reagan years, also suggested real progress, as did the failure of the United States to support the military in Haiti following the overthrow of the Aristide government in 1991.

Such examples of real yet limited progress best summarize the new directions in U.S. human rights policy toward authoritarian regimes. The United States no longer systematically ignores human rights in favor of ideological objectives. But there is no necessary connection between such a decline in what might be called negative human rights policies and the emergence of positive international human rights policies. To date there have been few new positive developments of significance. Neither the Bush administration nor Congress was willing to expend substantial political or financial capital on behalf of international human rights. Bush's opening to the PRC, despite a total lack of human rights progress and a government that flouts the global trends of recent years, is a striking example of the characteristic U.S. unwillingness to take human rights seriously when they conflict with other policy objectives (see Figure 6.1).

POWER AND INTERDEPENDENCE

A similar picture of limited progress is apparent if we turn from cold war ideological rivalry to the underlying international balance of power. Russia retains the capability to destroy life on this planet. The United

FIGURE 6.1 President George Bush, former U.S. ambassador to China, responds to the Tienanmen Massacre. Copyright 1992 by *The Miami Herald*. Reprinted with permission.

States has arguably become the world's only military superpower: the Gulf War underlined the unrivaled U.S. capability to project power at a great distance. Both countries, however, are forced to confront the fact that military power today is not so easily translated into other forms of power as it has been in many other times.

Although the fungibility of power—the ability to use one type of power to acquire other types of power—has often been overemphasized, in the past it was significant. States with high power on one dimension regularly used that power to increase their holdings in other dimensions of power. Today, however, states are increasingly unable or unwilling to achieve such transformations. In particular, the control of military power is increasingly irrelevant to the acquisition of economic power. The old dominant military powers today are being joined at the center of the international stage by second- and even third-rate military powers. Japan and Germany are emerging as central political actors in the new multipolar world order, based on their immense and still-growing economic power, despite their (relatively) paltry military power. And all indications are that they intend to remain secondary military powers.

"Power" is no longer a simple, undifferentiated capacity, even as a first-order approximation. The "great powers" of the emerging world order are powers in very different senses of the term. And some states, such as Saudi Arabia, are significant powers in some international issues, but negligible actors in most others.

As a result, international politics is increasingly issue specific. International political processes and outcomes vary dramatically from issue to issue. This situation may create new opportunities for progressive international action, by freeing issues from the dominance of security and ideological concerns. It also means, though, that we cannot automatically generalize from one issue area to another. In particular, the growing recognition of the need for international economic cooperation does not necessarily imply similar conclusions about human rights.

Some developed states are increasingly willing to relinquish significant elements of economic sovereignty. We see this both in formal multilateral organizations (most notably in the European Community) and in less-formal modes of international cooperation, such as the coordination symbolized by the annual economic summits. In addition, Third World and formerly Communist states are increasingly relinquishing economic sovereignty through IMF-imposed structural adjustment packages— although often out of dire necessity rather than genuine desire.

More-complex and less-state-centric patterns of order and cooperation, based on new and relatively deep conceptions of international interdependence, are also emerging in some noneconomic issue areas. A striking example is the surprisingly rapid success in regulating ozone-depleting emissions through the 1985 Vienna Convention and its 1987 (Montreal) Protocol. In security relations, however, interdependence has not penetrated very far, especially in U.S. policy. In fact, sovereignty remained at the core of President Bush's vision of the new world order, which, as he was at pains to note, "does not mean surrendering our national sovereignty or forfeiting our interests."[4]

A state-centric, sovereignty-based conception of international order remains central in the field of international human rights as well. Most states today still jealously guard their sovereign prerogatives in the field of human rights. For example, the multilateral human rights procedures discussed above are much weaker than the IMF or the General Agreement on Tariffs and Trade (GATT). Even in Europe, the relatively strong regional human rights system pales in comparison to the restrictions on state sovereignty achieved through regional economic institutions.

The persisting strength of sovereignty in the field of human rights rests in part on their inherent sensitivity. Even relatively rare or isolated human rights violations can be sufficiently embarrassing to deter some states from accepting strong international procedures. For example, the

United States continues to refuse to ratify almost all international human rights treaties, despite the fact that in most particulars American law and practice already conform to their requirements.

Another part of the explanation for the continuing attachment to sovereignty in the field of human rights is a qualitative difference between the material interdependence that underlies international economic cooperation and the moral interdependence that underlies international cooperation in human rights. Although neither less real nor less important than material interdependence, moral interdependence does typically lead to different sorts of national and international political processes, which make international cooperation more difficult to achieve.

Economic interdependence has a relatively tangible impact on daily life. The incentives to cooperate are immediate and concrete and thus are more readily recognized and more easily included in foreign policy. Furthermore, material interdependence means that each side has at least some unilateral power to prevent the enjoyment of the benefits of cooperation. An injured party is thus likely to find it relatively easy to retaliate against violations of international norms. This is especially important given the absence of effective multilateral enforcement mechanisms.

The moral interdependence underlying human rights, however, is not a tangible part of daily life for most Americans (nor for most ordinary citizens elsewhere). Furthermore, other states are not directly harmed by a government's failure to respect human rights. The moral sensibilities of foreign citizens and leaders may be offended, but human rights violations rarely cause direct or material harm to foreigners. Therefore, the incentives to retaliate are largely intangible—which in practice usually means low.

In addition, retaliatory enforcement of international human rights norms is inherently problematic. Moral suasion, which responds directly to the nature of the international offense, is notoriously weak. Any other type of retaliation, however, must be imported from another issue area, with the risk of escalating the dispute. Furthermore, because the means of retaliation are not clearly and directly tied to the violation, their legitimacy may appear more questionable.

Taken together, these observations on the character of power and interdependence in the post–cold war world suggest that progress in the field of international human rights remains substantially constrained by deep structural forces. The end of bipolarity, as opposed to the end of cold war ideological rivalry, is likely to have few significant short- or medium-run implications for international human rights. The impediments to international action on behalf of human rights rooted in the states system remain essentially unchanged in the post–cold war world. The best that we should hope for is slow incremental progress.

THE GULF WAR:
CONTINUITY IN THE MIDST OF CHANGE

The international response to the Iraqi invasion of Kuwait, "the first crisis of the new world order," vividly illustrates this mix of continuity and change. Although human rights were only peripherally involved in the decision to go to war, the example is still useful.

Most commentators have (rightly) emphasized the elements of change. The United States and the Soviet Union, which for decades had ritually chosen opposing sides in regional conflicts, were on the same side in this crisis. Although the Gulf coalition was dominated by the United States, the Bush administration exerted immense diplomatic efforts to involve Europe and Japan and to neutralize the PRC, Israel, and Syria. In addition, policy was coordinated through the United Nations. Although hardly collective security in a strong sense of the term, the international response to the invasion of Kuwait was in sharp contrast to the cold war pattern of superpower unilateralism—compare Grenada and Panama—which itself reflected the underlying cold war international order of bipolar ideological struggle.

The principle at stake, however, was the political independence and territorial integrity of Kuwait. Questions can be raised about the connection between many of the targets of U.S. bombing and the expulsion of Iraq from Kuwait. Nonetheless, soon after the Iraqis were expelled, the fighting did halt—to the dismay of many who preferred a holy war against the devil incarnate in Baghdad. The Gulf War was primarily about restoring the territorial status quo ante. Iraqi sovereignty has been subjected to extraordinary restrictions (most notably in the security zone in the North), continuing trade restrictions, and the almost-unparalleled restrictions on armament. Nonetheless, Iraq retains its prewar borders, its prewar dictator, and its prewar human rights problems. Despite the hysterical rhetoric calling Saddam Hussein worse than Hitler, the furthest the United States has been willing to go on behalf of the human rights of Iraqis living outside the security zones has been to prevent the Iraqi air force from operating in certain areas of southern Iraq.

The Gulf War was also about protecting the economic and strategic interests of the most powerful states in the system. It is unlikely that Kuwait would have been rescued but for its oil and strategic location. Furthermore, the war was prosecuted by sovereign states, rather than a supranational political organization or some other representative of the global community of humankind. Desert Storm was an operation of a temporary coalition of states, led by the state with the greatest military power, using the United Nations as a flag of convenience.

The international response was genuinely multilateral, in recognition of the decreased international political freedom of action of the United States. In addition, other countries covered much of the bill, reflecting declining U.S. economic power. Nonetheless, what ultimately counted was the power of sovereign states. A multipolar world certainly will function differently than a bipolar world. The United States, which has usually followed a unilateral approach to international relations, will have much to learn and some difficult adjustments to make. The post–cold war world, however, is still ordered by and around the power of states. Certain old forms and causes of conflict have been laid to rest. The new order, however, certainly will not be one of harmony either within or between states.

Still another way to underscore the continuing centrality of the state is to compare the collective intervention in northern Iraq with the situation in Sudan, less than a thousand miles away. When Sudan received independence in 1956, it was already embroiled in a civil war between the largely Arabized, Muslim north, which controlled the government, and the largely black, Christian and animist south (which itself was divided between the dominant Dinka and a number of smaller ethnic groups). Half a million people had died in this conflict by the time a regional autonomy agreement finally restored peace in 1972. The institution of *sharia*, strict, traditional Muslim law in September 1983, however, touched off a new round of civil war, which has intensified since the June 1989 military coup by fundamentalist officers.

Independent political parties, newspapers, trade unions, and professional associations are banned in Sudan and all forms of opposition are roughly repressed. Women's rights have been eliminated. Torture has for the first time become a regular technique of repression. Disappearances into clandestine "ghost houses" are another new weapon in the government's arsenal.

Drought and famine have turned a bad situation into a disaster, and both sides have used food as a political weapon. The government regularly bombs civilian targets in the South, including food relief centers, and has prevented food aid from entering rebel-controlled regions. The rebels for their part attack food shipments to government-held towns. Since 1988, over 500,000 people have died from starvation or the war, and today more than 5 million people are at risk of starvation. The government, however, refuses to admit that there is a food supply problem. In fact, in 1990 it traded 300,000 tons of grain to Libya and Iraq for arms and exported grain again in 1991!

Western governments and nongovernmental organizations have tried to avert famine despite the obstacles raised by both the government and the rebels. In frustration, however, the European Community has halted even humanitarian aid. The United States has also diverted humanitarian assistance, although less systematically. The United States, however, was Sudan's major backer from 1969 through 1985, largely as a counterweight to Libya and Soviet-backed Ethiopia. Between 1975 and 1985, the United States provided $1.5 billion in aid. Nonhumanitarian assistance to the government of Sudan was halted only in February 1990. In fact, some critics have charged that the Bush administration did not take the matter very seriously until after Sudan backed Iraq in the Gulf War, and even then, not because of human rights.

More Sudanese have died than even the most pessimistic estimates of the fate of the Kurds at the hands of a largely unchecked Saddam Hussein. The United States, however, along with the rest of the international community, can barely muster public criticism of Sudan's government. This is but one more reminder of the exceptional nature of the Gulf War and its aftermath (see Figure 6.2). Humanitarian intervention has indeed helped to protect Iraqi Kurds from the Baghdad government. But the security zone in northern Iraq owes its existence largely to nonhumanitarian considerations. Western intervention on behalf of Iraqi Kurds is more the exception that proves the rule than a model of humanitarian politics for the new world order.

MULTILATERAL HUMAN RIGHTS REGIMES IN THE 1990S

Before moving on to discuss the trend toward democratization over the past decade, we need to pause to consider what has been occurring in the multilateral human rights regimes discussed in Chapter 4. Here too, I will suggest, the pattern is one of modest incremental change, rather than radical transformation. We can frame the central issue here as whether power and authority are being transferred from states to the international community. The evidence so far, at least as I read it, is largely negative.

There has been modest progress at the regional level. The Council of Europe's new program of human rights assistance for the countries of Central and Eastern Europe is clear evidence of a desire to begin to prepare the former–Soviet bloc states for entry into the European human rights regime. And because good human rights practices are a major condition of acceptance into "Europe," with the associated symbolic and material benefits, the efforts of the Council of Europe are likely to have a significant impact, at least in the more progressive states of Central Europe. This represents a geographical expansion of the coverage of the existing European human rights regime rather than an increase in its powers.

In the Americas, the overall environment has improved dramatically: Elected (although not necessarily democratic) governments were in office in all the mainland countries of the hemisphere throughout 1991. The

FIGURE 6.2 ROB ROGERS reprinted by permission of UFS, Inc.

OAS General Assembly, which in the early 1980s refused to discuss the practices of gross and persistent human rights violators, has become willing to act on behalf of human rights. In addition to the embargo against Haiti, the rapid and concerted criticism of the suspension of parliamentary government in Peru in the spring of 1992 is a promising sign.

It is too early to say whether such actions represent a new pattern or a temporary interlude. The overall picture, though, is one of modest progress, with the realistic possibility of continued incremental growth throughout the rest of the decade.

Much the same is true of the CSCE. In Chapter 4 we noted the progress represented by the Copenhagen and Paris meetings. There have also been proposals to make the CSCE a much more active human rights supervisory body. The United States, however, is strongly opposed to such a qualitative transformation of the organization, and there seems to be little enthusiasm for that idea among the major states of Western Europe.

At the global level, however, not all the signs are positive. Consider, for example, the 1990 session of the Commission on Human Rights, the first in many years in which the clear majority of delegates were from countries with more or less freely elected governments. In addition to the defeat of a very mild resolution on the PRC, noted in Chapter 4, the Group of 77, the caucusing bloc of Third World states, tried (but ultimately failed) to eliminate the existing independent thematic procedures and replace them with politicized working groups of professional diplomats. And the enlargement of the commission to fifty-three members will make it even more difficult for it to function as a working body, while the addition of four African, three Asian, and three Latin American and Caribbean members shifts the balance of power in a way that is likely to preclude any significant enhancement of the powers of the commission.

The one unambiguous sign of human rights progress in the United Nations is the creation of the observer group in El Salvador. As part of the UN-mediated settlement that ended the Salvadoran civil war, a temporary observer group has been sent to El Salvador with unprecedented authority to engage in extensive on-site monitoring of human rights practices. This intrusion on Salvadoran sovereignty, however, was voluntarily accepted. There is little indication that many other states will choose to allow similar interventions. Furthermore, it is only a temporary measure, agreed to as part of a broader political settlement, intended to help smooth the transition to a new government. Although still of great importance, it should not be confused with human rights monitoring in more settled situations. In particular, the political dynamics that make a UN monitoring role acceptable, or even desirable, in such transitional situations are not likely to be replicated once a supervised election has been held.

This distinction between "normal" and transitional or other extraordinary situations raises broader questions about the international human rights significance of some other often-cited examples of transfers of authority or power from states to the international community. Consider the ultimately quite aggressive efforts to provide humanitarian assistance in Somalia, which have had at most the grudging consent of those with (although not legally in) power in the country. These efforts have come in a situation in which the Somali state has largely disintegrated into a struggle between warring clans and factions. They thus represent not so much a transfer of authority to the international community as an international response to a breakdown of national political authority. Although the result is the same—the UN now has authority in Somalia that it did not have a year ago—the political process by which this authority was obtained is unlikely to be replicated in more-settled situations.

Such new activities, along with the (far less successful) UN operation in Cambodia that seeks to end that country's civil war, are strikingly similar to the UN's efforts during the era of decolonization. The UN role was politically possible only because of gaps or breakdowns in standard patterns of sovereignty. In the case of decolonization, the transition involved a fundamental formal change in legal status.[5] In Somalia and El Salvador, civil war created a breakdown of authority. The UN has stepped into that void, providing humanitarian assistance in Somalia and transitional monitoring in El Salvador. But just as the decolonization activities of the 1960s had no direct spillover into new human rights activities of a more standard type, there is little reason to expect such a spillover today.

Where sovereignty has become problematic, the UN may (although will not necessarily) have an opportunity to intervene coercively. We should not belittle the importance or local impact of such interventions. But what has changed is not so much the balance of power between states and the international community as the opportunities for action. The end of the cold war has made it possible for states to allow the UN to act in such former areas of superpower rivalry. This does indeed result in greater authority for the international community. But the transfer of authority is of a peculiarly limited sort, with no necessary spillover into progress in other areas.

Somalia also reminds us of the distinction between humanitarian assistance and broader international human rights policies. Emergency aid to victims of natural or man-made disasters is a noble and important international activity. The Somalia case does involve an unprecedented augmentation of the authority of the international community in the field of humanitarian assistance. But we have no reason to expect a spillover into international human rights activities, as they have been conventionally understood.

Even during the cold war, massive famine usually provoked an international response that largely transcended politics. The Reagan administration's assistance to Ethiopia, then governed by one of the world's most reprehensible Marxist-Leninist regimes, is perhaps the most striking example. But there has been a huge gulf between disaster relief and providing even food aid, let alone international human rights intervention, once the immediate crisis is over. We have no reason to believe that there has been any fundamental change in perceptions or behavior in the so-called new world order. Therefore, the value of Somalia as a precedent for human rights activity by the UN is likely to be negligible.

The recent interventions in Iraq and Bosnia also seem likely to remain important exceptions rather than become precedents for a general expansion of international human rights monitoring and implementation activities. In each case, the international community has treated the conflict as an interstate conflict, despite the assertions to the contrary of Iraq and Serbia. The UN security zone in northern Iraq is the result of a cease-fire agreement. It has the consequence of protecting the human rights of Iraqi Kurds. But it provides absolutely no precedent for multilateral military protection of endangered minorities in more-normal circumstances. Likewise, the Bosnian intervention has been conceived of as assistance against aggression rather than human rights intervention, even if the result is to protect the lives of many Bosnians from a force that claims to be their government.

I do not want to belittle the importance of these new initiatives. Lives are being saved in ways that just a few years ago would not have seemed possible to most observers. I do, however, want to insist that these cases have few broader implications for international human rights policies. I see no evidence to suggest that the international community is willing to undertake major new initiatives to deal with direct violations of internationally recognized human rights by governments in control of their states. We may be witnessing modest expansions of the authority of regional communities in Europe and the Americas (but not in Africa, Asia, or the Middle East). I see little or no evidence, however, of any transfer of power or authority in the post–cold war world from states to the international community.

LIBERALIZATION, DEMOCRATIZATION, AND RIGHTS-PROTECTIVE REGIMES

Besides the end of the cold war, the other trend in the 1980s and early 1990s with special relevance to human rights was the collapse of authoritarian and totalitarian regimes. Here too, however, we face an immense gap between getting rid of old forms of human rights violations and establishing rights-protective regimes.

As we saw in Chapter 1, liberalization and democratization have been extensive and relatively deep in Latin America and Central and Eastern Europe and somewhat more uneven in Asia. More recently, long-entrenched authoritarian regimes in Africa have collapsed or been forced to liberalize.

Such changes, in addition to their immediate local impact, have contributed to a deeper international normative consensus. A dramatic, and undoubtedly progressive, change in the past few years has been the demise of "three worlds of human rights" arguments (see Chapter 2). The shallow cold war normative consensus on the interdependence and indivisibility of all human rights has become significantly deeper. In Central and Eastern Europe, the so-called socialist conception of human rights is in shambles, revealed to be largely a cover for the systematic violation of human rights. We can see in many Third World countries a similar rejection of old arguments that equated the struggle for self-determination and development with human rights. And in most countries, human rights advocates have become relatively immune from the charge that they are advocates of inappropriate foreign ideologies.

Cuba, North Korea, and the PRC do indicate that old modes of repression can persist in insular societies. Nonetheless, radical cultural-relativist human rights arguments today seem to carry little conviction or persuasive power, either internally or internationally. The terms of debate have changed. The universality of the Universal Declaration and the Covenants is now the real starting point for discussion.

We must be careful, however, not to overestimate the extent to which international human rights ideas have penetrated national human rights practices. In particular, we must be careful not to confuse decreased tolerance for old forms of repressive rule with support for, let alone institutionalization of, rights-protective regimes.

Very roughly, we can distinguish three levels of political progress toward respect for internationally recognized human rights. I call the first "liberalization," which decreases human rights violations and opens political space for at least some previously excluded groups. By "democratization" I mean the process of establishing a regime characterized by universal suffrage, responsible government, and relatively free and open political participation.[6] As we shall see, though, democratic regimes, thus understood, need not protect all internationally recognized human rights. That requires what I will call a "rights-protective regime," a political system that makes the protection of internationally recognized human rights a central element of its mission and justification, and that through extensive, intense, and sustained effort has had considerable success in realizing this aspiration.

Today, most proponents of nondemocratic government have been forced to change (at least the public expression of) their view, or to retreat from politics. Many recent liberalizations, however, have led to only modest human rights progress. For example, in Bulgaria and Romania in 1990 the most notorious of the old guard were purged and a few new faces brought in. For the most part, though, last year's Communists were elected as this year's new and improved noncommunists. The Russian legislature also remains largely under the control of only partially reformed Communists.

In Africa in particular, the state of "democratic transitions" is often confusing and precarious. Since the spring of 1990, national conferences to negotiate the end of one-party and military regimes have been held in a number of African countries, including Benin, Congo, Gabon, Ghana, Niger, Mali, Togo, and Zaire. The results range from great success in Benin to nearly total failure in Zaire. Some countries, such as Guinea, have not even reached this stage of political opening. Likewise, where multiparty elections have been held in Africa, the results have also been mixed, as we saw in Chapter 1.

Furthermore, in many countries semidemocratic liberalizations have become frozen. There is no necessary or automatic progression toward full democratization. For example, opposition political activity still remains a dangerous enterprise in Guatemala (see Figure 6.3).

Liberalizations present especially serious foreign policy challenges. It seems appropriate and perhaps even necessary to reward the human rights progress that liberalizations represent. But rewarding human rights performance that is still not good may perversely impede further progress. And at some point not too far down the road, praise and support must again turn to reproof if further progress is not forthcoming.

There is nothing inherently corrupt or inconsistent in treating the same violations differently in different countries or in the same country at different times. It does, however, require a fairly subtle and coherent international human rights policy in order to avoid the appearance of partisan inconsistency. Such a policy has usually been lacking in the United States, and in most other countries as well.

The Bush administration, like its predecessors, failed to translate a general verbal commitment to human rights into a coherent human rights policy. Even granting that there are good grounds for Bush's recent kindness to vicious, unreconstructed regimes in the PRC and Syria, the administration has failed to present its actions as part of a carefully conceived human rights policy. Beneath the fine-sounding rhetoric of democracy and human rights, Bush, like his predecessors, in practice combined extravagant vilification of the latest American enemy with embarrassing docility toward strategically significant countries and displayed an ad hoc approach to most other cases. In the post–cold war world, as in the past, U.S. human rights rhetoric has been supported by only fitful and inconsistent practice.

There are, of course, many countries that can justly be labeled new democracies making progress toward establishing rights-protective regimes. Czechoslovakia—more precisely, the newly created Czech Republic—provides a striking example of a fairly complete change not only of personnel but also of regime. Argentina under both Alfonsin and Menem presents a slightly less thorough but no less striking example of profound social and political transformation.

One of the notable features of most recent liberalizations and democratizations, however, has been the modest or even negligible role of international action. In Central and Eastern Europe, the end of Soviet support for repression was crucial to the fall of Communist governments. The positive steps toward liberalization and democratization, however, were almost entirely domestic. This points to a fundamental and widespread asymmetry in the ability of outside actors to help and to harm human rights.

The negative human rights impact of foreign forces has often been primary. Although events in Vietnam, Afghanistan, and Central and Eastern

FIGURE 6.3 Funeral procession in March 1990 following the death of a thirteen-year-old street child in Guatemala. Amnesty International photo.

Europe suggest that even massive outside military force may ultimately fail to maintain repressive rule, those countries also provide striking examples of the capacities of foreign powers, in the short and medium term, to tip the political balance in favor of forces of repression. Foreign intervention, however, has rarely been central in establishing a strong and stable rights-protective regime. Even Japan and West Germany, in some ways exceptions, confirm the rule: transformation came only after total defeat in a devastating war that completely discredited the prior regime.

Human rights cannot be given. They must be earned—and maintained—through hard and persistent domestic political work. Rights-protective regimes are almost always the product of domestic, not international, political forces.

Furthermore, the work of establishing rights-protective regimes is much more difficult than that of maintaining or reestablishing repression. Repressive regimes need only mobilize relatively small numbers of powerful or well-placed supporters and require only a passive, not a supportive, population. In addition, the kinds of financial and political support that foreign forces can provide is more easily put to effective use by repressive forces that already have considerable control over or access to politics, the economy, or the military.

It is thus both relatively easy for a powerful outside actor to contribute in a major way to serious human rights violations and relatively difficult for both internal and international forces to establish rights-protective regimes. The post–cold war reduction in foreign support for repression is a significant advance in the international struggle for human rights. This has opened political space for human rights advocates and helped to create a more-level domestic political playing field. It will not, however, automatically result in comparable levels of international support for newly democratic countries.

Even where a democratic transition has been real, it may remain incomplete. Consider, for example, "impunity" (*impunidad*) for the military in Argentina, Uruguay, and Chile, where the armed forces have accepted (varying degrees of) real civilian control but have largely refused to allow their members to be prosecuted for human rights violations. As we saw in Chapter 3, the new civilian governments in all three countries have largely been forced to accept the pardons that the armed forces granted themselves just before leaving power.

If the military is willing to exclude itself from politics and accept true civilian control in all other areas, impunity remains unjust but relatively unproblematic. The demonstrated political power of the military on this one issue, however, may be used in the future in other issue areas. The danger is especially great if the old forces of repression remain within the military, biding their time.

Even where all parts of the state apparatus are controlled by freely and fairly elected civilian governments, human rights are not necessarily secure. Democratization may leave a country far short of enjoying a rights-protective regime. Genuinely democratic governments may systematically use their power in ways that violate, threaten, or fail to defend internationally recognized human rights. In the post–cold war world we can already see at least two important types of democratic human rights violations: refusal to accept the limits on state power implied by human rights, which will be our focus in the next section, and insufficient attention to economic and social rights, a problem that will be addressed further on in this chapter.

OLD HABITS IN NEW DEMOCRACIES: LEARNING TO LIVE WITH LIMITS

Machiavelli, among many others, stressed "how difficult it is for a people accustomed to live under a prince to preserve their liberty, should they by some accident acquire it."[7] They are, he argued, like a wild beast that has been domesticated and then abruptly released. The confused and helpless creature quickly and willingly falls victim to the first person who will restore it to captivity. Although Machiavelli was characteristically extreme in his formulation, the problem is a serious one in the post–cold war world. A people that has known only arbitrary rule or elite domination faces an immense problem of resocialization.

Consider the former Czechoslovakia, where democratization has been relatively thorough. As part of the process of coming to grips with the legacy of the Communist past, a parliamentary commission was charged with exposing as many as 150,000 informants for the old secret police. The commission, however, has operated without even the appearance of due process. Often the accused have not even been allowed to see the "evidence" against them. This is the old system of denunciations and the presumption of guilt, in an updated (and somewhat less devastating) form. There may be a certain "poetic justice" in treating informers to a bit of their own medicine. It is, nevertheless, a clear violation of human rights.

Establishing a rights-protective regime requires developing an appreciation of the profound limits on government posed by individual human rights. Investigatory procedures with procedural safeguards are indeed slow and cumbersome. Their purpose, however, is to protect the rights of all individuals against abuses of state power, not to maximize the number of the guilty that are caught. Not only are human rights inherently "inefficient," but in a democratic society they are of greatest importance precisely when considerations of efficiency would set aside individual rights and dignity to pursue a social good. Until this is appreciated and accepted, human rights are likely to remain insecure.

Even if not a single innocent person were to be wrongly "exposed" as an informer, the procedure remains profoundly unjust. All human beings, including the guilty, have the same human rights, which they are entitled to enjoy equally. In fact, the way that the guilty and despised are treated provides one of the best indications of the extent to which human rights ideas and practices have penetrated a society and its political system. It is (relatively) easy to seek redress for victims of injustice or to accept the burden of respecting the rights of those who appear to be innocent. To be solicitous of the rights of the apparently guilty, the immoral, or the corrupt is a more difficult, sometimes even a distasteful, task. It is, however, of even greater importance to the long-term security of human rights. The enjoyment of human rights is precarious until the state intervenes to protect, rather than restrict or infringe, the rights of the unpopular and the immoral.

Communist party state regimes, by contrast, established differential rights for the pure, the impure, and those with unclear credentials—with the pure (those in power) doing the classifying. The Czech investigatory commission retains this fundamentally anti–human rights premise and procedure, simply reassigning the labels.

In October 1991, the Czechoslovak parliament went even further. Not only informers, but also members of the national security forces or Peoples' Militia, most Party officials, and activists in certain other bodies, were excluded from participating in the state administration, army, police and security forces, the media, or state-owned enterprises (including banks, railroads, and foreign trade corporations). Although the restriction is temporary, expiring at the end of 1996, the "crime" is troubling and the penalty significant.

Consider the contrast with the prosecution of torturers and the leaders of Argentina's military juntas. They were prosecuted and punished, not for their political views, associations, or offices, but for particular acts—kidnapping, torture, and murder—that were well-established crimes in Argentina and in virtually all other states. In Czechoslovakia, people were punished simply for working in or for core institutions of the old repressive regime, not for any particular acts that they committed. In some cases, such as minor informers, even the immorality of their actions was of relatively modest proportions.

Again, there is a certain poetic justice in denying people public opportunities on the basis of political associations that previously brought them special advantages. The analogy with the old regime, though, is cause for concern. As in the Communist persecution of "class enemies," people were punished by an ex post facto law for past immoral associations. The probability of such abuses spreading in the Czech Republic is relatively low (although not entirely negligible). In some other countries, however, we can readily imagine such understandable excesses becoming the first step toward a reentrenchment of rights-abusive practices.

Croatia, for example, has denied full citizenship rights to those who do not have three generations of Croatian parents on both sides. Particularly as ethnic animosity intensifies, it is easy to imagine increasingly severe denials of rights to non-Croats. And once one group or one right is excluded, it is relatively easy to add new groups or new rights. Much the same is true of restrictions on the rights of ethnic Russians in the Baltic republics.

In the old Soviet bloc, the assignment of differential rights to the pure and the impure was associated with the concentration of essentially arbitrary powers in the top leadership. In noncommunist states as well, entrenched dictatorships usually have concentrated arbitrary power in the hands of one individual or a relatively small corporate body. This suggests that another important measure of progress toward a rights-protective regime is the willingness of new governments to relinquish extraordinary powers of arbitrary rule. Again the key is accepting political limits in the name of the rights of each citizen.

Of particular importance is the way in which new leaders behave. One of the essential steps toward establishing a rights-protective regime is the widespread institutionalization of procedures that assure respect for individual human rights. The personalistic politics of a Boris Yeltsin may be a useful, even a necessary, step on the way toward a rights-protective regime. But it may also prove to be a repressive dead end, especially in conditions of crisis.

The issue here is not whether leaders are freely chosen or even whether they speak for the people, but whether human rights are secure. Democracy may simply mean tyranny of the majority. Particularly when a "democratic" (rights-protective?) political culture is not well established, the difference between what I have called democratic and what I have called rights-protective regimes may be considerable.

Human rights are fundamentally nonmajoritarian. They are concerned with each, rather than all. Human rights aim to protect each and every person, against majorities no less than against minorities. In fact, in democratic societies, where the majority is relatively well positioned to care for its own rights and interests, one of the most important functions of human rights is precisely to constrain the majority.

Even where populist leaders do in fact speak for the people, human rights remain threatened. Protofascist demagoguery is one natural outgrowth of populist politics in times of crisis. Consider, for example, Croatia's revival of the symbols of the wartime Nazi-puppet regime, which massacred a half million Serbs, and the no-less-ominous rhetoric and actions of the Milosovic regime in Serbia.

Free popular participation in politics can easily lead to violations of human rights. Many people, both individually and in groups, want to use their political power to harm their enemies or to gain advantage themselves unfairly. Even free elections may bring rights-abusive governments to power, a point that Americans in particular have had difficulty understanding.

NATIONALISM AND HUMAN RIGHTS

The collapse of the old order has also unleashed or created new threats to human rights, most notably nationalism. Internationally recognized human rights rest on the idea that individuals, simply because they are human beings, not only have certain basic rights but also have (and ought to enjoy) these rights equally. Aggressive, exclusive nationalism challenges the notion of equality that lies at the root of international human rights norms.[8]

Asserting national identity has often been an important element in struggles against outside domination. Self-determination, however, hardly guarantees the implementation or protection of internationally recognized human rights. The dreary decades following decolonization in Sub-Saharan Africa remind us that self-determination may simply substitute local despots for foreign ones. More recently, in Georgia Zviad Gamsakhurdia was freely and overwhelmingly elected president as a nationalist hero May 1991. By August, he was dealing with political opponents through arbitrary arrest, censorship, and other familiar dictatorial techniques. In September, he imposed a state of emergency. In late December, the opposition violently besieged Gamsakhurdia in the parliament building and forced him from the country in early January 1992. But a week later, those who removed him from power were firing on peaceful demonstrators seeking Gamsakhurdia's reinstatement.

The threats to human rights posed by nationalism, however, go well beyond the change in the nationality of dictators. A sense of national difference may progress to a rights-threatening sense of national superiority or ethnic privilege. This is especially problematic in the post–cold war period because of the suppression of nationalism in recent decades.

Communist rule in Central and Eastern Europe typically suppressed ethnic rivalry. It often did so by establishing the political hegemony of one ethnic group—most dramatically, of ethnic Russians in the Soviet Union. Nonetheless, the extreme persecution of ethnic Albanians in Yugoslavia and ethnic Turks in Bulgaria were relatively rare exceptions, at least after Stalin died.

Today, however, ethnic rivalry and discontent have moved to the fore. Some previously dominant groups, such as Serbs in the former Yugoslavia, have become much more aggressively overbearing. Other previously dominant groups, such as Russians in the other former Soviet republics, now fear nationalist retribution. Some previously subordinate groups, such as Slovaks in the former Czechoslovakia and Croats in Bosnia, seem more concerned with addressing old ethnic grievances than with establishing a new democratic order. Many other minorities remain subordinated, with their interests still ignored (e.g., ethnic Hungarians in Slovakia) or actively under attack (e.g., ethnic Turks in Bulgaria). And still other minorities, such as Ossetians in Moldova and Georgia, have simply seen new ethnic oppressors replace the old.

The human rights problems raised by nationalism are likely to be at least as severe in Sub-Saharan Africa, where many countries have ethnically diverse populations with strong senses of group identity and loyalty, as they are in Eastern and Central Europe. In Sub-Saharan Africa, too, political repression often helped to contain ethnic conflict. For example, in Nigeria in the late 1980s, military rule was seen by many observers as the only viable alternative to a steadily degenerating civilian politics of ethnic competition. Liberalization and democratization are certain to release pent-up ethnic discontents. For example, ethnic-religious riots in Katsina and Bauchi states in Nigeria in April 1991 killed as many as 1,000 people, and new riots broke out in Kaduna in May 1992. Likewise, the December 1992 elections in Kenya seem to have been concerned with ethnic rivalry as much as anything else.

Especially in conditions of economic scarcity, where an expanding supply of goods and services cannot be used to help to defuse intergroup rivalries, there is a relatively high probability that group competition will lead to ethnic conflict, and in some cases even violence. Rapid economic growth allows grievances to be addressed by directing a greater share of new resources to disadvantaged groups. In times of scarcity, however, especially in poor countries, politics tends to turn into a zero-sum contest for shares of an inadequate pie. Given the continent-wide decline in per capita income over the past decade, we should expect particularly severe problems in Africa in the coming years.

Separatism has been a solution of sorts in parts of the former Soviet Union and Yugoslavia. But "balkanization," the breakup of larger political units into small, fragile, and hostile nationalist states, presents serious economic, political, and human rights problems. There were good (although perhaps not sufficient) reasons for trying to create a multiethnic Yugoslavia. Much the same is true of Czechoslovakia, which Slovak nationalists succeeded in (peacefully) dissolving. And the likely costs of fragmentation are even greater in much of Africa, where the problems of political transition and economic development are severe enough without opening up the possibility of years, even decades, of tumults that may lead to nothing more than nationalist repression or the creation of new, and even more feeble, states.

Nonetheless, separatist demands for self-determination do seem well worth taking seriously even where dominant nationalities are not oppressive, and of course, where they are. Both internally and internationally, there is a genuine dilemma. The next several years are likely to see a succession of crises, many of which will be concluded after great financial, political, and human cost, to the satisfaction of no one.[9]

Formulating international human rights policy in such cases is by no means easy. Resolving competing ethnic claims is difficult enough for those whose rights and interests are directly at stake. It is virtually impossible for outsiders. How should foreign actors balance the competing demands of national self-determination, other human rights, and economic and political viability, as well as their own national interests in that area? What right do they have to become involved at all?

International human rights issues are inherently problematic in a world structured around sovereign states. Self-determination questions, however, are the most problematic of all because they are about defining the very units that are entitled to participate in international relations. From a moral point of view, self-determination is no less problematic, raising the question of determining the community within which human rights are to be pursued and protected. It is unclear whether foreign actors have a right to do anything at all beyond encouraging the peaceful resolution of disputes and attempting to moderate the severity of conflicts that lead to violence.

However important nationalism was to the collapse of oppressive rule in the Soviet bloc, the short- and medium-term human rights implications are largely negative. And foreign actors are in a particularly weak position to deal with these new threats to human rights.

MARKET-ORIENTED REFORMS, ECONOMIC CRISIS, AND ECONOMIC AND SOCIAL RIGHTS

The transition to market economies represents a very different sort of new human rights problem—or, rather, an old problem that is now re-emerging. The economic failure of Soviet-style command economies played a major part in the fall of the Soviet empire because of dissatisfaction with resulting conditions of life and because economic failure undercut the justification for totalitarian repression. In much of the Third World as well, developmental dictatorships have gone through a similar process of economic failure and political delegitimation. The failures of command economies, however, should not blind us to the human rights problems created by market economies.

Markets may be economically efficient: with a given quantity of resources, market systems of allocation and distribution, if they operate effectively, usually will maximize the total quantity of goods and services produced. But a market system also distributes production on the basis of efficiency. Markets are structured to respond to the interests and demands of those with "market power" (income, wealth, and information). They are not intended to respond to human needs (at least in the short and medium run). Although markets may produce more overall, they do not necessarily produce more *for* all. In fact, free markets typically produce gross inequalities in income, wealth, and living conditions.

We have here a different version of the conflict between perspectives that focus on each and those that focus on all. Arguments of economic efficiency deal with aggregate production. They focus on *average* incomes (per capita gross national product). Economic and social human rights, by contrast, are concerned with distributing certain basic goods, services, and opportunities to each and every person. Even if we grant the claim of efficiency—and many markets in the Second and Third Worlds are not, and in the short run cannot be, efficient—the resulting system may systematically violate the economic and social rights of many, or even most, individuals.

In Central and Eastern Europe, we are already beginning to see some of the negative human rights consequences of markets. Consider unemployment. Although the Communist alternative of systematic underemployment was undeniably unattractive, to many it is beginning to seem preferable, even in eastern Germany, where an excellent social security system is in place. Or consider health care. Soviet bloc consumers for many years had to provide gifts, gratuities, and outright bribes to doctors and other health care workers. Market-based health care systems, however, will lead to price rationing that will exclude many who previously had at least minimal access. The United States, in which literally tens of millions of people cannot afford adequate health care, presents a dismal picture of the consequences of a free market in medicine even in an extremely wealthy society.

In the Third World, with country after country engaged in market-oriented "structural adjustment" programs, social services are being cut from already-inadequate levels. Even if the costs of structural adjustment are primarily short term, as their defenders usually assert, these costs are heavy, and weigh most heavily on women, the poor, the elderly, and the disadvantaged. Moreover, when the transition to a market-oriented economy has been completed, there is no guarantee that large numbers of people will not be left behind. And, of course, there is no guarantee that reforms will be successful, that there will be any real social payoff for the massive sacrifices being forced on the poor and disadvantaged in the name of efficiency.

All this is particularly troubling because we have considerable, and disquieting, experience with development schemes that have relied on growth, or efficiency, alone. The new market orthodoxy of the 1990s is disconcertingly similar to the old orthodoxy of modernization theory, in which it was argued that the benefits of growth would automatically be redistributed throughout society. Unfortunately, those praising markets today almost completely ignore the fact that a significant proportion of the state economic intervention now under attack was provoked by the dismal failure of traditional growth-oriented, "trickle down" modernization strategies.

In conditions of absolute scarcity, the efficiency of markets may be essential to creating enough to go around in a reasonably short period of time. There may be no realistic choice other than radical privatization of the economy and of social services. Nonetheless, from a human rights perspective, markets are the lesser evil, not an intrinsic good.

This is a particularly important point for U.S. foreign policy. We tend to forget how heavily the U.S. government, as well as other Western governments, is involved in regulating markets and attempting to counteract the social inequities they produce. Not even Reagan or Thatcher ever seriously proposed returning to a true free market economy. Marx may have been wrong about many other things, but he was in many ways brutally accurate about the consequences of "free" markets for the lower classes. Unless we keep this firmly in mind, we may allow markets to be a new ideological justification for human rights abuses. For example, just as privatization and free markets were part of the assault on the poor and the workers in Chile during military rule, it is not hard to see "free markets" as the banner for new attacks on Central American peasant and working-class organizations, which have long been the principal victims of repression in the region.

The focus on economics is also important because of the American tendency to think that once a free election has been held, the human rights situation is under control. Even if we ignore the cases in which the elected government does not in fact control the country, in many countries economic, social, and cultural rights remain unaddressed. These human rights are intrinsically important, although many Americans persist in disparaging them. Furthermore, a country's performance on economic, social, and cultural rights can have an important impact on the fate of civil and political rights. Consider the rise of neo-Nazi violence in Germany, which ominously links ethnic conflict and economic dislocation. And when market reforms take place in an environment of economic crisis and failure, the threat to human rights is likely to be especially severe.

Economic failure tends to weaken whatever government is in power. In the 1980s this worked in favor of human rights, undermining numerous repressive regimes. Today, however, it threatens many newly liberalized and democratic regimes. For example, some Russians are beginning to express publicly nostalgia for the good old days. Within days of Russia's January 1992 price increases, Yeltsin's popularity began to erode.

These dangers are particularly great because in numerous countries the underlying economic problems that contributed to the collapse of the old regime persist. It is no coincidence that the past decade of liberalizations and democratizations began in the wake of the global recession of the early 1980s. Most observers in the late 1970s felt that South America's bureaucratic authoritarian regimes were very secure and stable. Torture, disappearances, and the systematic denial of virtually all civil and political rights did not seem to threaten their rule until the economic crises of the early 1980s. Economic failure was also essential to the collapse of the Soviet empire and has been no less central to the current wave of liberalizations and multiparty elections in Africa.

In addition, many of the economic problems faced by these new governments are outside of their control. For example, it will be years, and perhaps decades, before an alternative economic structure can be established in the countries of Central and Eastern Europe. The external economic dependence of many Third World countries is considerable. And the decade-long, continent-wide crisis in Africa powerfully illustrates the interaction of internal and external structural forces.

Restoring—or in some countries, initially instituting—civil and political rights may yield sufficient legitimacy to help a new government ride out severe economic problems. For example, despite Argentina's deteriorating economy, when Raul Alfonsin turned over power to Carlos Menem in July 1989, Alfonsin became the first elected president in Argentine history to complete his term of office and pass the presidency to an elected successor from an opposing party. If a government can create a sense that it is acting decisively and with some prospect of success, it may also increase its perceived legitimacy. If a human rights–oriented political culture does develop and become institutionalized, prospects are even more promising. Nonetheless, with virtually all new democracies and recently liberalized regimes today facing severe economic problems, it would be dangerous to underestimate their vulnerability.

This would seem to be one area in which external assistance could have a significant positive impact. Although foreign actors can usually play only a supporting role in establishing rights-protective regimes, at crucial turning points, and in the stage of democratic consolidation, the right kind of external support can indeed make a difference. For example, foreign technical and financial assistance can in many cases not only directly improve the enjoyment of economic and social rights but also indirectly strengthen new governments, whose legitimacy is likely to be enhanced by demonstrated economic efficacy. Such assistance is also attractive because it is likely to avoid charges of intervention.

Real support, however, will require more than just words of encouragement and a reprogramming of already-appropriated aid. It will require a willingness to pay for further international human rights achievements. No state, and certainly not the United States, seems willing to make the sizable financial investment required.[10] Even forgiving past debt, let alone providing substantial new resources, seems more than most countries are willing to do. Simply retaining U.S. foreign aid at its already pitifully low levels will require substantial work.

Opposing systematic human rights violations is no longer enough. As we have already seen, ending old forms of abuse is only a first step on the way to protecting human rights. Unfortunately, there is no evidence that the new human rights needs and opportunities of the 1990s are being seriously explored, let alone exploited, by the United States, the Europeans, or the international community.

INTERNATIONAL HUMAN RIGHTS
POLICY IN A NEW WORLD ORDER

What could be done, if there was the political will? On what basis should we fashion an international human rights policy for the post–cold war world? I will stress the importance of limited expectations, continued commitment, moral clarity, and integrating human rights with other foreign policy concerns. Although my comments will focus on U.S. foreign policy, most are more generally applicable.

Even well-intentioned and well-designed international human rights policies face immense national and international barriers. This deserves special emphasis today because in most countries we have already reaped the positive, sometimes dramatic, results of withdrawing support from repressive regimes. The heady days of the fall of entrenched dictators is largely past (although a few, such as Castro and Mobutu, still cling to power). The struggle has shifted to the often slow and laborious—and certainly far less exhilarating—work of building new institutions and expectations that will provide entrenched, long-run protections for internationally recognized human rights. In some countries, simply holding the line at current levels of respect for or abuse of human rights will count as great success.

The constraints on achieving a decisive impact, however, do not excuse reduced efforts, smug satisfaction, or inaction. The often-repeated claim that the United States "won" the cold war suggests that the international struggle for human rights is largely over. In fact, it has just begun. Continued, even redoubled, national commitment is required from new governments, which may themselves be fragile. And the international contribution, even if secondary, remains important.

The prospects for a sustained U.S. effort, however, are not bright. Both public attention and U.S. foreign policy have typically lurched from crisis to crisis, separated by long stretches of neglect. Consider, for example, the dramatic swings in U.S. policy toward Central America over the past four decades or the tendency for Sub-Saharan Africa to be in the news only when there is a coup, famine, or civil war. In the absence of dramatic short-term successes, the risks of lapsing into disinterest are great. Hard economic times at home further deflect attention. None of the candidates in the 1992 presidential election had much to say about human rights, and few people in the public or the media criticized this.

Human rights NGOs may be able to contribute to counteracting these tendencies. Over the past fifteen years, groups such as Amnesty International and Human Rights Watch have become accepted as authoritative sources of information, both in the media and in important congressional committees. Such groups have also developed networks of relationships with important legislators and staff members. There is now a significant (if severely underfunded) human rights lobby in Washington. And like other special interest groups, their attention will not be deflected by other issues, nor are their efforts likely to be sapped by past partial successes.

In addition to this private-sector human rights "infrastructure," the public-sector infrastructure has also been significantly enhanced over the last fifteen years. Although human rights remains a secondary concern in the corridors of Foggy Bottom, the Bureau of Human Rights and Humanitarian Affairs in the State Department has grown in size and become increasingly professional. In addition, human rights monitoring has become a well-institutionalized part of the activities of most U.S. embassies. Such bureaucratic entrenchment may help to mitigate the tendency toward reduced attention. In countries other than the United States, which participate in regional and international human rights–monitoring systems, an even broader infrastructure is present, providing further reminders of the necessity of continued efforts.

Continued commitment will be easier if we can clarify and highlight the moral fundamentals underlying international human rights policy. U.S. policy must recapture—or, perhaps, capture for the first time—a clear sense of the meaning and importance of the international struggle for human rights. It is not (and never has been) equivalent to the struggle against communism, which is but one model of systematic human rights violations. Human rights are about guaranteeing, through the institution of equal and inalienable rights for all persons, the conditions necessary for a life of dignity in the contemporary world. They are universal rights. Systematic violations therefore demand our concern and condemnation, wherever they occur.

Human rights, of course, are only one part of foreign policy. In some circumstances, other policy objectives appropriately take priority. Political "necessity" may require or justify cooperating with a repressive regime. In such a case, though, we must continue to condemn—not excuse—the human rights violations that are taking place, and we must remain painfully aware of the evil with which we are consorting or to which we are perhaps contributing.

Foreign policy is in part a moral undertaking. It is not, however, an entirely moral enterprise. The task we face is to *integrate* human rights (and other moral concerns) into foreign policy rather than occasionally tack them on, as has been the American norm. Although this is a difficult and complex political task, some orienting guidelines can be suggested.

We must go beyond general rhetorical flourishes and give human rights a clear and explicit priority in U.S. foreign policy. The best way to do this, I would suggest, is to treat gross and systematic violations of human rights as establishing a prima facie case for ending direct U.S. support of the regime in question and for reducing cultural exchanges, trade, and other voluntary cooperative ties. This would shift the burden of proof to advocates of maintaining (or improving) relations with rights-abusive regimes.

Rather than ask, in effect, Is the human rights situation bad enough that we can no longer allow business as usual? we should ask, Are there other, precisely defined, interests that are sufficiently important to excuse cooperating with a rights-abusive regime? The United States has already adopted a similar approach with respect to states that support international terrorism or contribute to the proliferation of nuclear weapons. There is no good reason not to do the same for international human rights.

Establishing a (rebuttable) presumption against close relations with repressive regimes, however, is only the first step toward integrating human rights concerns into foreign policy. Because of the realities of limited funds, time, interest, and attention, international human rights policy must selectively focus on some countries. Four criteria should be central in choosing the cases that will receive special attention and action: severity, trends, responsibility, and efficacy.

Although the severity of human rights violations in a country must be a central concern, it should not be the sole criterion. We should also examine trends in patterns of respect for and abuse of human rights. Consider, for example, the problem of responding to two dozen death-squad killings in a year. In Guatemala in the mid-1980s, this would have represented a reduction of over 99 percent from the level of the early 1980s. It would have merited a different level of concern and a different type of response than in Costa Rica, which had almost entirely avoided the phenomenon of death squads.

Few systematic violations of even a single right can be stopped all at once, not to mention halting all violations in a country with a long record of repression. The criterion of severity responds to the universality of human rights. The criterion of trends recognizes the political particularities of establishing rights-protective practices and attitudes.

A focus on trends may also encourage an international response before the situation gets entirely out of hand. International human rights policies should aim at halting the descent into repression before it reaches crisis levels rather than waiting until a particularly brutal regime is wreaking mass havoc. Such preventive human rights diplomacy is likely to be especially important in the post–cold war world because of the various temptations and risks of regression discussed above.

In choosing countries for special attention, we should also consider the likely effects of our efforts. Foreign policy is not only about setting ends but also about matching means to those ends. The symbolic act of criticizing violations even in a country where one has little or no economic or political influence remains important (because it is morally demanded, because avoiding even the appearance of complicity is an important minimum objective, and because words and symbolic acts may not be entirely without long-run impact). Nonetheless, we should also consider the actual short- or medium-term impact on human rights practices.

This may sometimes suggest the seemingly paradoxical strategy of focusing attention on countries where the underlying human rights problems are less severe, because the task of improving human rights practices in such cases often is less difficult. It may also suggest focusing on "friends" more than either "enemies" or countries with which we do not have close relations, because we have greater influence with our friends. The Reagan administration's nearly exclusive focus on human rights violations in Soviet-bloc countries, where U.S. influence was at a minimum, was perhaps the clearest sign of its largely rhetorical approach to international human rights; that is, of the absence of a real international human rights *policy.*

In choosing countries for priority attention, one's own responsibility for creating or fostering rights-repressive policies or regimes ought to be an important consideration. This too may suggest a focus on "friends," or special efforts on behalf of recent enemies. Conversely, past support for recently removed repressive regimes may require a less-forceful public diplomacy than might otherwise be demanded.

Looking at trends, efficacy, and responsibility will lead to treating comparably severe violations differently in different countries. Rather than a sign of debilitating inconsistency, however, this is necessary and desirable. True consistency means treating like cases in like manner. "Like cases," however, cannot be specified simply by the number and type of human rights violations. Consider a legal analogy. Not every thief deserves the same punishment, even if the particulars of the crime are the same. We also look, for example, at past behavior, typically treating first-time offenders more leniently than hardened criminals.

Severity, trends, influence, and responsibility provide only rough guidelines. These guidelines may point in different directions in particular cases. Nonetheless, they provide relatively clear guidance and the basis for constructing a coherent and defensible policy. The danger, though, is that "balancing" various and at times competing considerations may degenerate into incoherent, ad hoc decisions or partisan inconsistency. Unfortunately, this has been, and remains, the rule in U.S. international human rights policy.

The international human rights challenge for the United States (and other countries) in the post–cold war world is to develop a realistic, committed, morally sound international human rights policy and to truly integrate this into the rest of U.S. foreign policy. The end of the cold war has removed one major impediment. The presence of numerous recently liberalized or democratized countries creates a variety of (limited) opportunities. The work of crafting a new international human rights policy to meet these new conditions, however, has not been a major concern of the Bush administration, the Congress, or any of the major presidential candidates in 1992.

The Bush administration, which claimed credit for much of the new world order, like its predecessors, failed to translate an abstract verbal commitment to human rights into a coherent human rights policy. For example, even if we allow that there were good grounds for Bush's post–Gulf War kindness to Syria, which had not even liberalized, the administration did not present its actions as part of a carefully conceived human rights policy.

Rather than join in the difficult work of consolidating and deepening progress, the United States seems content to gloat over "winning the cold war," bombing Iraq into temporary submission, and praising the virtues of elections and markets. This is a significant improvement from the cold war era, when the United States was a major contributor to human rights violations. Nonetheless, it is a culpable moral failure and a shameful betrayal of the idea of international human rights. With no other country or organization coming forward to assert international leadership, we are likely to look back on the early 1990s as a period of tragically missed opportunities.

□ □ □

Appendix: Universal Declaration of Human Rights

General Assembly Resolution 217A (III), 10 December 1948.

Whereas recognition of the inherent dignity and of the equal and inalienable rights of all members of the human family is the foundation of freedom, justice and peace in the world,

Whereas disregard and contempt for human rights have resulted in barbarous acts which have outraged the conscience of mankind, and the advent of a world in which human beings shall enjoy freedom of speech and belief and freedom from fear and want has been proclaimed as the highest aspiration of the common people,

Whereas it is essential, if man is not to be compelled to have recourse, as a last resort, to rebellion against tyranny and oppression, that human rights should be protected by the rule of law,

Whereas it is essential to promote the development of friendly relations between nations,

Whereas the peoples of the United Nations have in the Charter reaffirmed their faith in fundamental human rights, in the dignity and worth of the human person and in the equal rights of men and women and have determined to promote social progress and better standards of life in larger freedom,

Whereas Member States have pledged themselves to achieve, in co-operation with the United Nations, the promotion of universal respect for and observance of human rights and fundamental freedoms,

Whereas a common understanding of these rights and freedoms is of the greatest importance for the full realization of this pledge,

Now, therefore,

The General Assembly

Proclaims this Universal Declaration of Human Rights as a common standard of achievement for all peoples and all nations, to the end that every individual and every organ of society, keeping this Declaration constantly in mind, shall strive by teaching and education to promote respect for these rights and freedoms and by progressive measures, national and international, to secure their universal and effective recognition and observance, both among the peoples of Member States themselves and among the peoples of territories under their jurisdiction.

Article 1. All human beings are born free and equal in dignity and rights. They are endowed with reason and conscience and should act towards one another in a spirit of brotherhood.

Article 2. Everyone is entitled to all the rights and freedoms set forth in this Declaration, without distinction of any kind, such as race, colour, sex, language, religion, political or other opinion, national or social origin, property, birth or other status.

Furthermore, no distinction shall be made on the basis of the political, jurisdictional or international status of the country or territory to which a person belongs, whether it be independent, trust, non-self-governing or under any other limitation of sovereignty.

Article 3. Everyone has the right to life, liberty and the security of person.

Article 4. No one shall be held in slavery or servitude; slavery and the slave trade shall be prohibited in all their forms.

Article 5. No one shall be subjected to torture or to cruel, inhuman or degrading treatment or punishment.

Article 6. Everyone has the right to recognition everywhere as a person before the law.

Article 7. All are equal before the law and are entitled without any discrimination to equal protection of the law. All are entitled to equal protection against any discrimination in violation of this Declaration and against any incitement to such discrimination.

Article 8. Everyone has the right to an effective remedy by the competent national tribunals for acts violating the fundamental rights granted him by the constitution or by law.

Article 9. No one shall be subjected to arbitrary arrest, detention or exile.

Article 10. Everyone is entitled to full equality to a fair and public hearing by an independent and impartial tribunal, in the determination of his rights and obligations and of any criminal charge against him.

Article 11.—1. Everyone charged with a penal offence has the right to be presumed innocent until proved guilty according to law in a public trial at which he has had all the guarantees necessary for his defence.

2. No one shall be held guilty of any penal offence on account of any act or omission which did not constitute a penal offence, under national or international law, at the time when it was committed. Nor shall a heavier penalty be imposed than the one that was applicable at the time the penal offence was committed.

Article 12. No one shall be subjected to arbitrary interference with his privacy, family, home or correspondence, nor to attacks upon his honour and reputation. Everyone has the right to the protection of the law against such interference or attacks.

Article 13.—1. Everyone has the right to freedom of movement and residence within the borders of each state.

2. Everyone has the right to leave any country, including his own, and to return to his country.

Article 14.—1. Everyone has the right to seek and to enjoy in other countries asylum from persecution.

2. This right may not be invoked in the case of prosecutions genuinely arising from non-political crimes or from acts contrary to the purposes and principles of the United Nations.

Article 15.—1. Everyone has the right to a nationality.

2. No one shall be arbitrarily deprived of his nationality nor denied the right to change his nationality.

Article 16.—1. Men and women of full age, without any limitation due to race, nationality or religion, have the right to marry and to found a family. They are entitled to equal rights as to marriage, during marriage and at its dissolution.

2. Marriage shall be entered into only with the free and full consent of the intending spouses.

3. The family is the natural and fundamental group unit of society and is entitled to protection by society and the State.

Article 17.—1. Everyone has the right to own property alone as well as in association with others.

2. No one shall be arbitrarily deprived of his property.

Article 18. Everyone has the right to freedom of thought, conscience and religion; this right includes freedom to change his religion or belief, and freedom, either alone or in community with others and in public or private, to manifest his religion or belief in teaching, practice, worship and observance.

Article 19. Everyone has the right to freedom of opinion and expression; this right includes freedom to hold opinions without interference and to seek, receive and impart information and ideas through any media and regardless of frontiers.

Article 20.—1. Everyone has the right to freedom of peaceful assembly and association.

2. No one may be compelled to belong to an association.

Article 21.—1. Everyone has the right to take part in the Government of his country, directly or through freely chosen representatives.

2. Everyone has the right of equal access to public service in his country.

3. The will of the people shall be the basis of the authority of government; this will shall be expressed in periodic and genuine elections which shall be by universal and equal suffrage and shall be held by secret vote or by equivalent free voting procedures.

Article 22. Everyone, as a member of society, has the right to social security and is entitled to realization through national effort and international co-operation and in accordance with the organization and resources of each State, of the economic, social and cultural rights indispensable for his dignity and the free development of his personality.

Article 23.—1. Everyone has the right to work, to free choice of employment, to just and favourable conditions of work and to protection against unemployment.

2. Everyone, without any discrimination, has the right to equal pay for equal work.

3. Everyone who works has the right to just and favourable remuneration insuring for himself and his family an existence worthy of human dignity, and supplemented, if necessary, by other means of social protection.

4. Everyone has the right to form and to join trade unions for the protection of his interests.

Article 24. Everyone has the right to rest and leisure, including reasonable limitation of working hours and periodic holidays with pay.

Article 25.—1. Everyone has the right to a standard of living adequate for the health and well-being of himself and of his family, including food, clothing, housing and medical care and necessary social services, and the right to security in the event of unemployment, sickness, disability, widowhood, old age or other lack of livelihood in circumstances beyond his control.

2. Motherhood and childhood are entitled to special care and assistance. All children, whether born in or out of wedlock, shall enjoy the same social protection.

Article 26.—1. Everyone has the right to education. Education shall be free, at least in the elementary and fundamental stages. Elementary education shall be compulsory. Technical and professional education shall be made generally available and higher education shall be equally accessible to all on the basis of merit.

2. Education shall be directed to the full development of the human personality and to the strengthening of respect for human rights and fundamental freedoms. It shall promote understanding, tolerance and friendship among all nations, racial or religious groups, and shall further the activities of the United Nations for the maintenance of peace.

3. Parents have a prior right to choose the kind of education that shall be given to their children.

Article 27.—1. Everyone has the right freely to participate in the cultural life of the community, to enjoy the arts and to share in scientific advancement and its benefits.

2. Everyone has the right to the protection of the moral and material interests resulting from any scientific, literary or artistic production of which he is the author.

Article 28. Everyone is entitled to a social and international order in which the rights and freedoms set forth in this Declaration can be fully realized.

Article 29.—1. Everyone has duties to the community in which alone the free and full development of his personality is possible.

2. In the exercise of his rights and freedoms, everyone shall be subject only to such limitations as are determined by law solely for the purpose of securing due recognition and respect for the rights and freedoms of others and of meeting the just requirements of morality, public order and the general welfare in a democratic society.

3. These rights and freedoms may in no case be exercised contrary to the purposes and principles of the United Nations.

Article 30. Nothing in this Declaration may be interpreted as implying for any State, group or person any right to engage in any activity or to perform any act aimed at the destruction of any of the rights and freedoms set forth herein.

□ □ □

Discussion Questions

CHAPTER ONE

1. Why should Americans be concerned with human rights practices abroad? Why should *states* or intergovernmental organizations be concerned? Anyone under thirty probably takes it for granted that states pursue human rights in their foreign policies. As we have seen, however, this is historically unusual. Whether you think the traditional practice of not pursuing international human rights objectives is good or bad, it is important to understand the logic underlying it. How can it be justified? In your opinion, why were people in the past willing to treat human rights violations as a purely national affair?

2. By the same token, it is important to understand why these traditional views have been replaced. Consider the following possibilities.

Changing moral sensibilities: *Are* our moral views all that much different from those of other generations? (If so, what does that suggest about the universality of human rights?) Or is it that we now feel more free to act on these values? If so, why? *Can* changes in ideas, by themselves, have such an impact on policy?

Other changes in the character of international relations: Are these reasons for changes in views of human rights? Peace and prosperity. Growing international interdependence. Cold war and detente. Decolonization.

Changes in *national* human rights practices: Have attitudes toward human rights changed?

3. We might also ask just how deeply changing views toward international human rights have penetrated. We talk often about international human rights, but action often falls far short of rhetoric. Why? Is it lack of *real* interest? Constraints on our ability to achieve our objectives? Competing objectives?

4. *Should* international agencies like the United Nations be involved in enforcing internationally recognized human rights? Why? What would be sacrificed by a greater international role? What would be gained? Can international organizations be trusted to make the sorts of sensitive political choices involved in dealing with human rights?

5. If you think that there should be a larger international role, why do you think that this has not come about? What would be required to overcome the existing impediments? How costly—economically, politically, and in human terms— would this be? Would these costs be worthwhile? Do you think that change is

likely in the next few years? The next few decades? What factors would lead one to expect continuity? What factors suggest change?

6. What kind of actor is best suited to pursue international human rights: individuals, NGOs, states, or intergovernmental organizations? What are the strengths and weaknesses of each?

CHAPTER TWO

1. *Are* there such things as human rights? Where do they come from? How would you go about trying to convince someone who answers these questions differently from you? Do you find my claim that human rights rest on a moral account of human possibility to be plausible? Persuasive? Satisfying? Why?

2. In the body of the text, I emphasize the differences between rights and other sorts of moral principles and practices. Do you think that I overemphasize the difference? What are the ways in which rights are similar to considerations of righteousness (or utility)?

3. Should we really prefer to protect human rights when it conflicts with social utility? Should the rights of the individual or the few take priority over the happiness of the many? In particular, should *governments* act on any principle other than social utility?

4. How do we know what things are on a justifiable list of human rights? How would you go about trying to convince someone who proposes a radically different list? Would it be easier or harder if the list were less radically different?

5. What is the status of the principle of equal concern and respect, which I draw on to justify the list of human rights in the International Bill of Human Rights? Should this principle be preferred to others? What are some other plausible grounds that might underlie this particular list?

6. I proceeded on the assumption that some sort of justification of human rights is possible. Does this suggest that the particular justification makes no real difference for the purposes of international relations? Is such a view sound? Does it really make no difference why people believe that there are human rights?

7. Are economic, social, and cultural rights human rights? Why? What explains the general reluctance of many Americans to consider them *really* human rights? Are the reasons philosophical? Is anything more involved than the generally poor performance of the United States on these rights? Just how different are such arguments from the old Soviet claims that civil and political rights really are not so important as economic, social, and cultural rights?

8. Does the "positive"/"negative" distinction really make no moral difference at all? Is there really no difference between killing someone and failing to help someone who then dies? Does it make any difference whether we are thinking about personal morality or the activity of governments?

9. What is the relation between philosophical theory and international legal norms in the case of human rights? Can we legitimately evade philosophical difficulties by pointing to international consensus? What are the costs of such a strategy? What are the costs of *not* following the consensus? And speaking of consensus, am I correct about the *moral* irrelevance of consensus? Does it make no

difference at all to the validity of a moral principle or proposition whether there is widespread agreement or disagreement about it?

10. *Should* human rights function as an international standard of legitimacy? If yes, what else, if anything, is required for international legitimacy? If a government meets all the other criteria but violates human rights, why should it be seen as *internationally* (rather than morally or nationally) illegitimate?

11. Sovereignty certainly has gotten in the way of international human rights policies. But is it really such a bad thing? Do you want other countries and international organizations inquiring into the human rights practices of *your* country? International anarchy has its obvious drawbacks, but do you *really* want a higher political authority telling your country how to behave in such important areas?

12. The United States is not a party to most international human rights treaties. Can a country that refuses to allow international scrutiny of its human rights practices speak with moral authority about human rights practices elsewhere? Why should other countries take U.S. international human rights rhetoric seriously (even disregarding domestic human rights problems in the United States)? Does the April 1992 decision of the United States to ratify the International Covenant on Civil and Political Rights (but not its first optional protocol) change matters significantly?

13. Which of the three models of international human rights do you find most attractive (issues of their current descriptive accuracy notwithstanding)? Why? What are the greatest strengths of your preferred model? How and why might others find it defective?

14. Even if realists overstate their case, don't they have one? How frequently are states really able to pursue international human rights concerns? Have recent international changes made it harder or easier?

15. How often do states use "realism" as little more than an excuse for not doing what they know they ought to do but would prefer not to? Imagine personal moral relations if "realist" arguments were allowed. Are the differences between interpersonal and international relations really so extreme that we can allow such radically different standards to apply? Conversely, are the similarities so great that we can apply the same standards without major modifications across the two realms?

16. *Are* human rights ideas truly universal? Are the differences between cultures and countries really primarily concerned with secondary human rights issues? Do recent changes in international relations have anything to tell us about the universality of human rights? Consider, for example, the fall of the Communist bloc and democratization in much of the Third World. Then consider Islamic fundamentalism and the rise of nationalist hostilities.

17. Make a list of all the arguments you can think of that can be made for cultural relativism. Which of these actually refer to *cultural* factors and which to political, economic, or ideological factors? Are arguments of political relativism as persuasive as arguments of cultural relativism? Why? What about economic relativism? Is the distinction between culture, politics, and economics helpful or revealing? Why?

18. Are differences in human rights ideas, whatever their nature, relatively permanent and static, or are they relatively fluid and changing? Does this make a dif-

ference to your evaluation of claims of relativism? If the relevant practices are changing (or even just capable of change), should international human rights policy be directed more to respecting the way they are now or trying to make them more consistent with international human rights standards? What are the strengths and weaknesses of each approach?

19. Suppose that there are indeed major cultural differences with respect to human rights in the world today. *Should* we take those into account? Why? Should we allow them to alter our international human rights policies and practices? If so, don't we in effect end up acting on other peoples' values? If not, what right do we have to impose our values on others?

CHAPTER THREE

1. Are there situations in which torture or disappearances could be justified? (Don't answer too quickly, whatever your initial inclination.)

2. How can people become torturers? Even if they are not applying the electric shocks to the victims, how can people work in, for, or around institutions that regularly practice torture or arbitrary execution? Consider the following possibilities.

Sadism: They enjoy it.

Commitment: They believe it is necessary to achieve a higher good.

Self-interest: They see an opportunity to get ahead.

Coercion: They are forced to participate.

Cowardice: They find themselves in a system they are afraid to resist.

Denial: They try to convince themselves that things are other than they appear.

Inertia: They simply do it because it is there.

Does why people do it make a difference? Does it make a *moral* difference?

3. Chile and Uruguay had long and relatively well-established democratic traditions. Nonetheless, they still endured over a decade of extraordinarily repressive military rule. How can this be explained? Although you probably lack the factual information to make a truly informed judgment, speculating on possible reasons can be useful, particularly if we want to use these cases to think about prospects for democracy elsewhere.

4. Is it easier to build or to destroy a democracy? Once it is destroyed, how (and how easily) can it be fixed? Does the way, and the length of time, it was destroyed have a significant impact on the prospects for recovery or repair? Does the particular way that democracy was (re-)instituted have an impact on its future prospects?

5. It obviously makes sense to distinguish between larger and smaller numbers of human rights violations. But does it make sense to distinguish between different types of violations? If so, which ones are especially heinous? Why?

Is there a qualitative difference between a regime that tortures people but feeds everyone well and one that allows people to suffer from malnutrition but tortures no one? Or between a regime that allows free political participation but requires everyone to work sixty-hour weeks and one that provides thirty-five-hour work weeks but no political participation? There are differences certainly, and they are likely to be of considerable political importance. But are the differences of any *moral* significance?

Are the only important (moral) distinctions between human rights violations ultimately quantitative? This would seem to be the implication of the claim that all human rights are interdependent and indivisible. But is the moral difference really just the number of people and the number of rights violated?

6. However you have answered the preceding set of questions, you can construct a list of human rights violators and rank them from more to less severe. Having done that, what foreign policy implications can you draw? Suppose we concentrate on the worst cases. The reasons to do so are fairly obvious. But are there drawbacks? Suppose someone were to suggest that we actually should focus on *less*-severe violators because the chances for improving practices there are greater. Or consider the claim that we should focus on the trend in a given country. Even if we accept this, should an improving or a declining trend receive greater weight? What other relevant considerations can you think of? States clearly cannot concentrate on all human rights violators equally. But how should they choose priority cases? (We will return to these questions at the end of Chapter 6.)

7. How should new governments deal with former torturers, dictators, and the members of the repressive apparatus of the old regime?

Suppose that there are no political constraints imposed by the continuing power of these forces. Who should be punished, for what, how severely? How should vengeance, justice, mercy, and reconciliation be balanced?

Now suppose that the old forces of repression do still hold considerable power. How far should the demands of justice be pressed? At what point does bowing to power corrupt or undermine the new political order? Is there a real, practical alternative to accepting the lesser of two evils? Are real, practical alternatives the only ones that should be acted upon?

8. Although economic, social, and cultural rights received some attention in this chapter, the central focus was on violations of civil and political rights. This reflects the focus of international discussions of human rights violations in the Southern Cone. Is that focus the best one? Was the distinctive character of human rights violations in the Southern Cone significantly connected with economic, social, and cultural rights? Even if the distinctive nature of the repression concerned civil and political rights, should there have been greater international attention to economic, social, and cultural rights?

CHAPTER FOUR

1. You have read in this chapter about a large number of multilateral human rights regimes. What kind of overall evaluation would you draw? Clearly there is a reasonably large amount of international activity. What sort of impact has it had? Is that impact worth all the effort?

2. There are a diverse array of multilateral human rights bodies: global and regional, comprehensive and single issue, individual and situation oriented, political and legal. What are the strengths and weaknesses of each type? Is there, in

your view, some best type? What is the relationship between the best and the possible in this area?

3. How would you assess international reporting schemes in particular? Again, be sure to ask not only what they have (and have not) accomplished, but also what the costs have been, and what alternatives there are.

4. Make an inventory of alternative multilateral approaches that either have not yet been tried or in your view have not been adequately exploited. Then ask yourself why they haven't been used and whether these impediments are likely to persist in the future.

5. In this chapter, the argument is advanced that international human rights procedures are likely to have their greatest impact where the situation is relatively good (or at least less bad). What do you think of this? What does it suggest about the most effective forms of international action? Are you comfortable with the idea of writing off the worst cases (which some may draw as the central policy implication of this argument)? Is there a practical alternative?

6. One of the striking facts about the multilateral human rights machinery is its heavy concentration on civil and political rights. While there has been much general political talk in the UN about economic, social, and cultural rights, when it comes to treaties and monitoring systems, the focus has been largely on civil and political rights. (At the global level, the Committee on Economic, Social, and Cultural Rights is the exception that proves the rule, as is the ILO in single-issue regimes). What are the reasons for this? Is this a defensible allocation of resources and attention? What kinds of things would have to change to bring about a more comprehensive system of international human rights monitoring?

7. Even when we consider only civil and political rights, there is a strong concentration on a relatively small number of rights, especially rights to nondiscrimination and particularly egregious violations of personal liberty and bodily integrity. There has been very little attention to the *political* aspects of civil and political rights. How can this be explained? How should it be evaluated? What are the alternatives, both theoretical and practical?

CHAPTER FIVE

1. Should we accept the description of postwar U.S. foreign policy as dominated by anticommunism? Suppose that we do. Was it a bad thing? Should anticommunism have had a less-overriding priority? Or was the problem that anticommunism was pursued with excessive zeal? Is there something special about an ideological (or moralistic) foreign policy that leads to such excess? If so, does that force us to reconsider some arguments of the realists?

2. Should the United States be able to define for itself which internationally recognized human rights it wishes to recognize or pursue?

If so, why? If we can pick and choose, how can we justify an international human rights policy if others pick and choose differently?

If not, why? Why should the United States (or any other sovereign state) have to follow international human rights norms, no matter how widely accepted they are?

3. The United States has a relatively active and aggressive bilateral international human rights policy but refuses to participate in most multilateral international human rights regimes. (It wasn't until April 1992 that the United States ratified the International Covenant on Civil and Political Rights, and even then it did not ratify the optional protocol.) Can such a double standard be justified? Why should others countries take U.S. international human rights policy seriously when the United States is not open to the international human rights policies of other countries and multilateral agencies?

4. In reviewing the evidence of U.S. policy toward South Africa, Central America, and the Southern Cone, what strikes you more, the continuities or the changes between different U.S. administrations? When all is said and done, just how different was Carter's policy from that of either Ford or Reagan? Were the differences largely symbolic? Even if they were, how serious a criticism is that? Is symbolism a negligible part of foreign policy? Of international human rights policy?

5. The same question might be asked about the differences between the international human rights policies of the United States and the so-called like-minded countries. When it comes to making the difficult choices, when it comes to sacrificing their own interests, just how different are countries such as Canada, Norway, and the Netherlands? Consider, for example, the differences between Dutch policy toward Indonesia and Suriname. Is the difference one of quality or merely a matter of degree?

6. Whether the differences are large or small, "real" or "symbolic," there are differences between the international human rights policies of these countries. How can these be explained? What are the factors considered in the chapter? What additional possible explanations can you advance?

7. Consider the emphasis of the like-minded countries on economic, social, and cultural rights. Is their approach better than or just different from that of the United States? Why? Does your answer change if you look at the issue from the perspectives of foreign policy, foreign aid policy, or international human rights policy?

CHAPTER SIX

1. How would you evaluate my argument that the structure of the international system remains fundamentally the same? Is a (more) multipolar system really as similar to a bipolar one as I suggest? Is the state really still as central as I claim? Is interdependence in one area really likely to remain relatively insulated from other areas?

2. Trying to assess the future after a momentous change such as the end of the cold war is in part an exercise in figuring out what evidence we should be focusing on. I stressed evidence of continuity and called for limited expectations. Is there evidence of change that I ignored or downplayed?

3. "Current" cases date very quickly. When I finished the final draft of this book, Croatia had been replaced in the public eye by Bosnia, and Somalia was only beginning to receive considerable international publicity. When I made the final

editorial revisions, the U.S. military was relatively well ensconced in Somalia. By the time you read this, other cases may be grabbing the headlines. Whatever they are, take two or three and ask whether the international response shows evidence primarily of continuity or of change.

4. How would you evaluate the distinction drawn between liberalization, democratization, and creating a rights-protective regime? Am I correct in saying that this distinction points to important long-term concerns that should lead us to moderate some of the early optimism associated with the fall of the Soviet Union? Am I correct that this distinction is especially important for Americans, who tend to focus on the formalities of democratization, often to the exclusion of the real substance of protecting human rights?

5. The picture of nationalism painted in this chapter is extremely bleak. Is nationalism in itself a bad thing? Or is it that nationalism, a good or neutral thing, has gotten out of control? Even if nationalism is not ultimately the answer, does it begin to address the (excessive?) individualism of a human rights perspective?

6. Are markets, from a human rights point of view, really just (at best) the lesser evil? Am I correct in suggesting that questions of economic, social, and cultural rights have in recent years often gotten lost in the rush toward market-oriented economic reforms? Even if that is true, is this a necessary first step toward sustained progress on economic, social, and cultural rights? If it is, though, how can we assure that later steps are taken?

7. Can a viable international human rights policy be constructed by responding to violations according to the principles of severity, trends, responsibility, and efficacy? Are there other principles that are as important? Is this list too long? Is the problem of "inconsistency" really as easily resolved as I suggest?

8. Throughout this book, the focus has been on describing what has taken place. Even when prescriptive arguments have been advanced, the emphasis has been as much on the possible as on the desirable. Whatever one may have to say about such an approach in thinking about the past and the present, is it the best one for thinking about the future? Even if it is, doesn't it need to be supplemented by innovative, perhaps even visionary thinking? What would that look like in the case of international human rights? What explains the distance between the desirable and the possible?

□ □ □

Notes

CHAPTER ONE

1. Participation in the league's Minorities System, however, was forced upon a defeated Germany and on the new states of Central and Eastern Europe as the price of international recognition. The victorious powers conspicuously refused to be covered, even in their European territories, let alone in their colonial empires. The countries of Latin America also refused to join. And the United States was not a member of the League of Nations.

2. Although there were no negative votes, the Soviet Union and its allies abstained, claiming that insufficient emphasis was given to economic and social rights. In addition, South Africa abstained because of the provisions on racial discrimination and Saudi Arabia abstained because of the provisions on gender equality.

CHAPTER TWO

1. This is not exactly correct. Although children are human beings, they usually are not thought to have, for example, a right to vote. This is typically justified on the grounds that they are not fully developed human beings. But once they reach a certain age, they must be recognized to hold all human rights equally. Similarly, those who suffer from severe mental illness are often denied the exercise of many rights— but only until they regain full use and control of their faculties. Furthermore, both children and the mentally ill are denied the protection or exercise only of those rights for which they are held to lack the necessary requisites. They still have, and must be allowed to enjoy equally, all other human rights.

2. Some other languages stress a different multiplicity of meaning in their parallel terms. For example, Spanish, French, and German all use terms—*derechos humanos, droits de l'homme, Menschenrechte*—that contain words meaning both law and rights. Were we working in one of these languages, our discussion at this point might take a slightly different route.

3. Alan Gewirth, *Human Rights: Essays on Justification and Application* (Chicago: University of Chicago Press, 1984).

4. Jack Donnelly, *Universal Human Rights in Theory and Practice* (Ithaca, N.Y.: Cornell University Press, 1989), chap. 1–3.

5. For a more extensive development of this argument, which derives from the work of Ronald Dworkin, see Rhoda E. Howard and Jack Donnelly, "Human Dignity, Human Rights, and Political Regimes," *American Political Science Review* 88 (September 1986), pp. 801–817.

6. Maurice Cranston, *What Are Human Rights?* (New York: Basic Books, 1964), p. 50.

7. Maurice Cranston, *What Are Human Rights?* (London: The Bodley Head, 1973), pp. 66–67.

8. For an extended discussion of this idea, see Hedley Bull, *The Anarchical Society* (New York: Columbia University Press, 1977).

9. Robert Gilpin, "The Richness of the Tradition of Political Realism," in Robert O. Keohane (ed.), *Neo-Realism and Its Critics* (New York: Columbia University Press, 1986), p. 305.

10. Hans Morgenthau, *Politics Among Nations,* 2d ed. (New York: Alfred A. Knopf, 1954), p. 9.

11. George F. Kennan, "Morality and Foreign Policy, " *Foreign Affairs* 64 (Winter 1985–1986), p. 206; and *Realities of American Foreign Policy* (Princeton: Princeton University Press, 1954), p. 48.

12. George F. Kennan, *The Cloud of Danger: Current Realities of American Foreign Policy* (Boston: Little, Brown, 1977), p. 45.

13. Herbert Butterfield, *Christianity, Diplomacy and War* (London: The Epworth Press, 1953), p. 11.

14. Robert J. Art and Kenneth N. Waltz, "Technology, Strategy, and the Uses of Force," in Art and Waltz (eds.), *The Use of Force* (Lanham, Md.: University Press of America, 1983), p. 6.

15. Kennan, "Morality and Foreign Policy," p. 207.

16. Perhaps the best version of this argument is Adamantia Pollis, "Liberal, Socialist, and Third World Perspectives of Human Rights," in Peter Schwab and Adamantia Pollis (eds.), *Toward a Human Rights Framework* (New York: Praeger, 1982). A revised version appears in Richard P. Claude and Burns Weston (eds.), *Human Rights in the World Community,* 2d ed. (Philadelphia: University of Pennsylvania Press, 1992).

17. Rhoda Howard, in an unpublished paper, has labeled this perspective "cultural absolutism."

18. This may be just slightly too strong. Indigenous peoples who live in traditional societies relatively unchanged by states and markets may have a plausible claim to radically different treatment. Only a tiny fraction of the world's population, however, live in such societies today.

CHAPTER THREE

1. Marcelo Cavarozzi, "Political Cycles in Argentina Since 1955," in Guillermo O'Donnell, Philippe C. Schmitter, and Laurence Whitehead (eds.), *Transitions from Authoritarian Rule: Latin America* (Baltimore: Johns Hopkins University Press, 1986).

2. Quoted in Amnesty International USA, *Disappearances: A Workbook* (New York, 1981), p. 9.

3. Guatemala was the first country to use disappearances systematically as a means of repression, in the 1960s. The practice seems to have been introduced into South America through the example of the Brazilian military in the late 1960s. For a good general introduction, see ibid.

4. Americas Watch, *Truth and Partial Justice in Argentina: An Update* (New York, 1991), p. 6. In Uruguay, however, as we will see, most of the disappeared reappeared. Chile fell somewhere in between. But the basic strategy was similar in the three countries.

5. Ian Guest, *Behind the Disappearances: Argentina's Dirty War Against Human Rights and the United Nations* (Philadelphia: University of Pennsylvania Press, 1990), p. 41.

6. V. S. Naipaul, *The Return of Eva Peron* (New York: Vintage Books, 1981), pp. 170, 162.

7. Roberta Cohen, "Human Rights Diplomacy: The Carter Administration and the Southern Cone," *Human Rights Quarterly* 4 (May 1982), p. 214.

8. Lawrence Weschler, *A Miracle, a Universe: Settling Accounts with Torturers* (New York: Pantheon Books, 1990), p. 145.

9. John Simpson and Jana Bennett, *The Disappeared: Voices from a Secret War* (London: Robson Books, 1985), p. 225.

10. See ibid.

11. Quoted in ibid., p. 66.

12. In fact, one of the tragic ironies in Uruguay was that the Tupamaros had already been destroyed by the end of 1972, that is, before the coup. (See Weschler, *A Miracle, a Universe,* pp. 107–111; Martin Weinstein, *Uruguay: Democracy at the Crossroads* [Boulder, Colo.: Westview Press, 1988], pp. 51, 203.) And in Chile there was no guerrilla threat at all.

13. Guest, *Behind the Disappearances,* p. 29.

14. See, for example, David Pion-Berlin, *The Ideology of State Terror: Economic Doctrine and Political Repression in Argentina and Peru* (Boulder, Colo.: Lynne Rienner Publishers, 1989), pp. 119–122.

15. Lawyers' Committee for International Human Rights, *The Generals Give Back Uruguay* (New York, 1985), p. 57; Weschler, *A Miracle, a Universe,* p. 112; Inter-Church Committee on Human Rights in Latin America, *Violations of Human Rights in Uruguay* (Toronto, 1978), p. 7; Weinstein, *Uruguay,* pp. 44, 52.

16. Pion-Berlin, *The Ideology of State Terror,* p. 101.

17. The following summer, similar groups from several Latin American countries joined to form FEDEFAM (Federation of Families of Disappeared Persons and Political Prisoners). Its first president was Lidia Galletti, one of the leaders of the mothers. Patrick Rice, the Irish priest mentioned above who survived his trip to ESMA, became its volunteer secretary, operating out of a small office with a borrowed typewriter in Caracas, Venezuela. FEDEFAM became an important source of information and a focus for concerted international action by relatives' groups throughout Central and South America.

18. Simpson and Bennett, *The Disappeared,* p. 110.

19. For a good brief overview of the activities of the Vicaría, see Americas Watch, *The Vicaría de la Solidaridad in Chile* (New York, 1987).

20. Ibid., p. 35.

21. Jinny Arancibia, Marcelo Charlin, and Peter Landstreet, "Chile," in Jack Donnelly and Rhoda E. Howard (eds.), *International Handbook of Human Rights* (Westport, Conn. : Greenwood Press, 1987), p. 62.

22. Lawyers' Committee for International Human Rights, *The Generals Give Back Uruguay*, pp. 32–35.

23. An English edition was published in 1986, under the same title.

24. For a review of the entire process of prosecutions and pardons, as well as further information on the actions of the Menem government, see Americas Watch, *Truth and Partial Justice*.

25. See Weschler, *A Miracle, a Universe*, pp. 173–236.

26. Hannah Arendt, *The Human Condition* (Chicago: University of Chicago Press, 1958), p. 241.

27. From Zbigniew Herbert, "Mr. Cogito on the Need for Precision," quoted in Weschler, *A Miracle, a Universe*, p. 191.

CHAPTER FOUR

1. Stephen D. Kranser, "Structural Causes and Regime Consequences: Regimes as Intervening Variables," in Kranser (ed.), *International Regimes* (Ithaca: Cornell University Press, 1982), p. 2.

2. This section draws heavily on Howard Tolley's authoritative book, *The U.N. Commission on Human Rights* (Boulder, Colo.: Westview Press, 1987).

3. Additional special rapporteurs have been appointed on religious intolerance (in 1986) and human rights violations by mercenaries (in 1987), but their activities have been much less significant. A promising Working Group on Arbitrary Detention was also created during the 1991 session.

4. Chapter 3 deals with human rights conditions in Chile. The reasons for Chile's prominence in international human rights discussions are complex. They certainly include genuine shock over the nature of the violations and special outrage, given Chile's long and relatively deep democratic tradition. Chile was also seen by at least some in the international human rights community as providing the United Nations a foot in the door for broader monitoring in general. But the complicity of the United States in the overthrow of Allende and the strong support of the military regime by the Nixon and Ford administrations injected a considerable element of politics into the situation, as did the fact that Allende was the world's only freely elected Marxist leader.

5. Optional procedures for complaints by one state against another have never been used. The other major activity of the Human Rights Committee is to issue "general comments" that seek to interpret particular provisions of the covenant or to improve the reporting process. A second optional protocol, on abolition of the death penalty, has not yet entered into force.

6. In addition, earlier decisions were taken in cases concerning Canada, Colombia, Finland, Italy, Madagascar, Mauritius, Sweden, Uruguay, and Zaire.

7. The International Covenant on Economic, Social, and Cultural Rights establishes no supervisory body. It does, however, require parties to submit periodic reports to the Economic and Social Council. For several years these reports were considered by an ECOSOC Sessional Working Group. In 1986, ECOSOC created a new expert committee, the Committee on Economic, Social, and Cultural Rights, in an effort to improve the reporting system. The committee's review of reports is very similar to that of the Human Rights Committee.

8. The 1989 Convention on the Rights of the Child will be the basis for the development of a new regime in the 1990s. In addition, it is possible, perhaps even likely, that various strands of concern with the rights of indigenous peoples will in the next few years coalesce into something that might be called a regime. The five single-issue regimes considered here, however, cover all the major cases to date.

9. These racial designations, however, did not necessarily have any connection to previously existing facts. For example, in 1956 and 1957, Sophiatown, a black freehold section of Johannesburg, was rezoned white and the residents forcibly removed. In 1966, District Six of Capetown was declared white, although the population was 90 percent Coloured. Since 1960, over 3.5 million blacks have been removed from white areas, and more than a million forced to relocate within designated black areas.

10. This was no coincidence. In fact, one could largely plot economically worthless land by looking at a map of the Homelands. For example, Bophuthatswana was made up of nineteen separate pieces, and KwaZulu contained twenty-nine major and forty-one minor pieces of unconnected territory, assuring that the best agricultural land was reserved for whites. And mineral rights were not even formally placed under the control of the Homeland governments.

11. All of this is in addition to the officially sanctioned violence of South Africa's system of corporal punishment. For example, between July 1987 and June 1988, approximately 40,000 people, mostly juveniles, were punished by whippings after their convictions for a variety of offenses. See J. Sloth-Nielsen, "Legal Violence: Corporal and Capital Punishment," in Brian McKendrick and Wilma Hoffmann (eds.), *People and Violence in South Africa* (Cape Town: Oxford University Press, 1990).

12. Newell M. Stultz, "Evolution of the United Nations Anti-Apartheid Regime," *Human Rights Quarterly* 13 (February 1991), pp. 22–23.

13. Other important treaties include the 1952 Convention on the Political Rights of Women, which had ninety-six parties at the start of 1990, and ILO Convention No. 100 concerning Equal Remuneration for Women and Men Workers for Work of Equal Value, which had only eleven parties.

14. Andrew C. Byrnes, "The 'Other' Human Rights Treaty Body: The Work of the Committee on the Elimination of Discrimination Against Women," *Yale Journal of International Law* 14 (Winter 1989), p. 56.

15. The principal source for the remainder of this section is Cecilia Medina Quiroga, *The Battle of Human Rights: Gross, Systematic Violations and the Inter-American System* (Dordrecht: Martinus Nijhoff, 1988). Readers should consult her book for more detail on this subject. For a discussion of human rights in Chile under Pinochet, see Chapter 3.

16. There were fifteen votes in favor of including the paragraph on Chile, two opposed (Chile and Haiti), and ten abstentions (Brazil, Costa Rica, Dominica, Ecuador, El Salvador, Panama, Paraguay, Peru, Suriname, and the United States). This total in favor was one short of the sixteen votes required.

17. Medina, *The Battle of Human Rights*, p. 312.

18. For a detailed account of Argentina's efforts in the United Nations, see Ian Guest, *Behind the Disappearances: Argentina's Dirty War Against Human Rights and the United Nations* (Philadelphia: University of Pennsylvania Press, 1990), pt. 2.

19. See Robert Pastor, *Condemned to Repetition: The United States and Nicaragua* (Princeton: Princeton University Press, 1987), pp. 149–151.

20. Unfortunately, the Tunisian league, perhaps the most respected human rights NGO in the Arab world, was forced to close down in the spring of 1992.

21. Adib Al-Jadir, "Human Rights in the Arab World," *Journal of Arab Affairs* 9 (Spring 1990), p. 3.

22. Quoted in Helsinki Watch Committee, *The Moscow Helsinki Monitors: Their Vision, Their Achievement, the Price They Paid, May 12, 1976–May 12, 1986* (New York, 1986), p. 5. The following discussion draws principally on this report.

23. We should also note that repression of human rights activists in CSCE countries has not been entirely restricted to the Soviet bloc. In Turkey, twenty-three members of the Executive Committee of the Turkish Peace Association, formed in response to the security provisions of the Helsinki accords, were imprisoned for their activities.

CHAPTER FIVE

1. For a slightly different, but generally consistent, periodization, see David P. Forsythe, *The Internationalization of Human Rights* (Lexington, Mass.: Lexington Books, 1991), pp. 121–127.

2. The domestic and international sides of this arrogance come together in the refusal of the United States to ratify the International Human Rights Covenants, as well as most other international human rights treaties. (In the spring of 1992, however, the United States finally did ratify the International Covenant on Civil and Political Rights, more than a quarter century after it was adopted. But even then, there was no serious consideration given to ratification of the International Covenant on Economic, Social, and Cultural Rights, reflecting a further element of American exceptionalism that is discussed later in the chapter.) The United States has characteristically held other countries to international human rights standards and procedures that it has refused to allow to be applied to itself.

3. The theoretical basis of such arguments has been discussed and criticized in Chapter 2.

4. David Carleton and Michael Stohl, "The Foreign Policy of Human Rights," *Human Rights Quarterly* 7 (May 1985), pp. 205–229. Compare Stephen B. Cohen, "Conditioning U.S. Security Assistance on Human Rights Practices," *American Journal of International Law* 76 (April 1982), pp. 246–279.

5. Liisa Lukkari North, "El Salvador," in Jack Donnelly and Rhoda E. Howard

(eds.), *International Handbook of Human Rights* (Westport, Conn.: Greenwood Press, 1987), pp. 125–126.

6. Most independent observers put the figure significantly higher. See, for example, Lawyers Committee for International Human Rights and the Watch Committees, *The Reagan Administration's Record on Human Rights in 1985* (New York, 1986), pp. 53–54. Americas Watch estimated almost 2,000 murders by death squads and the security forces in 1985. See North, "El Salvador," p. 119, and Americas Watch, *El Salvador's Decade of Terror: Human Rights Since the Assassination of Archbishop Romero* (New Haven: Yale University Press, 1991).

7. This section is largely a revised version of the introductory section of Rhoda E. Howard and Jack Donnelly, "Confronting Revolution in Nicaragua: U.S. and Canadian Responses," Carnegie Council on Ethics and International Affairs, New York, 1990, mimeographed.

8. For most of the second half of 1992, radical conservatives in the U.S. Senate, led by Jesse Helms, blocked desperately needed foreign aid in an attempt to force Chamorro to purge many remaining Sandinistas. This had at least some impact. For example, in September 1992 the government reorganized the national police, removing many former Sandinistas from high positions. Such an example suggests that even in the changed international environment of the post–cold war world, democratically elected governments that came to power with massive U.S. support are not immune to U.S. interference in their internal affairs. It is also a reminder that anticommunism remains a powerful political force in the United States, although there are few Communists left to combat.

9. Lars Schoultz, *National Security and United States Policy Toward Latin America* (Princeton: Princeton University Press, 1987), p. xi.

10. Jeane J. Kirkpatrick, "Dictatorships and Double Standards," *Commentary* 68 (November 1979).

11. The Committee of Santa Fe, *A New Inter-American Policy for the Eighties* (Washington, D.C.: Council for Inter-American Security, 1980), p. 37.

12. See, for example, Americas Watch Committee and the American Civil Liberties Union, *As BAD as Ever: A Report on Human Rights in El Salvador* (New York, 1984).

13. Americas Watch, *Annual Report, June 1984–June 1985* (New York, 1985), p. 4.

14. Cynthia Brown (ed.), *With Friends like These: The Americas Watch Report on Human Rights and U.S. Policy in Latin America* (New York: Pantheon Books, 1985), p. 20. Compare the Watch Committees and Lawyers Committee for Human Rights, *The Reagan Administration's Record on Human Rights in 1986* (New York, 1987), pp. 49 and 92–99, and *The Reagan Administration's Record on Human Rights in 1987* (New York, 1987), p. 106. On the Reagan administration's systematic misrepresentation of the facts, see Americas Watch, *Managing the Facts: How the Administration Deals with Reports of Human Rights Abuses in El Salvador* (New York, 1985).

15. This is not to suggest that human rights ought to have been at top, or even necessarily that they ought not to be at the bottom. The point here is simply to describe the place human rights concerns actually held in the policies of two administrations toward Central America.

16. Christopher Coker, *The United States and South Africa, 1968–1985*: *Con-*

structive Engagement and Its Critics (Durham, N.C.: Duke University Press, 1986), p. 105.

17. On the role of international financial pressure, see Robert M. Price, "Majority Rule in South Africa: The Role of Global Pressure," in Harvey Glickman (ed.), *Toward Peace and Security in Southern Africa* (New York: Gordon and Breach Science Publishers, 1990).

18. Another Dutch institutional innovation of interest is the independent Human Rights Advisory Committee, created in 1983 to provide advice to the foreign minister on practical issues of human rights policy. The advisory committee has taken its independence very seriously, even issuing unsolicited advice to the minister and, in 1984 in the case of Suriname, advice that the minister explicitly said that he did not want to receive.

19. Norway and the Netherlands are usually the world's two leading aid providers on a per capita basis, providing more than 1 percent of GNP in foreign aid. In recent years, the United States has provided less than one-fifth of 1 percent. For example, in 1986 Norway, a country of 4.2 million people, provided $800 million in foreign aid, while the United States, with 240 million people, provided $9.8 billion. The United States, with nearly sixty times the population, provided only about twelve times as much aid.

20. Quoted in Charles Cooper and Joan Verloren van Themaat, "Dutch Aid Determinants, 1973–85: Continuity and Change," in Olav Stokke (ed.), *Western Middle Powers and Global Poverty: The Determinants of the Aid Policies of Canada, Denmark, the Netherlands, Norway and Sweden* (Uppsala: Almquist and Wiksell International, 1989), p. 119.

21. Quoted in Olav Stokke, "Norwegian Aid: Policy and Performance," in Stokke (ed.), *European Development Assistance* (Oslo: Norwegian Institute of International Affairs, 1984), pp. 328–329.

22. Quoted in Olav Stokke, "The Determinants of Norwegian Aid Policy," in Stokke, *European Development Assistance*, p. 170.

23. The behavior of the like-minded countries in multilateral human rights forums has been in sharp contrast to that of the United States. Those countries have unusually high rates of ratification of international human rights treaties, and they have given multilateral human rights a high priority in their foreign policies, whereas the United States has given at best secondary emphasis to multilateral human rights activities. For example, Canada and the Netherlands played leading roles in the revival of the Commission on Human Rights in the late 1970s and early 1980s. The Carter administration was a supporter of these efforts, but the Reagan administration did its best to undo them and attempted to turn the commission into an instrument in the new cold war.

24. Jan Egeland, *Impotent Superpower—Potent Small State: Potentialities and Limitations of Human Rights Objectives in the Foreign Policies of the United States and Norway* (Oslo: Norwegian University Press, 1988), pp. 3, 5.

25. Ibid., p. 15.

26. *Statements and Speeches* 82/12, Ottawa: Bureau of Information, Department of External Affairs. Quoted in Howard and Donnelly, "Confronting Revolution in Nicaragua."

27. Egeland, *Impotent Superpower*, p. 23.

28. Students of comparative politics usually refer to this as a "corporatist" system. Each well-defined segment of society—each "corporate" group—is seen as *entitled* to have its interests taken into account, even if it is at the moment politically out of power. The United States, by contrast, tends to operate with a more "winner take all approach," as the early years of the Reagan revolution demonstrated particularly clearly.

CHAPTER SIX

1. Speech of April 13, 1991, at Maxwell Air Force Base, *Vital Speeches of the Day* 57, no. 15 (May 15, 1991), pp. 450–452.

2. By "antihumanitarian intervention," I mean intervention that has the consequence of harming human rights. It is the opposite of the familiar notion of humanitarian intervention.

3. Such an argument, clearly, is but one person's interpretation. It is one possible (informed) guess about the next several years, and you should read it as such. In fact, you should be warned that at times I have consciously presented points in an extreme fashion in order to provoke thought and reaction. You may also want to pay special attention to the discussion questions for this chapter, which largely suggest alternative ways of viewing the changes of the last few years and their implications for the future.

4. Speech of April 13, 1991, *Vital Speeches,* p. 450.

5. There are certainly a number of possible areas for UN or regional action of a very precisely analogous character, most notably in the former states of Yugoslavia and the Soviet Union. These, though, are clearly special cases that have no obvious implications for other kinds of international human rights activities.

6. This is a fairly common definition of formal or institutional democracy. It should not be confused with what might be called substantive democracy (which has been variously characterized as involving an egalitarian distribution of power, opportunities, or goods) and is much closer to what I call a rights-protective regime.

7. Niccolo Machiavelli, *The Discourses* (Harmondsworth: Penguin Books, 1970), p. 153 (Book I, Discourse 16).

8. Note that I do not say nationalism in all its forms has this consequence. When it leads to the political expression of group superiority, however, nationalism often does.

9. We should also note that separatist nationalism underscores the continuing centrality of the state in the new world order. What people are demanding is a state of their own. To the extent that there are appeals to the international community, it is usually to acquire a state or to protect a group against a state from which it has seceded or desires to secede, as in the former states of Yugoslavia. Only in the most severe cases, such as Somalia, is there serious international consideration given to intervening to avert a humanitarian crisis. And even Somali sovereignty has been infringed only after the complete collapse of internal order pushed literally millions of people to the brink of starvation.

10. Only in the former German Democratic Republic (GDR—East Germany) has there been a massive influx of money, an "exception" that in fact strongly confirms the rule of no major increase in *foreign* assistance.

□ □ □

Suggested Readings

CHAPTER ONE

Although the literature on human rights has become rather large in the past decade, there are few good general introductory overviews of international human rights policies. The best (and the book most comparable to this volume) is David P. Forsythe, *Human Rights and World Politics* (Lincoln: University of Nebraska Press, 2d ed., 1989). Forsythe emphasizes U.S. foreign policy, but there are also good discussions of international law and organization and theoretical and ideological perspectives on human rights. Also useful is R. J. Vincent, *Human Rights and International Relations* (Cambridge: Cambridge University Press, 1986). Vincent offers good discussions of the theory of human rights, cultural relativism, and the implications of human rights for contemporary international theory and practice (although the chapter on East-West relations is now dated). Jack Donnelly, *Universal Human Rights in Theory and Practice* (Ithaca: Cornell University Press, 1989), is somewhat narrower in focus. Richard Pierre Claude and Burns H. Weston (eds.), *Human Rights in the World Community*, 2d ed. (Philadelphia: University of Pennsylvania Press, 1992), is probably the best general collection of essays currently available.

Students in particular are likely to find much useful information in Walter Laqueur and Barry Rubin (eds.), *The Human Rights Reader* (New York: New American Library, 2d ed., 1989). A very different, but quite comprehensive, volume is Edward Lawson (ed.), *Encyclopedia of Human Rights* (New York: Taylor & Francis, 1991). Attention should also be drawn to the journal *Human Rights Quarterly*. This interdisciplinary journal is generally considered to be the best scholarly journal in the field, but its articles typically are quite accessible to the average reader.

Those interested in the activities of human rights NGOs can get a pretty good sense of the range and diversity of their activities through the *Human Rights Internet Reporter*. For a good analytical overview, see Laurie S. Wiseberg and Harry M. Scoble, "Recent Trends in the Expanding Universe of NGOs Dedicated to the Protection of Human Rights," in Ved P. Nanda, James R. Scarritt, and George W. Shepherd, Jr. (eds.), *Global Human Rights: Public Policies, Comparative Measures, and NGO Strategies* (Boulder: Westview Press, 1980). On Amnesty International, see Marie Staunton and Sally Fenn (eds.), *Amnesty International Handbook* (Claremont, Calif.: Hunter House, 1991). This short and very accessible book includes information for those interested in becoming actively involved in the work of Amnesty International. They may also write to Amnesty International USA, 322 Eighth Avenue, New York, N.Y. 10001, or call (212) 807-8400 or (800) 55AMNESTY.

CHAPTER TWO

The single most important, and most cited, theoretical work on human rights is Henry Shue, *Basic Rights: Subsistence, Affluence, and U.S. Foreign Policy* (Princeton: Princeton University Press, 1980). Shue provides a subtle and powerful argument for the equal and overriding priority of rights to security, subsistence, and liberty; an extended discussion of the duties that flow from these rights; and a sensitive application of these theoretical ideas to U.S. foreign policy. (A shorter version of the core of the argument is available in Shue's essay "Rights in the Light of Duties," in Peter G. Brown and Douglas MacLean [eds.], *Human Rights and U.S. Foreign Policy: Principles and Applications* [Lexington, Mass.: Lexington Books, 1979].) For an alternative perspective on economic, social, and cultural rights, see Maurice Cranston, "Are There Any Human Rights?" *Daedalus* 112 (Fall 1983), pp. 1–18, and Hugo Adam Bedau, "Human Rights and Foreign Assistance Programs, " in Brown and MacLean, *Human Rights and U.S. Foreign Policy.*

The most ambitious effort to develop a contemporary philosophical theory of human rights is Alan Gewirth, *Human Rights: Essays on Justification and Applications* (Chicago: University of Chicago Press, 1982). Gewirth's main argument, however, is dense and rather technical (although some of the later essays in the volume do provide accessible applications of the theory). For critiques of Gewirth, and good examples of other philosophical perspectives, see J. Roland Pennock and John W. Chapman (eds.), *Human Rights* (New York: New York University Press, 1981).

Chapters 1 and 2 of Jack Donnelly, *Universal Human Rights in Theory and Practice* (Ithaca: Cornell University Press, 1989), present a more modest, and much more accessible, theory. For a good book-length discussion that emphasizes the similarities between rights and other grounds of action (in contrast to Donnelly's emphasis on the special features of rights), see James W. Nickel, *Making Sense of Human Rights: Philosophical Reflections on the Universal Declaration of Human Rights* (Berkeley: University of California Press, 1987). Chapter 1 of R. J. Vincent, *Human Rights and International Relations* (Cambridge: Cambridge University Press, 1986), provides a good, if necessarily brief, overview of some of the central theoretical issues. Vincent's "The Idea of Rights in International Ethics," in Terry Nardin and David R. Mapel (eds.), *Traditions of International Ethics* (Cambridge: Cambridge University Press, 1992), usefully links ethical issues with international relations theory in the case of human rights.

The literature on cultural relativism and human rights is large. Vincent, *Human Rights and International Relations,* Chapter 3, provides a good general overview of the issue. For a further development of the weak relativist position defended in this chapter, see Donnelly, *Universal Human Rights in Theory and Practice,* Parts 2 and 3 (especially Chapters 3 and 6). A very similar argument, applied to contemporary Africa, is developed in Chapter 2 of Rhoda E. Howard, *Human Rights in Commonwealth Africa* (Totowa, N.J.: Rowman and Littlefield, 1986). For a radical relativist account, see Alison Dundes Renteln, "The Unanswered Challenge of Relativism and the Consequences of Human Rights," *Human Rights Quarterly* 7 (November 1985), pp. 514–540. (Renteln develops this argument in much greater detail in *International Human Rights: Universalism Versus Relativism* [Newbury Park: Sage Publications, 1990].) A slightly less radical relativist argument is presented in Adamantia Pollis and Peter Schwab, "Human Rights: A Western Construct with Limited Applicability," in Pollis and Schwab (eds.), *Human Rights: Cultural and Ideological Perspectives* (New York: Praeger Publishers, 1980).

There are several useful readers that deal entirely or principally with issues of cultural relativism. I list them here in chronological order of publication: UNESCO, *Human Rights: Comments and Interpretations* (London: Allan Wingate, 1949); Pollis and Schwab (ed.), *Human Rights: Cultural and Ideological Perspectives;* Kenneth W. Thompson (ed.), *The Moral Imperatives of Human Rights: A World Survey* (Washington, D.C.: University Press of America, 1980); Claude E. Welch, Jr., and Virginia A. Leary (eds.), *Asian Perspectives on Human Rights* (Boulder: Westview Press, 1990); Jan Berting et al. (eds.), *Human Rights in a Pluralist World: Individuals and Collectivities* (Westport, Conn.: Meckler, 1990); Abdullahi Ahmed An-Na'im and Francis M. Deng (eds.), *Human Rights in Africa: Cross-Cultural Perspectives* (Washington, D.C.: The Brookings Institution, 1990); Abdullahi Ahmed An-Na'im (ed.), *Human Rights in Cross-Cultural Perspectives: A Quest for Consensus* (Philadelphia: University of Pennsylvania Press, 1991).

CHAPTER THREE

Readers interested in more information on the Southern Cone should probably begin with Iain Guest, *Behind the Disappearances: Argentina's Dirty War Against Human Rights and the United Nations* (Philadelphia: University of Pennsylvania Press, 1990). Guest, a journalist who covered the United Nations Commission on Human Rights for a number of years, begins with an account of the repression following the coup in Argentina. His telling of the story is particularly powerful because of the effective use of personal accounts of some of the victims. Guest then moves on to the halting efforts of the United Nations to deal with disappearances in Argentina (and elsewhere), followed by an extended discussion of U.S. policy during both the Carter and the Reagan years. Somewhat narrower, but even more moving for being a first-person account by a journalist victim of the Dirty War, is Jacobo Timerman, *Prisoner Without a Name, Cell Without a Number* (New York: Knopf, 1981).

John Simpson and Jana Bennett, *The Disappeared: Voices from a Secret War* (London: Robson Books, 1985), is another useful example of political journalism, providing detailed information on the internal politics of the Dirty War. A much more idiosyncratic, but penetrating, analysis by a cynical external observer can be found in V. S. Naipaul, *The Return of Eva Peron* (New York: Vintage Books, 1981). For a more general discussion of disappearances as a technique of human rights violations, see Amnesty International USA, *Disappearances: A Workbook,* New York, 1981.

The horror of the Dirty War is difficult to capture fully even in good journalism (let alone in dry academic prose). Literary representations thus can be particularly useful. Among fictional accounts, perhaps the best is Lawrence Thornton,

Imagining Argentina (New York: Doubleday, 1987), a novel in the "magic realist" tradition of García Márquez. Among poets, one might begin with Marjorie Agosin, *Zones of Pain/Las Zonas del Dolor* (Fredonia, N.Y.: White Pine Press, 1988), a short bilingual collection of poems on the human consequences of military rule in Chile.

Another journalistic account, Lawrence Weschler, *A Miracle, A Universe: Settling Accounts with Torturers* (New York: Pantheon Books, 1990), is perhaps the best place to begin further reading and reflection on the difficult process of overcoming the legacy of repression. The second half of the book, which began as two articles in the *New Yorker*, is a brilliant and moving discussion of the system of repression in Uruguay and the politics of the amnesty referendum. The first half, which deals with Brazil and thus is strictly speaking outside the scope of this chapter, is also valuable.

Readers interested in additional country case studies of the sort presented in this chapter should consult Jack Donnelly and Rhoda E. Howard (eds.), *International Handbook of Human Rights* (Westport, Conn.: Greenwood Press, 1987). Although a number of the chapters have become somewhat dated, there is no other readily available source of such case studies.

CHAPTER FOUR

The bulk of the literature on international human rights regimes is written by international lawyers. As a result, much of it is more technical and legalistic than the average reader of this book would desire. Three comprehensive edited volumes, however, should be noted: Karel Vasak and Philip Alston (eds.), *The International Dimensions of Human Rights* (Westport, Conn.: Greenwood Press, 1982); Theodor Meron (ed.), *Human Rights and International Law: Legal and Policy Issues* (Oxford: Clarendon Press, 1984); and Hurst Hannum (ed.), *Guide to International Human Rights Practice*, 2d ed. (Philadelphia: University of Pennsylvania Press, 1992). These volumes, which are structured primarily in terms of particular international organizations, cover all the international human rights regimes discussed in this chapter. For a legal approach focusing more on the work of lawyers, with a special emphasis on the United States, see Frank Newman and David Weissbrodt (eds.), *International Human Rights: Law, Policy, and Process* (Cincinnati: Anderson Publishing Co., 1990).

Two good summary overviews of the human rights work of the United Nations in its first four decades are David P. Forsythe, "The Politics of Efficacy: The United Nations and Human Rights," in Lawrence S. Finkelstein (ed.), *Politics in the United Nations System* (Durham, N.C.: Duke University Press, 1988), and Tom J. Farer, "The United Nations and Human Rights: More Than a Whimper, Less Than a Roar," *Human Rights Quarterly* 9 (November 1987), pp. 550–586. (An abbreviated version of the Farer essay can be found in Richard Pierre Claude and Burns H. Weston [eds.], *Human Rights in the World Community* [Philadelphia: University of Pennsylvania Press, 1989].) Howard Tolley's *The United Nations Commission on Human Rights* (Boulder: Westview Press, 1987) is the definitive book on this central institution of the global human rights regime. It also provides a good general account of the ups and downs of the human rights work of the United Nations. For a somewhat more jaundiced perspective, focusing on the problem of political bias, see Jack Donnelly, "Human Rights at the United Nations, 1955–1985: The Question of Bias," *International Studies Quarterly* 22 (September 1988), pp. 275–303.

Burns H. Weston, Robin Ann Lukes, and Kelly M. Hnatt, "Regional Human Rights Regimes: A Comparison and Appraisal," in Claude and Weston (eds.), *Human Rights in the World Community*, provides a useful brief summary. For more depth, consult A. Glenn Mower, Jr., *Regional Human Rights: A Comparative Study of the West European and Inter-American Systems* (New York: Greenwood Press, 1991). Although often highly technical, Cecilia Medina Quiroga, *The Battle of Human Rights: Gross, Systematic Violations and the Inter-American System* (Dordrecht: Martinus Nijhoff, 1988), is an excellent resource on the Inter-American regime. On the Helsinki process, see Arie Bloed and Pieter Van Dijk (eds.), *Essays on Human Rights in the Helsinki Process* (Dordrecht: Martinus Nijhoff, 1985).

CHAPTER FIVE

Stanley Hoffmann, "Reaching for the Most Difficult: Human Rights as a Foreign Policy Goal," *Daedalus* 112 (Fall 1983), pp. 19–49, provides an excellent and subtle discussion of some of the fundamental problems and possibilities in pursuing human rights in foreign policy. Equally useful as a general introduction to the issue is Charles Frankel, *Human Rights and Foreign Policy* (Headline Series, No. 241, October 1978). Another good, short introductory discussion, with an especially thorough presentation of the means available for use on behalf of human rights, is Evan Luard, *Human Rights and Foreign Policy* (Oxford: Pergamon Press [for the United Nations Association of Great Britain and Northern Ireland], 1981). (An abbreviated version of this essay is available in Richard Pierre Claude and Burns H. Weston [eds.], *Human Rights in the World Community* [Philadelphia: University of Pennsylvania Press, 1989].)

Arthur Schlesinger, Jr., "Human Rights and the American Tradition," *Foreign Affairs* 57, no. 3 (1979), pp. 503–526, presents a lively version of a standard, mainstream U.S. liberal approach. Richard Falk ("Ideological Patterns in the United States Human Rights Debate: 1945–1978," in Natalie Kaufman Hevener [ed.], *The Dynamics of Human Rights in U.S. Foreign Policy* [New Brunswick, N.J.: Transaction Books, 1981], and Chapter 2 of *Human Rights and State Sovereignty* [New York: Holmes and Meier, 1981]) offers a more radical view. William F. Buckley, Jr., "Human Rights and Foreign Policy: A Proposal," *Foreign Affairs* 58 (Spring 1980), pp. 775–796, presents a clear statement of the traditional conservative approach. Jeane J. Kirkpatrick, "Dictatorships and Double Standards," *Commentary* 68 (November 1979), pp. 34–45, is the authoritative presentation of the Reagan position. Tracy Strong, "Taking the Rank with What Is Ours: American Political Thought, Foreign Policy, and Questions of Rights," in Paula R. Newburg (ed.), *The Politics of Human Rights* (New York: New York University Press, 1980), provides an excellent, and somewhat more neutral, discussion of human rights ideas in the American tradition of political thought. Although all these articles were written in response to Jimmy Carter's introduction of human rights into the mainstream of U.S. foreign policy, they remain valuable statements of the basic perspectives that still dominate

American discussion. The same is true of Hans Morgenthau's essay *Human Rights and Foreign Policy* (New York: Council on Religion and International Affairs, 1979), a classic statement of the realist perspective. For another classic realist analysis, see Henry A. Kissinger, "Continuity and Change in American Foreign Policy," in Abdul Aziz Said (ed.), *Human Rights and World Order* (New York: Praeger Publishers, 1978).

Said (ed.), *Human Rights and World Order*, is just one of several edited volumes on human rights and U.S. foreign policy produced in the later 1970s. The best is Peter G. Brown and Douglas MacLean (eds.), *Human Rights and U.S. Foreign Policy: Principles and Applications* (Lexington, Mass.: Lexington Books, 1979). This volume combines theory and policy analysis in a stimulating way. Although many of the examples, as well as the case studies in the final part of the volume, are now pretty dated, most of the volume remains surprisingly timely. David P. Kommers and Gilburt D. Loescher (eds.), *Human Rights and American Foreign Policy* (Notre Dame: University of Notre Dame Press, 1979), and Hevener, *The Dynamics of Human Rights in U.S. Foreign Policy*, have held up a bit less well, but many of the individual essays remain worth reading.

[David Heaps], *Human Rights and U.S. Foreign Policy: The First Decade, 1973–1983* (New York: American Association for the International Commission of Jurists, 1984), is perhaps the best short historical overview of U.S. policy. It also sharply draws the contrast between the Carter and the Reagan approaches. The discussion of U.S. policy in David P. Forsythe's introductory text *Human Rights and World Politics* (Lincoln: University of Nebraska Press, 2d ed., 1989) is excellent. For more detail, see A. Glenn Mower, Jr., *Human Rights and American Foreign Policy: The Carter and Reagan Experiences* (Westport, Conn.: Greenwood Press, 1987). The chapters on the United States in David P. Forsythe, *The Internationalization of Human Rights* (Lexington, Mass.: Lexington Books, 1991), are extremely useful. Forsythe's *Human Rights and U.S. Foreign Policy: Congress Reconsidered* (Gainesville: University of Florida Press, 1988) is the only extended discussion of the much understudied congressional role in U.S. international human rights policy.

For essays dealing with some of the basic theoretical and practical problems of linking human rights and foreign aid, see Brown and MacLean (eds.), *Human Rights and U.S. Foreign Policy*. Stephen B. Cohen, "Conditioning U.S. Security Assistance on Human Rights Practices," *American Journal of International Law* 76 (April 1982), pp. 246–279, provides a detailed account of the loopholes and inadequacies in the U.S. policy process. Two articles by David Carleton and Michael Stohl ("The Foreign Policy of Human Rights: Rhetoric and Reality from Jimmy Carter to Ronald Reagan: A Critique and Reappraisal," *Human Rights Quarterly* 7 [May 1985], pp. 205–229, and "The Role of Human Rights in U.S. Foreign Assistance," *American Journal of Political Science* 31 [November 1987], pp. 1002–1018) show that there is little statistical correlation between the human rights practices of recipient states and U.S. foreign aid disbursements. Also useful is David P. Forsythe, "US Economic Assistance and Human Rights: Why the Emperor Has (Almost) No Clothes," in David P. Forsythe (ed.), *Human Rights and Development: International Views* (London: Macmillan, 1989).

Roberta Cohen, "Human Rights Diplomacy: The Carter Administration and the Southern Cone," *Human Rights Quarterly* 4 (May 1982), pp. 212–242, is the best brief discussion of this subject. Iain Guest, *Behind the Disappearances: Argentina's Dirty War Against Human Rights and the United Nations* (Philadelphia: University of Pennsylvania Press, 1990), provides much more detail, covering both the Carter and the Reagan years. Lars Schoultz's book *Human Rights and United States Policy Toward Latin America* (Princeton: Princeton University Press, 1981) is one of the few works that looks in detail at the actual operation of the U.S. foreign policy process in the field of human rights. On U.S. policy toward South Africa, see Christopher Coker, *The United States and South Africa, 1968–1985: Constructive Engagement and Its Critics* (Durham, N.C.: Duke University Press, 1986).

There has been very little written on human rights and foreign policy in countries other than the United States. The two principal exceptions are Robert O. Matthews and Cranford Pratt (eds.), *Human Rights in Canadian Foreign Policy* (Kingston and Montreal: McGill–Queen's University Press, 1988), and Jan Egeland, *Impotent Superpower—Potent Small State: Potentialities and Limitations of Human Rights Objectives in the Foreign Policies of the United States and Norway* (Oslo: Norwegian University Press [distributed by Oxford University Press], 1988). The Matthews and Pratt volume is particularly useful for its comprehensive scope, covering the domestic Canadian policy context and Canadian policy in both multilateral and bilateral contexts. On the aid policies of the like-minded states, see Olav Stokke (ed.), *Western Middle Powers and Global Poverty: The Determinants of the Aid Policies of Canada, Denmark, the Netherlands, Norway and Sweden* (Stockholm: Almquist & Wiksell International, 1989). Wolfgang S. Heinz, "The Federal Republic of Germany: Human Rights and Development," and Peter R. Baehr, "Human Rights, Development and Dutch Foreign Policy: The Role of an Advisory Committee," in Forsythe (ed.), *Human Rights and Development*, are useful brief discussions of countries that have adopted some unusual institutional mechanisms.

The general issue of the justifiability of humanitarian intervention, although not pursued in this chapter, is worth additional reading and reflection. The starting point for contemporary discussions is Michael Walzer, *Just and Unjust Wars* (New York: Basic Books, 1977), pp. 53–63, 101–108. Walzer argues that in a world of sovereign states, humanitarian intervention is likely to be morally justifiable only in extremely narrow and rare instances. See also Michael Walzer, "The Moral Standing of States: A Response to Four Critics," *Philosophy and Public Affairs* 9 (Spring 1980), pp. 209–229. For a variety of less restrictive accounts, see the critics to whom Walzer responds in "The Moral Standing of States," and Terry Nardin and Jerome Slater, "Non-Intervention and Human Rights," *Journal of Politics* 48 (February 1986), pp. 86–96. For an argument that comes to conclusions similar to Walzer's, but primarily through legal and political, rather than moral, analysis see Jack Donnelly, "Human Rights, Humanitarian Intervention, and American Foreign Policy: Law, Morality and Politics," *Journal of International Affairs* 37 (Winter 1984), pp. 311–328. (An abbreviated version of this essay is available in Richard Pierre Claude and Burns H. Weston [eds.], *Human Rights in the World Community* [Philadelphia: University of Pennsylvania Press, 1989].)

CHAPTER SIX

The pace of change in contemporary international relations is so fast that any suggested readings for this chapter have a relatively high probability of seeming outdated, if not positively anachronistic, when this book appears—let alone during its useful life. When I started writing, the Berlin Wall had not yet fallen. When the first draft was completed, Croatia was only beginning to appear in the news and few ordinary Americans knew anything at all about Bosnia. When I delivered the final draft to the publisher, the Soviet Union had been dissolved, but Somalia was still largely unknown to most Americans, and few experts seriously contemplated large-scale military intervention. In making the final corrections to the copyedited manuscript in December 1992, I had to alter references to the soon-to-be-partitioned country of Czechoslovakia. The reader should therefore treat with care the following suggestions, which have been kept to a bare minimum.

David P. Forsythe, "Human Rights in a Post–Cold War World," *Fletcher Forum of World Affairs* 15 (Summer 1991), pp. 55–70, is one of the earliest attempts to make sense of the human rights implications of the end of the cold war. Forsythe's account is somewhat more optimistic than the one I have presented in this chapter. On Central and Eastern Europe, see Allan Rosas and Jan Hegelsen (eds.), *Human Rights in a Changing East-West Perspective* (London: Pinter Publishers, 1990), and Vojtech Mastny and Jan Zielonka (eds.), *Human Rights and Security: Europe on the Eve of a New Era* (Boulder: Westview Press, 1991).

We are now at the beginning of a flood of volumes on international relations in the post–cold war world. Although they do not explicitly deal with human rights issues, two that are of interest are Thomas G. Weiss (ed.), *Collective Security in a Changing World* (Boulder: Lynne Rienner Publishers, 1993), and Graham Allison and Gregory F. Treverton (eds.), *Rethinking America's Security: Beyond Cold War to New World Order* (New York: W. W. Norton, 1992).

□ □ □

Glossary

American exceptionalism is the belief that the United States is culturally and politically different from, and usually superior to, other countries. It can be traced to the colonial period and the biblical image of the city on the hill. In the area of human rights it tends to be expressed in the common American view that the United States in some important sense defines international human rights standards.

Anarchy, the absence of political rule, is characterized by the lack of authoritative hierarchical relationships of superiority and subordination. In international relations, anarchy refers to the fact that there is no higher authority above states. Anarchy, however, need not involve chaos (absence of order). Thus, international relations has been called an anarchical society, a society in which order emerges from the interactions of formally equally sovereign states.

Apartheid, an Afrikaans term meaning separateness, was the policy of systematic, official racial classification and discrimination in South Africa. Building on a long tradition of racial discrimination, white South African governments in the 1950s and 1960s developed an unusually extensive, highly integrated system of official discrimination touching virtually all aspects of public life and many aspects of private life as well. The policy was officially renounced following a (whites only) plebiscite in March 1992.

The **categorical imperative** is Kant's fundamental principle of morality. Kant argues that there is one and only one fundamental moral principle: Act so that you always treats other people as ends, never as means only. This principle is an imperative (a command), and it is categorical (it applies without exception, in all times, places, and circumstances). It is a classic example of deontological ethics, moral systems that focus on the inherent character of an act (and the intentions of the actor) rather than on the consequences of acts.

Civil and political rights are one of two principal classes of internationally recognized human rights. They provide protections against the state (such as rights to due process, *habeus corpus*, and freedom of speech) and require that the state provide certain substantive legal and political opportunities (such as the right to vote and to trial by a jury of one's peers). They are codified in the International Covenant on Civil and Political Rights and in Articles 1–21 of the Universal Declaration of Human Rights (see Table 1.1).

Cold war is the term used for the geopolitical and ideological struggle between the Soviet Union and the United States following World War II. It began in earnest roughly in 1948, waxed and waned over the following forty years, and finally ended with the collapse of the Soviet bloc in 1989.

Cosmopolitan and **cosmopolitanism** refer to a conception of international relations that views people first and foremost as individual members of a global political community (*cosmopolis*) rather than as citizens of states.

Disappearances are a form of human rights violation that became popular in the 1970s. Victims, rather than being officially detained or even murdered by the authorities or semiofficial death squads, are "disappeared," taken to state-run but clandestine detention centers. Torture typically accompanies disappearance, and in some countries the disappeared have also been regularly killed.

Economic, social, and cultural rights are one of two classes of internationally recognized human rights. They guarantee individuals socially provided goods and services (such as food, health care, social insurance, and education) and certain protections against the state (especially in family matters). They are codified in the International Covenant on Economic, Social, and Cultural Rights and in Articles 22–27 of the Universal Declaration of Human Rights (see Table 1.1).

The **1503 procedure** is an investigatory procedure (established by ECOSOC Resolution 1503) of the United Nations Commission on Human Rights that deals with situations of gross, persistent, and systematic violations of human rights.

The **Helsinki process** is an informal description of the human rights activities undertaken within the Conference on Security and Cooperation in Europe (CSCE). The term derives from the Helsinki Final Act of 1975, which defined the terms of reference of the CSCE.

Human rights, the rights that one has simply because one is a human being, are held equally and inalienably by all human beings. They are the social and political guarantees necessary to protect individuals from the standard threats to human dignity posed by the modern state and modern markets.

The **International Bill of Human Rights** is the informal name for the Universal Declaration of Human Rights and the International Human Rights Covenants, considered collectively as a set of authoritative international human rights standards. This title underscores the substantive interrelations of these three documents.

The **International Human Rights Covenants** comprise the International Covenant on Economic, Social, and Cultural Rights and the International Covenant on Civil and Political Rights, which were opened for signature in 1966 and entered into force in 1976. Along with the Universal Declaration of Human Rights, these are the central normative documents in the field of international human rights.

An **international regime** is a set of principles, norms, rules, and decision-making procedures accepted by states (and other relevant international actors) as binding in an issue area. The notion of a regime points to patterns of international governance that are not necessarily limited to a single treaty or organization.

Internationalist and **internationalism** refer to a conception of international relations that stresses both the centrality of the state and the existence of social relations among those states.

The **like-minded countries** are a group of about a dozen small and medium-sized Western countries, including Canada, the Netherlands, and the Nordic countries. They often act in concert in international organizations and generally pursue foreign policies that are more "liberal" than those of the United States, Japan, or the larger Western European countries. The like-minded countries particularly emphasize development issues, and they have tried to play an intermediary role between the countries of the South and the larger northern countries.

A **nongovernmental organization (NGO)** is a private association of individuals or groups that engages in political activity. International NGOs (INGOs) carry on their activities across state boundaries. The most prominent human rights INGOs include Amnesty International, Human Rights Watch, the International Commission of Jurists, and the Minority Rights Group.

Nonintervention is the international obligation not to interfere in matters that are essentially within the domestic jurisdiction of a sovereign state. This duty is correlative to the right of sovereignty and expresses the principal practical implications of sovereignty, viewed from the perspective of other states.

Quiet diplomacy is the pursuit of foreign policy objectives through official channels, without recourse to public statements or actions. A standard mechanism for pursuing virtually all foreign policy goals, it became a political issue in the United States in the late 1970s and 1980s when conservative critics of the policy of the Carter administration and defenders of the policy of the Reagan administration argued that U.S. international human rights policy toward "friendly" (anticommunist) regimes should in most cases be restricted *solely* to quiet diplomacy.

Realism (realpolitik) is a theory of international relations that stresses international anarchy, human egoism, the priority of power and security, and the need to exclude considerations of morality from foreign policy.

A **relativist** believes that values are not universal but a function of contingent circumstances. **Cultural relativism** holds that morality is significantly determined by culture and history. Marxism is another form of **ethical relativism**, holding that values are reflections of the interests of the ruling class. **Radical relativism** sees culture as the source of all values.

Sovereign and **sovereignty** refer to the absence of obligation to a higher authority. International relations over the past three centuries has been structured around the principle of the sovereignty of territorial states.

Statist and **statism** refer to a theory of international relations that stresses the centrality of sovereign states. Realism usually is associated with a statist theory of international relations.

A **treaty** is an agreement between states that creates obligations on those states. Treaties are one of the two principal sources of international law, along with custom (regularized patterns of action that through repeated practice have created expectations and thus acquired an obligatory character). The two most important international human rights treaties are the International Covenant on Economic, Social, and Cultural Rights and the International Covenant on Civil and Political Rights.

The **Universal Declaration of Human Rights** is a 1948 General Assembly resolution that provides the most authoritative statement of international human rights norms. Together with the International Human Rights Covenants, it is sometimes referred to as the International Bill of Human Rights.

Universalism is the belief that moral values such as human rights are fundamentally the same at all times and in all places. It is the opposite of relativism.

Utilitarianism is a moral theory (most closely associated with Bentham and Mill) that holds that the right course of action is that which maximizes the balance of pleasure over pain. This is the most common form of consequentialist ethics, which focus on the consequences of acts rather than their inherent character.

□ □ □

Chronology

1890 Treaty abolishing the slave trade adopted at Brussels Conference.
1919 International Labor Organization founded. First multilateral organization to deal with human (in this case, workers') rights.
1920 League of Nations begins discussing minority rights in Central and Eastern Europe.
1926 Slavery Convention opened for signature.
1945 United Nations Charter affirms protection of human rights as a principal goal of the organization.
Nuremberg War Crimes Trials introduce charge of crimes against humanity to international law.
1946 United Nations Commission on Human Rights meets for first time.
1948 Convention on the Prevention and Punishment of the Crime of Genocide opened for signature.
Universal Declaration of Human Rights adopted by United Nations General Assembly.
1950 European Convention for the Protection of Human Rights and Fundamental Freedoms opened for signature.
1953 Draft International Human Rights Covenant tabled in UN Commission on Human Rights because of cold war rivalry.
1954 U.S.-backed military overthrow of freely elected government of Jacobo Arbenz in Guatemala.
1956 Soviet invasion of Hungary.
1959 Inter-American Commission of Human Rights established.
1960 Sharpeville Massacre places apartheid permanently on international agendas.
UN General Assembly adopts resolution 1514 (Declaration on the Granting of Independence to Colonial Countries and Peoples).
1965 International Convention on the Elimination of All Forms of Racial Discrimination opened for signature.
1966 International Human Rights Covenants opened for signature.
1969 American Convention on Human Rights opened for signature.
1970 ECOSOC resolution 1503 adopted, giving the Commission on Human Rights authority to investigate systematic human rights violations.

1973   Military coup in Chile overthrows government of Salvador Allende. U.S. Congress recommends linking foreign aid to the human rights practices of recipient countries.

1976   International Human Rights Covenants enter into force. Human Rights Committee established.

1977   Amnesty International receives Nobel Peace Prize.

1979   White Paper formally incorporates human rights into the foreign policy of the Netherlands.
International Convention on the Elimination of Discrimination Against Women opened for signature.

1980   Working Group on Disappearances established by UN Commission on Human Rights.

1981   African (Banjul) Charter on Human and Peoples' Rights opened for signature.

1982   Special Rapporteur on Arbitrary Executions appointed by Commission on Human Rights.

1984   Report of the Argentine National Commission on Disappearances published.
Convention Against Torture and Other Cruel, Inhuman, or Degrading Treatment or Punishment opened for signature.

1985   Special Rapporteur on Torture appointed by Commission on Human Rights.

1986   UN General Assembly adopts Declaration on the Right to Development.
ECOSOC creates Committee on Economic, Social, and Cultural Rights.

1989   Tienanmen Massacre in Beijing.
Fall of Berlin Wall marks the end of the cold war and the dissolution of the Soviet bloc.
Peaceful transfers of power following elections in Argentina, Brazil, El Salvador, and Uruguay.
Convention on the Rights of the Child opened for signature.

1991   Dissolution of the Soviet Union.
Working Group on Arbitrary Detention created by Commission on Human Rights.

1992   Plebiscite in South Africa completes official repudiation of apartheid.
End of civil war in El Salvador and deployment of UN human rights monitoring force.
"Ethnic cleansing" in Bosnia leads UN to authorize new international war crimes tribunal.

About the Book and Author

Human rights, now a regular part of international relations, were not recognized as a legitimate subject of diplomatic concern prior to 1945. Jack Donnelly traces the rise of human rights issues after World War II, through the Universal Declaration of Human Rights, the dark days of the cold war, the resurgence of interest during the Carter presidency, and the Reagan administration's resistance, up to the current post–cold war era.

Although concerned primarily with the international politics of human rights, the book includes a chapter on theoretical issues, including the moral basis of human rights, problems of cultural relativism, and the place of human rights in the contemporary international society of states. Case studies of human rights violations in Chile, Argentina, South Africa, El Salvador, and Nicaragua, as well as extensive illustrations drawn from other parts of the world, lend concreteness to the discussion. Throughout the volume, Donnelly gives attention not only to the realist emphasis on power and international anarchy but also to the reality and impact of moral concerns, interdependence, international organizations, and nongovernmental organizations.

There is an extensive discussion of multilateral human rights activity, both throughout the UN system and in regional organizations. A chapter on the bilateral politics of human rights supplements the expected discussion of U.S. initiatives with a comparative analysis of the international human rights policies of other Western democracies, including Canada, Norway, and the Netherlands. The final chapter, "International Human Rights in a Post–Cold War World," shows the human rights implications of the decisive changes in international relations sparked by the revolutions of 1989 and highlights the opportunities for and the constraints on progressive action on behalf of internationally recognized human rights in the remainder of the 1990s.

Tables, boxes, photos, cartoons, and essential human rights documents accompany the text, along with features common to all Dilemmas in World Politics books—discussion questions, suggested readings, a chronology, and a glossary. *International Human Rights* is ideal for all levels of students in international relations, foreign policy, peace studies, international organizations, and law.

201

Jack Donnelly is the Andrew W. Mellon Professor of International Relations at the Graduate School of International Studies at the University of Denver. He has written numerous articles on human rights theory and practice that have appeared in journals such as *American Political Science Review, World Politics,* and *Human Rights Quarterly.* He is also the author of *Universal Human Rights in Theory and Practice.*

Index